Mr Fezziwig's Ball.

Frontispiece. "Mr Fezziwig's Ball", illustration for A Christmas Carol *by Charles Dickens, 1843.*

JOHN LEECH
and the
VICTORIAN SCENE

Simon Houfe

ANTIQUE COLLECTORS' CLUB

ISBN 0 907462 44 8

British Library CIP data
Houfe, Simon
  John Leech and the Victorian Scene.
  1. Leech, John   2. Illustrators — England
  — Biography
  I. Title
  741′.092′4   NC978.5.L/

Published for the Antique Collectors' Club
by the Antique Collectors' Club Ltd.

Printed in England by Baron Publishing, Woodbridge, Suffolk

In Memory of My Mother
Kathleen Byers Houfe
July 30th, 1983

"Leech is the sort of man that appears once in a century."

W.M. Thackeray

"Caricatures help to make history — and they are history also — in the matter of costume, fashions, and social usages, the only history which is clear, entertaining, and to the point."

Samuel Lucas

Acknowledgements

In preparing this biography of John Leech I have received generous help from many quarters. Leech's natural friendliness and conviviality seems to have extended itself to all those who admire him and his works, and it has been a real pleasure to be welcomed into homes where his oil sketches decorate the walls and his illustrated books line the shelves. First of all I must thank the descendants of Leech's friends Dean Hole and Charley Adams for their hospitality and goodness in letting me see so many things from their collections. I received great kindness from the late Tim Tallents who lent me transcripts of Leech's letters to Dean Hole and showed me many objects associated with Leech and his great-grandfather. His daughter, Mrs Virginia Dessain, also gave me assistance and I spent a happy day at Caunton Lodge talking to his aunt, Mrs Mary Hole. Mr Robert Dimsdale gave me unlimited access to the letters in his possession at Barkway and the Baron and Baroness Dimsdale allowed me to photograph some interesting family portraits.

The following kindly gave me permission to reproduce pictures in their possession or to inspect them: The Rt Hon The Viscount Leverhulme, Lady Flett, Martin Horrocks Esq, Mrs Virginia Surtees, Mrs Edward Norman-Butler, Lionel Lambourne Esq, the late Edward Croft-Murray, Mrs Mary Orme. I had invaluable help and hints from many colleagues and friends during the last three years including, Lady Mander, Lady Reid, Mrs Barbara Muir, Malcolm Warner Esq, Henry Markham Esq, Miss Hilarie Faberman, Timothy Matthews Esq and Professor Dudley Johnson.

As usual the staffs of record offices and libraries were indefatigable in aiding my researches, particularly The Bodleian Library; the Royal Library, Windsor Castle, and the Hon Mrs H. Roberts; The Victoria and Albert Museum Library; The Public Record Office; The City of Westminster Reference Library; The Houghton Library, Harvard University; The Armand Hammer Foundation, Los Angeles; the Royal Borough of Kensington and Chelsea Libraries; and the London Library. I had in addition much useful advice from the Bedfordshire, Nottinghamshire, Northamptonshire and Staffordshire Record Offices, as well as from the *Punch* Archives (Miss Mary Anne Bonney) and the Staffordshire Regiment Archives (Major M.K. Beedle Retd). Miss Margaret Christian of Christie's provided me with important catalogue material, Peter Day, curator of Chatsworth, lent his help and Dr Ernst Zillekens made the Charterhouse School Archives available to me for study. The Garrick Club and the City Art Gallery, Manchester, kindly let me reproduce pictures in their possession and the Barber Institute of Fine Arts, Birmingham, kindly loaned me photographs of their Leech pictures; the National Portrait Gallery allowed me to reproduce their fine drawing of Leech by Millais for the book. Both the Castle Museum, Nottingham, and the Department of the History of Art, Reading University, furnished me with information on their early Leech collections.

I wish to express particular thanks to Simon Richardson for his helpful research into the London Coffee House and of the Leech family's long connection with it. Once again thanks are due to my publisher John Steel and his able assistant on this project, Mrs Elizabeth Watson.

Simon Houfe

Avenue House
Ampthill.

March 1984

Contents

Colour Plates

Note on illustrations: *Interspersed throughout the book are sketches and* Punch *cartoons not all of which are referred to specifically in the text. Unless otherwise stated, all illustrations are the work of John Leech.*

Chapter One

LIFE ON LUDGATE HILL

In the early 1800s the heart of London was still the City. The fashionable drift westwards into Georgian crescents and squares had not turned the tide for the traditional haunts of trade and commerce; east of Temple Bar was still populous and bustling in daytime, lively and clamorous by night. Although the stage and mail-coaches now picked up their first class passengers in Piccadilly, the majority of them began and finished their long journeys within a square mile of St Paul's Cathedral. From the far west, the Exeter coach rolled into the yard of the Bull and Gate in Aldersgate Street, the "Dart" on its record-breaking runs completed its course from Brighton at the Spread Eagle, Gracechurch Street, and the "Princess Charlotte" at the White Horse, Fetter Lane. At 5 o'clock every morning "The Wonder" left the Bull and Mouth in St Martin's-Le-Grand to accomplish the journey to Shrewsbury in fifteen and three-quarter hours. Just over an hour later the "Telegraph" started for Manchester, reaching the capital of the North-West in just eighteen and a quarter hours. May Day was the great time for record runs, when proprietors vied with each other to improve performance and surprised even their own calculations. Whether it was the "Royal Clarence", the "Stamford Regent" or the "Tally-ho" the competition was intense and the beauty of the equipages, as well as the magnificent appearance of the teams, were only other words for their efficiency.

The Regency City, therefore, continued to be a place of transit; new arrivals from all corners of the country as well as from abroad, were set down and picked up within its confines. The banks, the mercantile houses and Lloyds were all there, but the population was not simply a work force of professionals, but still of ordinary Londoners connected with the markets, the river and the docks, as well as that huge, now vanished army of men, who slaved, served, and sweated over that four-legged idol — the horse.

In Ludgate Hill was to be found the perfect place for trade. Within easy reach of the lawyers' chambers at the Temple, the academicians of the Royal Academy at Somerset House and the booksellers' haunts of St Paul's Churchyard, its gentle incline in the shadow of the cathedral was a natural stopping place for traveller, businessman or fashionable dawdler from the West End. The Belle Sauvage Inn was a hive of activity and so was the coffee house opposite, hard by

HOW TO SUIT THE TASTE.

Waiter. " GENT. IN NO. 4 LIKES A HOLDER AND THINNER WINE, DOES HE? I WONDER HOW HE 'LL LIKE THIS BIN?"

the slender tower of Wren's St Martin's church, a punch house began in 1731 and variously described as "coffee house" and "Dorchester Beer and Welsh Ale Warehouse". It was most probably its promising position and its established custom that made it attractive to Mr James Rowley, who set up his new London Coffee House there in January 1771, having moved round the corner from his St Paul's Coffee House near Doctors' Commons. With him he brought the specialities of his house "Rowley's Herb Snuff and Tobacco" which were to become equally famous on Ludgate Hill.[1] Rowley ran No 24 Ludgate Hill as both coffee house and tavern, attracting to his establishment the small clubs of that day with their galaxies of notable members. James Boswell was frequenting the rooms in 1772 and John Wilkes in 1792, Dr Priestley and Benjamin Franklin also held meetings there.

Rowley's flair as a host, and his undoubted ability in attracting such an eminent clientele, could only be sustained if the purveyor of the famous "herb snuff" could find a younger man to carry on the business. His choice, a surprising one, fell on John Leech or Leach, a man of some ability who had worked his way up in the Rowley domain. Leech was a Londoner of Irish extraction who had been apprenticed to Bates Cook of St Paul's Churchyard and then taken on as a waiter at the London Coffee House in the 1770s.[2] Described as "good-natured" and "esteemed by his acquaintance",[3] Leech certainly had ample good fortune in being taken into partnership with James Rowley in 1790. During this time the reputation of the London Coffee House increased and the grandeur of its private rooms as well as the lavishness of its table became renowned. Three years after Leech's partnership began, it was described as "a large and superb mansion with a profusion of attendants, first rate cooks, the best of waiters, the smartest chambermaids, hair-dressers, porters and shoe blacks".[4] In February 1797, James Rowley died[5] and John Leech found himself the sole proprietor of this sizeable business, of its coffee rooms, dining-rooms and bedchambers, of its private apartments for meetings of jurors and masons, of its reputation as a market place for "gentlemen from the country".[6] Below ground he was master of its straw-strewn vaults, stacked with casks of French and Portugal wine, bottles of old brandy, East India madeira, pipes of port, tokay, and kilderkins of British wine, orange bitters and cordial cloves.

Leech was as able as his predecessor, if less of a publicist. The "herbal snuff", so long advertised, now took second place to elegant viands and fine victuals and *Feltham's London* 1805, could describe modern kitchens where "culinary articles" were "dressed by steam". It must have been during Leech's time that the building was refronted and a grand room created inside in the neo-classical taste to act as a sleeping room for the Old Bailey juries who stayed here during long sittings (see illustration opposite). By some architectural quirk one side of the coffee house, that to the left, was within the rules of the Fleet Prison, a fact that like the proximity of the Old Bailey brought Leech much custom.[7] A photograph taken in about 1870, gives a

1. *Public Advertiser,* 7 January, 1771.
2. *Fruits of Experience,* pp. 165-166 (Westminster Public Library).
3. ibid.
4. *Roach's London Pocket Pilot,* 1793.
5. *Gentleman's Magazine,* n.d.
6. *Feltham's Picture of London,* 1805.
7. *Farington Diary,* 19 October, 1804

THE JURORS' SLEEPING APARTMENT AT THE LONDON COFFEE-HOUSE.

The great room of The London Coffee House, 1856, often used by jurors as a sleeping apartment. These grand interiors were probably carried out for John Leech's great-uncle.

good indication of what the London looked like in Leech's day, a handsome Georgian house in London brick with a stucco front, very visible on its corner site to anyone climbing the hill to St Paul's, with cellarage below and blinds shading the glazed front windows of the coffee house part of the establishment (see illustration on page 14).

Leech Senior, though popular and fair, ruled the London with a firm hand. When in late 1793, a Dr Hudson and a Mr Pigott, having dined too well, began to give seditious toasts "May the Republic of France be triumphant" and to describe the Prince of Hesse Cassel as a "swine dealer", Mr Leech sent for the constable and had the gentlemen taken into custody. It was a piece of patriotic John Bullishness that he was to pass on to later members of his family![8]

By 1805, John Leech, approaching middle age, with a quarter of a century of experience behind him, took a Mr Dallimore into partnership in both the coffee house and wine merchant's business. This

8. *Gentleman's Magazine,* 1 October, 1793.

13

View of Ludgate Hill about 1870. The London Coffee House was the building on the left marked 'Family Hotel'. It has since been demolished.
National Monuments Record

connection was very successful throughout the Napoleonic Wars and the house was at its zenith in 1813 when the great topographer Brayley called it "a most extensive establishment".[9] Although Mr Dallimore was co-proprietor for fifteen years, Leech Senior must have been looking for a successor from his own family to carry on the name and tradition of the London. As the years passed, the most likely heir must have seemed to be a nephew, John Leech, the son of his brother who was then living in Ireland.[10] The nephew, a remarkably handsome young man with all the charm and ability to mix well that is essential for a publican and hotelier, was brought over from Ireland, established in Southwark and was adopted and trained by the uncle. When John Leech Junior married, he settled

9. Brayley, E., *Description of London and Middlesex,* Vol. 3, p. 632.

10. Leech albums, Bodleian Library, MSS Eng misc e 946/1-7.

14

SINGLE BLESSEDNESS.

Illustration from The Comic English Grammar, *1840.*

across the river in a trim house at No 28 Bennett Street, near Stamford Street. A further incentive to make Leech Senior hand on his commercial enterprises to his nephew was provided in the middle of 1817; on 29 August that year a son, yet another John, was born to John Leech Junior and his wife Esther in Southwark. News of the birth must have been reported with alacrity at the London Coffee House, and the old gentleman, in between letting superior rooms for an auction and inspecting the latest delivery of Madeira wine, would have preened himself that another generation might one day take its place on Ludgate Hill to serve and satisfy the public. But the young great nephew on the Surrey side of the river, gurgling and frothing in his cradle, was not destined to make the name John Leech famous for its wines, spirits and ales. It was to serve and satisfy the public in quite a new way, not from behind the counter but from behind the drawing-board, not in the intricacies of a bill of fare but in the rich varieties of human life and folly seen by a perceptive, yet compassionate, artist. Within twenty-five years this third John Leech would have transformed the style of humorous art in this country, and not only that, would have transformed completely the way people saw themselves.

* * * * *

Leech and Dallimore continued at 24 Ludgate Hill until 1819 when John Leech Junior joined them in the business as Leech, Dallimore and Leech. This triumvirate was short-lived; Dallimore perhaps thought better of remaining in a firm that was now so clearly a family concern, and he left before 1823. By that year Leech felt his nephew was well enough settled for him to retire from a trade that had occupied him for half a century, and he went to live at Chatham Place, Bridge Street. From 1823 the proprietorship is listed as John Leech Junior & Co.[11]

Little John Leech must have moved into the master's apartments of the London Coffee House with his father and mother before his third birthday, his earliest impressions, therefore, were of Ludgate Hill and its vicinity.[12] The Leech family now consisted of at least two other children beside John; several more were to follow. The London, under his father's management, was an exciting place to grow up in, the rabbit warren of rooms, staircases, cellars and attics would have endeared it to the heart of any small boy, but there was too the constant flow of people, arrivals and departures, strange men gabbling in foreign languages, the famous, the infamous and the anonymous rubbing shoulders for an instant in the wooden booths over chops and steaks. The ambience which Leech Senior had created was certainly not insular or prosaic, conversation flowed in the rooms, there was a frank exchange of ideas and above all the discussions ranged over, around and in the printed word. A passage from the *Epicures Almanack*, 1815, shows how metropolitan and how sophisticated was the world in which the young artist was growing up.

11. Lillywhite, Bryant, *London Coffee Houses,* 1963.

12. Caroline Leech in her correspondence with Evans (Houghton Library, Harvard MS Eng 1028) and in Leech albums (Bodleian Library, op. cit.) tries to stress the gentility of the family and their lack of direct connection with the London Coffee House. But the family must have lived there, at least prior to Leech Senior's death when the Bridge Street house became vacant, 1823.

Thomas Rowlandson after Woodward. A single sheet caricature, c.1800, typical of the prints which would have influenced Leech at an early age.

"The London Coffee House ... is on a most magnificent scale; the accommodations elegant, and the company numerous and respectable. In the Coffee Room dine a great number of small parties and single gentlemen daily. Upstairs the most sumptuous entertainments are frequently served up to large parties. To those parties who rarely visit such establishments, it is scarcely possible to conceive the quality of the plate, china and other essentials, requisite for the conduct of this vast concern, the number of cooks, waiters and domestics, as well as the order that reigns among them, are equally surprising and admirable. Almost all the British newspapers, and the most popular monthly journals are taken in; and the greatest facilities are afforded to the stranger for pursuing any plan he may conceive, either of business or pleasure ..."

The world of books and booksellers was very much part of the scene at the London. Old Leech must have encouraged it, because we find important book sales taking place here in the Regency[13] and as late as 1851, the Cadell Library was auctioned by Mr Hodgson on the premises. A philosophical society, dedicated to the study of chemistry and other scientific matters, held its first meeting there in 1807 and artists such as C.R. Leslie lodged there on first settling in London. Perhaps most important of all, some illustrated journals were actually issued from 24 Ludgate Hill. In 1796, "The Bond Street Lounge", a magazine containing illustrations and fashion plates, was published "from the London Coffee House".[14]

If this was not fertile ground enough for a keen-eyed young boy to grow up in, we know too that John Leech Junior, the new landlord, was bookish and a tolerable amateur artist with the pencil. It is hardly conceivable that in such an atmosphere, the latest caricatures "hot" from the presses of Tegg, McLean and Humphrey, were not brought in, read and laughed over, the works of Cruikshank, Rowlandson and "Paul Pry", bright with hand-colouring and full of the unbuttoned, ribald humours of the time. The small rather delicate boy would have found more than enough to occupy him in this adult world, the groups of people loitering round the door of the house, the shadows cast by the lamplight within, the city men and others poring over the latest journal, shoulders bent, heads craned. Ludgate Hill itself with its jingle of harness outside, its proliferation of books and magazines in the shop windows, its population of nomads and regulars indoors, provided the basic ingredients of John Leech's life. Horses were at once his passion and his paymasters, the smell of newsprint was his regular companion and his fellow Londoners, drab or dandified, pompous or pathetic, were to be his chief source of inspiration.

Few glimpses of John Leech's earliest years have come down to us. W.P. Frith, the artist's fullest and least satisfactory biographer, does mention family holidays in the 1820s, when little John with his brother Tom, and his five sisters, Mary, Caroline, Esther, Fanny and Polly, went with their parents to Brighton. It was the Brighton of the Regency, fashionable and busy, only just becoming a resort of stucco terraces and crescents. The young boy learnt to ride a pony there in

13. Catalogue of 1813 in Guildhall Library.

14. Ashton, J. *Old Times, Social Life at the End of the 18th Century*, 1885.

A contemporary engraving of the Great Hall, Charterhouse.

1823 under the personal instruction of one of George IV's stable servants from the Pavilion,[15] and the beach and hills behind held a lasting attraction for him for the rest of his life. It may have been at Brighton that he had the serious fall from a pony that damaged his arm, making him frail during his schooldays and unable to join in rougher games.[16]

A better insight is perhaps provided by the story of his meeting with John Flaxman, the Royal Academician. Most prodigies have some such tale of a meeting with a celebrated man who recognises their genius; this one seems to have a bit more credibility than most. From 1817 to 1825, Flaxman was constantly engaged in designs for the silversmiths, Rundell, Bridge and Rundell, whose premises were next door to the London Coffee House in Ludgate Hill. Nothing more natural surely, than that the artist should call in at the London for refreshment and see the child drawing with pencil and paper for his mother. Flaxman is reputed to have said "Do not let him be cramped by drawing-lessons; let his genius follow its own bent. He will astonish the world." Later on Flaxman, who had become a friend of the Leeches, looked at further drawings and pronounced "That boy must be an artist; he will be nothing else."[17] It seems more likely that both comments were made on the same occasion when John Leech was about nine. Flaxman himself died before the boy's tenth birthday, and however precocious he could scarcely have produced anything to give rise to extravagant comment before that age.

One juvenile drawing that survives at Charterhouse School is certainly a very spirited effort for a small boy (Colour Plate 1, page 19). It was done in 1823 when he was six years old and is, predictably enough for a dweller on Ludgate Hill, of a Royal Mail coach. Leech shows here, even at this early age, a tremendous sense of movement, a pleasant balance of coach and horses across the page, a deft use of watercolour washes and a nice sense of colour. Close scrutiny reveals the word "Bath" on the door of the machine and this is of course the Bath Mail that he would have seen, wide-eyed, as it left the gates of the Belle Sauvage Inn. It was that same Belle Sauvage Inn that was to have a more menacing meaning to the Leech family ten years later, but now it spelt out only the romance of the road, great distances and opportunities for using that first watercolour box, a present from proud parents.

John Leech Junior probably recognised that he could do more for his son's education than his uncle had done for him. Aware of his own inadequacies in learning, he determined on the best, and the best for a city man's son was Charterhouse. Charterhouse was a seventeenth century foundation of school, chapel and hospital, some way north of St Paul's and about half a mile from Ludgate Hill. By the 1820s its clerical origins had been left behind and it was emerging as one of the leading public schools. Young John Leech became a day boy at the school in January 1825 at the age of seven and a half, exchanging the familiar noise of the London Coffee House for the nearly medieval atmosphere of the Charterhouse, grey-walled, creeper-clad, with its courtyards, quadrangles, cloistered arches and

15. Frith, W.P., *John Leech His Life and Work,* 1891, Vol. 2, p. 93.

16. ibid., Vol. 1, p. 6.

17. ibid., Vol. 1, p. 5.

A contemporary engraving of the inner gateway, Charterhouse.

Great Hall. There was a period of eighteen months when the small boy made the daily trek through the city streets to the school and back again, but in September 1826 he became a boarder at Charterhouse, entering Churton's and joining the six hundred fellow pupils on a more permanent basis.

Immediately Leech would have felt himself part of a tradition and a community. The school was entered by a gatehouse with a top-hatted porter and inside it was like a citadel within a city. He would run through the low Stuart doorways of Wash House Court where tall brick chimneys were bitten into the stonework, dart through the austere Great Cloister and eat amid the clatter of pewter in the totally collegiate Dining Hall with its carved screen and Jacobean decoration. The 1820s were not the most enlightened era of public school life, it was the period to be satirised by Dickens in *Nicholas Nickleby,* characterised perhaps by the disciplinarian rule of Dr Keate at Eton and immortalised for its brutality in *Tom Brown.* According to Frith, Mrs Leech was over-fond of her eldest son and over-protective about his entry into the big school, taking a nearby room so that she could watch him playing. Whether she did or not, or whether the child knew it, the general tenor of the letters home is rather unhappy. In between the usual boyish references to wanting "cake", "small bladders to make balloons of" or "a penknife if you please" come the gloomy statements "I am so dull here" or "I feel quite unhappy here and miserable".[18] But there were opportunities for the busy coffee house proprietor to see his son, from noon till half-past two or from four till nine at night when visitors were allowed. His father sent him half a crown when he needed it and a small weekly allowance to keep him going.

> My Dear Mamma,
>   I understand that you came to see me yesterday, and me being in the green, you did not see me, so that made me still more unhappy, I beg you will come and see me on Saturday for I am very unhappy.
>   I want to see you or Papa very much indeed.
>   J. Leech [19]

> My Dear Papa,
>   You desired me to send you my report I have not had it since the last one. I went in to be examined by Dr Russell yesterday but did not get promoted but I did not lose more than one or two places, I will send you my next report. I hope you are quite well.
>   Mamma and Brother and Sisters the same
>   Your affectionate
>   Son
>   J. Leech [20]

It is strange that the artist who was to fill Victorian journals with schoolboy swells, schoolboy prigs, schoolboy snobs and schoolboy

18. Frith, op. cit., Vol. 1, pp. 10-13.
19. ibid., Vol. 1, p. 10.
20. ibid., Vol. 1, p. 14. The original letter is in the collection of Charterhouse School.

Colour Plate 1. A watercolour drawing of the Bath Mail, sketched by John Leech in 1823 when he was six years old. 4 x 7½ins.
Charterhouse School

gormandisers, should have been himself so untypical a schoolboy. Perhaps he was already the caricaturist at heart, the humorist, standing a little outside the rough and tumble, acutely observing the foibles and follies around him? Academically he was very average indeed; the reports sent home to Ludgate Hill read "generally attentive" or "does his best" observations on a conscientious tryer rather than a pupil of any great promise. But despite being only average and not very robust physically he was a universally popular boy, "gentle" one contemporary called him[21] and "the most popular boy in the school" was another's recollection.[22] The Charterhouse School list of 7 May, 1828, shows Leech, then nearly eleven years old, in the first division of the Tenth Form, W.M. Thackeray being on the same list in one of the senior forms. Thackeray later recalled him as "a small boy at the Charterhouse, in a little blue buttoned-up suit, set up upon a form and made to sing 'Home sweet home' to the others crowding about."[23] H.O. Nethercote, his school-friend, remembered that "the margins of his grammars were a delight to boyish eyes"[24] and another friend recollected that Leech had teamed up with a boy called Douglas who had a great power in caricature and had copied his work. The jolly decorations to the books must have been his only progress in Latin verse. Years later he confessed to having found the subject impossible and having always "got somebody to do them for him".

The only sheet of Latin exercise surviving is as blotchy and crossed out as one could expect, apparently part of a holiday task done at Brighton in about 1827. Leech was presumably staying at the Old Ship with friends and his tutor, whose letter to the father gives a pleasant glimpse of the boy on holiday.[25]

Brighton — Monday

Dear Sir,

I hope you will excuse John's not having written his exercise over fairly this evening because he has been out.

21. Frith, op. cit., Vol. 2, p. 93.

22. ibid., Vol. 2, p. 283.

23. Quoted by Lady Ritchie and cited in Gordon Ray's *The Letters & Private Papers of W.M. Thackeray*, 1945, Vol. 1, pp. cxliv-cxlvi.

24. Frith, op cit., Vol. 2, p. 283.

25. The Revd John Gough Clay, M.A., Leech's tutor and life-long friend. The original letter is in the collection of Charterhouse School.

The "Coach Tree" at Charter-house, from which Leech used to watch the mails passing. An illustration made by the artist for Once a Week, *1860.*

with the Pritchards nearly all day; immediately after breakfast we went up upon the Downs to fly a kite, and did not get home to the Old Ship to dinner till two o'clock. Then after dinner we took a long ride, for the whole of the afternoon. He has undertaken his exercise this evening much more willingly, and has done it in the rough pretty fairly. He sends his love to you and his mamma, and he bids me say that he will write to her tomorrow

Yours truly

J. Clay

Leech was sufficiently strong in the arm in the late 1820s to learn fencing with the celebrated Mr Angelo, who visited the school, and at

Contemporary engraving of the Old College of Physicians.

the same time to learn drawing under the resident master, Mr Burgess. Leech later confessed to learning nothing from this tuition, gaining much more from the fun of his carefree marginalia. A few surviving efforts are vital and amusing but not obvious precursors of great talent. In long afternoons, he loved to go to the corner of the quadrangle and climb the "Coach Tree", a tall old tree with spikes driven into its trunk, from which vantage he could watch the mails driving in and out of the City. His memories of Charterhouse were happy enough for him to return thirty years later and sketch this incident with his other self, aged thirteen, perched in the branches (see illustration on page 20).[26]

One holidays, the young Leech returned home to find that his pony was missing. It had been sold to pay debts![27] It was the first inkling for the youth that all was not well at home and a very bitter way to learn of it. But other distractions occupied him and specially the choice of a career. There seems to have been some understanding between Leech and his father that he should study medicine. Drawing was still a pleasant recreation, and Leech, always adaptable, apparently accepted the prospect of life as a doctor. Consequently in December 1831, he left Charterhouse at the age of fourteen and a half and moved in the autumn of 1832 the few hundred yards by Smithfield Market to St Bartholomew's Hospital.

* * * * *

Leech spent the years 1832 and 1833 in medical training, attending the lectures and associating with a band of lively, but far from attentive, fellow students. At St Bartholomew's he became acquainted with Arthur William à Beckett and with a witty would-be journalist, Percival Leigh. Neither the latter, nor John Leech, took their vocations very seriously and Dickens' famous sketch of the medical students Ben Allen and Bob Sawyer, one drinking brandy neat, the other with "a barrel o' oysters atween his knees" was probably true to life of the young artist and his author friend. Perhaps they would have been as pleased too with Pickwick's comments on these professional attitudes — "Eccentricities of genius, Sam".

There are no records of how Leech adapted to the wards, the discipline of the dissecting room with its terrible stench and grisly specimens. He was at least very lucky to be studying under a very remarkable doctor, Edward Stanley, later Principal Surgeon of Bart's and eventually Surgeon Extraordinary to Queen Victoria. At the time Leech arrived, Stanley was simply lecturer on anatomy, and it is on record that Leech "delighted" him by his excellent drawings of human limbs and his innate sense of proportion.[28] This study, virtually the only training that he had, was to stand him in good stead when he had to earn money with his pencil. Many of these sketches survived into the 1890s for Frith to see, and whether sections of muscle or just facetious portraits, no line was wasted.

26. *Once a Week,* 1860, Vol. 3, p. 98.
27. Evans letters, Harvard University, MS Eng 1028. Edmund Yates to Evans, 9 October, 1885.
28. Frith, op. cit., Vol. 1, p. 16.

John Leech's desk. It was on this desk that he drew while staying with Dr Thomas Smith at Crawley, Sussex in 1833-34.
Timothy Matthews Collection

It was customary for students who became Licenciates of the Society of Apothecaries to get themselves placed with a reputable doctor. Leigh, who was Leech's senior, qualified in 1834 at the age of twenty-two and another friend of the same age, Albert Smith, joined his father. It seems unlikely that Leech ever became L.S.A. His family had pinned their hopes on placing John with the Scottish physician, Sir George Ballingall. When this proved impossible, he was sent as assistant in succession to Mr Whittle, Dr Thomas Smith and Dr John Cockle.

Leech's apprenticeship with Bramley Whittle was celebrated more by its humour than its medical prowess. Whittle was a sort of Regency Bohemian, half quack, half retailer, who lived in a house in the vicinity of Hoxton, full of rabbits and pigeons which he bred. He indulged in gymnastics, impersonated Hercules and was adept at picking up stones with his mouth! Most useful for Leech was his meeting there another apprentice, Albert Smith of the Middlesex Hospital, an inveterate scribbler who hoped to get some of his work published. Leech and Smith became life-long friends and the result of their months with Whittle was some ludicrous passages in *The Adventures of Mr Ledbury,* which Smith wrote and Leech illustrated some years afterwards. After Whittle, Dr John Cockle, of 18, New Ormond Street, was a paragon of respectability (he later became Physician to the Royal Free Hospital). Leech mischievously remembered this benefactor in later years by incorporating "Cockles Pills" into some of his *Punch* cartoons!

During the year 1833 to 1834 Leech, by now sixteen years of age, tall and handsome with a lot of animal fun lurking below a somewhat shy manner, was placed with a Dr Thomas Smith at Crawley in Sussex. While in the Smith household, his interest in medicine was as strongly sublimated to his desire to draw as it had been at Bart's, the whitewashed walls of his room were covered with drawings of horses and he enjoyed making caricatures and comic sketches of Smith, his children and the pets in the house on his little wooden desk. In this happy rather boisterous atmosphere, his efforts were not received uncritically: "On being twitted about his horses' tails which were said to resemble *Bannister Brooms,* he would remark 'Oh, you wait and see I shall be a great artist some day'."[29]

In the Spring of 1833, the elder Leech wrote to Dr Smith to enquire about his son and to tell him of changes in his own life. The letter, almost the only one of Leech's father to survive, tells us much about the man, his mixture of gentlemanly sentiments and rather haphazard business arrangements.[30]

Andertons
Coffs Ho
Ap 24th 1833

My dear Sir,

Do not think the worst of me that I have not written you. I think I bid John tell you I should do so. I have been so occupied with alterations necessary to make here (in

29. MSS notes of Dr Timothy Martin, Matthews Collection.

30. ibid.

HOW TO GET RID OF A GRATIS PATIENT.

" SO, YOU'VE TAKEN ALL YOUR STUFF, AND DON'T FEEL ANY BETTER, EH ? WELL, THEN, WE MUST ALTER THE TREATMENT ; YOU MUST GET YOUR HEAD SHAVED ; AND IF YOU WILL CALL HERE TO-MORROW ABOUT ELEVEN, MY PUPIL HERE WILL PUT A SETON IN THE BACK OF YOUR NECK."

case my household are ill) that I have not had a moment, at least such a one as I could wish to devote to you. You are not a man to require a repetition of acknowledgements and I cannot heap them upon you to the extent that they are due and complain at the same time of wanting time. You must come up and live with me and bring the young ladies your sisters with you all. John is too happy I suppose to think much of home but we begin to think he ought soon to return. I sincerely hope he has been as little in your way as possible. Does he read hard? 'Woe betide me and my whole generation' I have doubts about it. You are too indulgent to him. I beseech you, however, never to let him be an interruption to you. In a week I hope to take him off your hands if till then you can accommodate him. May I say I begin to feel his intrusion here has been too.... Mrs Leach and my daughter Caroline will immediately write to Miss Smith. Caroline has been out of Town ever since we left Bernard Street. Let me have the pleasure of a line from you and believe me my dear Sir,

Ever obliged and faithfully yours
John Leach

This letter and even John's exile in Sussex, were partly the result of a great upheaval in the family that was to affect all the Leeches and alter the course of the young man's life. Mr Leech had decided to sell the London Coffee House and vacate Ludgate Hill altogether. It was a major break with the past and with upwards of fifty years of proprietorship at No 24. The reasons for this sudden decision can only be guessed at. Leech Senior, who had died in the mid-1820s had left an astonishing will with personal bequests of £10,000, but the residue of his considerable property to his only daughter. His nephew received £5,000 but probably insufficient assets to keep such a large concern running smoothly.[31] The great-uncle was a hard man and ruthless with his tenants, the nephew was a more accommodating fellow, not hasty in striking a bargain. As late as 1831, the culture loving Leech Junior had encouraged the City of London Artists and Amateurs conversaziones to take place in his private rooms, but it was not enough to combat the competition of the great clubs. Leech had had a short partnership with a Mr Buttel from 1826 to 1830, but money was scarce and it appeared that the greatest hope for his diminishing fortunes was to move westward. At the end of 1832, he sold the London to Mr Samuel Lovegrove and took over Anderton's Coffee House at 183 Fleet Street.

Anderton's was better situated but needed a great deal doing to it. A local builder Henry Nixon undertook the alterations and new furniture, fittings and utensils were installed and a considerable outlay of capital expended on wines, spirits and porter. The house must have opened in May 1833 but did not really prosper because it did not have that ancillary of a good coffee house, a supper room. Mr Leech decided to establish a table d'hôte, for which he had ample

31. Leech albums, op. cit.

experience at the London. It proved to be a fatal decision.

It appears that Mr Leech's gentle disposition and lack of commercial acumen were seen as weaknesses. They had made him enemies, probably before he had left Ludgate Hill. The move westwards had angered the other coffee house keepers of Fleet Street, in what was becoming an increasingly cut-throat line of business; the establishment of the table d'hôte was the last straw. His enraged competitiors met together at the Belle Sauvage Inn and formed a combination to drive Mr Leech out of business. They fixed an embargo on any tradesmen who supplied Anderton's, whether for cash or credit, with goods, threatening to withdraw *their* customer from these businesses. A great number of the smaller tradesmen and the two neighbouring breweries were coerced into this, fearing for their livelihoods. Mr Leech had no alternative but to purchase his ale and stout elsewhere and to retail it at scarcely any profit to himself. The only way out of this impossible situation was to take a partner who had capital, but Leech's amiable ways and poor judgement gained him a garrulous partner whom he had met for a few minutes in the supper room. This fickle gentleman lent him £400 and soon afterwards closed for repayment. Leech was caught and within a very short time the bailiff was in possession of the premises. Creditors, who had been prepared to wait, demanded payment and Leech was ruined.

All this had happened within seven or eight months of the coffee house opening, within seven or eight months that is of nearly £5,000 being spent on the building, £650 on the stock in trade and £428 in coals, oils and stationery. It was revealed that there were outstanding debts of £800 from the Ludgate Hill days and wine charges and taxes due to the tune of £1,555. A meeting of the creditors took place at Anderton's on January 3rd 1834, the builder Henry Nixon in the chair and a large number of others present, all favourably disposed towards Mr Leech. Nixon spoke of Leech's "industry and execution" at Anderton's and of the fact that the balance of money owed, some £2,665 10s 4d, "was considered by many persons a very small deficiency". Nevertheless he had no reserves to fall back upon and as Nixon remarked he would make no "proposition without the assistance of some private friend or relative" and he "had a family of eight children". A second meeting to investigate the money owed to the servants at Anderton's was held in February, an acrimonious letter from a local tradesman appeared in *The Times* and after that "Mr Leech's Bankruptcy" was forgotten.[32]

Forgotten that is by everyone except the family, for them its disgrace, its fouling of human relationships and its crushing burden on their lives was to track inexorably across the next generation. In June 1835, a further hearing at the Court of Bankruptcy brought Leech and his wife into open conflict. Mrs Leech's annuity which should have been given to her, had been appropriated by her husband in his difficulties and never repaid. The Court found against Mrs Leech's claim but it was not a verdict that was likely to improve the harmony of family life.[33]

32. *The Times,* 4 January, 1834.
33. ibid., 2 June, 1835.

Mr Leech was completely shattered by the circumstances and with increasing ineptitude and bitterness was quite unable to build a new life. Over forty years later Caroline Leech recalled that the memory of "his own wrong" never faded and she paints a picture of her father which could have come from the pen of Mrs Micawber. "...never was a man more qualified by natural disposition and attainments to do honour to any position in life, however exalted, than our beloved Father. Adverse circumstances, unhappily placed him in a position where there was no opportunity of distinguishing himself according to his abilities and the world's idea of distinction."[34]

For young John Leech, eighteen years old and for the first time enjoying the company of some rakish London friends, the sudden disappearance of a comfortable life, money, career and prospects, was cruel. Highly sensitive to change and desperately shy, the drop in the family income and the fall in their social status was something that rankled with him for the rest of his life. There was no future for him in medicine without money; Leigh could go on to become a member of the Royal College, Smith could join his father at Chertsey, but Leech's prospects were not bright in 1835. But the bankruptcy which had so coloured his life and was to continue to do so as his father became more dependant on him, brought out very quickly the genius for drawing. Without the impetus provided by his father's failure, he could have remained an amateur, a marvellous pencil artist no doubt, but without that cutting edge which is the touchstone of a pictorial journalist. The shabby genteel world of Micawberism which was now settling on his parents and himself was the greatest spur to new things. If he could no longer own horses and gigs and the things he loved, he could observe the world on paper, laugh gently at it, rebuke it a little; that was after all what the Leeches had done for two generations, please the public.

34. Leech albums, op cit.

THE STAG AT BAY.

Chapter Two

YOUNG CARICATURIST
1835 to 1841

ohn Leech's acquaintance in London was very much wider than that provided by the medical students at Bart's or the apprentices at the various quack doctors and apothecaries for whom he worked. At about the time that the family fortunes collapsed, Leech met a young Londoner who was to play quite an important part in his future life. Charles Adams, almost Leech's contemporary in age,[1] became his friend through their mutual love of horses. Adams, working his way up a precarious ladder in surveying, was employed in London, but put most of his energies and resources into a couple of horses that he hired. Unable to use them much during the day time, Adams used them at night. Leech admired horses, Adams knew about the mystique of horses; Leech drew horses in his peripatetic sketch books, Adams drove them tandem fashion through the sleeping countryside at break-neck speeds. Frith mentions almost *en passant* the riotous rides of the two young men and their high jinks in the semi-rural London of the 1830s.

Charles Adams was a good-looking, brawny young man of twenty when the artist Joseph Kenny Meadows painted a miniature of him in 1835 (see page 27). (It could have been Meadows, an established illustrator who provided the introduction between them.) There is a certain cheeky cockney charm in that face and nose, a certain flamboyance in the dress suggestive of both the dandy and the opportunist. Adams, full of daredevil youthful exuberance was obviously the leader in these escapades, watched, perhaps slightly in awe by his gentler and more timid friend. There were other differences too, which perhaps made an attraction of opposites. Whereas Leech was transparently honest, and almost naïvely so in business, Adams was a tough commercial man, not afraid on occasions to sail perilously close to the wind.

The friendship worked; Leech became familiar with the world of horse dealers, horse sales, ostlers, grooms and horseflesh in general under Adams' practised eye. Adams found evident enjoyment in Leech's instinctive love of the sporting life, his humorous eye and sense of the ridiculous. Frith's descriptions of these nocturnal forays "rousing sleepy toll-keepers and terrifying belated wayfarers"[2] lends an almost Myttonesque colour to Leech's early life. Perhaps in their milder way they were trying to mimic the lives of the Regency Corinthians, Tom and Bob, featured in Pierce Egan's *The Real Life*

1. Charles Adams was born on 18 April, 1815. His extensive correspondence with John Leech is in the collection of his descendant Robert Dimsdale.

2. Frith, W.P., *John Leech His Life and Work,* 1891, Vol. 1, p. 234.

Charles Adams by Joseph Kenny Meadows, 1838. Adams was Leech's oldest and closest friend.
Dimsdale Collection

in London of a decade earlier. This book, with its hand-coloured narrative pictures by the Alkens, was all the rage in London sporting circles, its recklessness and extravagance acting like a swan song to the libertine Georgians before the onset of Victorian respectability.

Leech was already aware of this set of artists who depicted the world of the hunt, the turf and the road; during the 1800s and 1820s there was a greatly invigorated school of equestrian artists and engravers, the printsellers' windows were filled by the coaching scenes of James Pollard, thoroughbreds by Ben Marshall and hounds in full cry by Alken.

Leech's gentlemanly recreation with Adams must have been a welcome relief from the family troubles, a happy escape from his pessimistic father and the unequal struggle of trying to make his living with a pencil. A sight of high stepping tandem ponies or sleek hunters, even if it was only at Tattersall's, must have brought some brightness to these cheerless days and in the last resort, Adams or "Charley" as Leech called him, was always there to lend him some money. It was during this difficult time that the relationship of these horse-mad young men was really cemented, Adams became his most intimate correspondent, the one to whom he was ever most open and frank.

If they could not always own these wonderful animals, they could always admire them in the hunting pictures of their greatest contemporary, Henry Alken. Both of them must have been struck by the life and panache of Alken's prints; Leech we know admired them. Some of his earliest surviving drawings, known from photographs at Charterhouse, were copies from Alken. They were executed in about 1835, before the artist was nineteen, and show those stretched out horses and arched legs, associated with Alken, and all equestrian art before the moving picture. What was the principal attraction of Alken for Leech? Was Alken or anybody else the main influence on this energetic and very receptive mind?

Leech, extraordinary genius as he was, nevertheless stood at the beginning of a whole series of new trends in art, which placed him in a most fortunate position. It may not have seemed like it in 1835 when he was drearily going from publisher to publisher with his portfolio, "hopes that brightened at a word of commendation, only to be scattered by a few stereotyped phrases...",[3] but that is in fact what was happening. His life coincided exactly with a shift of emphasis from personal to domestic satire, from symbolic to situational humour, from the scornful pillorying of the eighteenth century to the compassionate mockery of the nineteenth. It is perhaps worthwhile at this point, with Leech on the threshold of his career, to take stock of these changes which brought about that distinctive style that so many have come to love.

The tradition of British sporting art had a great deal to do with Leech's development as an artist, he was well aware of the engravings of Georgian times,[4] but Alken had a special place. Henry Alken's engravings introduced humour to the traditional sports; true Bunbury had featured some comic countrymen and Gillray had

3. Frith, op. cit., Vol. 1, p. 21.
4. Photographs of Leech's copies of Alken are in the collection of Charterhouse School.

satirised the hunt magnificently in 1800[5] (see illustration below), they were unusual. Alken's views were no longer pristine prints of the hunting party, immaculately attired, strung along frieze-like in perfect country, they were factual, unheroic, as much narrative as *The Real Life in London*. Alken introduced incident and accident to his horsemanship, nice gentlemen came croppers, nearly got drowned, were thoroughly soaked, caught in trees and were dismally unseated. The humour and interest of this broke entirely new ground and it was just one fresh departure that was to benefit Leech tremendously. From the early 1820s Alken was producing books of humorous sporting subjects, a few titles out of the score are *Humorous Specimens of Riding,* 1821, *Town Versus Country, Hunting or Six Hours Sport of Three Real Good Ones from the East End,* the latter being episodes of cockney sportsmen, a favourite of Leech and his predecessors. Alken's intensely amusing scenes only needed a personalising touch; Leech's pencil and temperament were perfectly attuned to give them this, but also ideally suited to the new climate in publishing.

The separately issued caricature print which had been circulated in London since Hogarth's day was coming to the end of its natural life.

5. Gillray's set includes "Hounds Finding", "Hounds in Full Cry", "Hounds Throwing Off" and "Coming in at the Death" published on 8 April, 1800.

Publish'd April 8th 1800 by H. Humphrey, No 27 St. James's Street, London.

R..... Esq.r del.t

HOUNDS IN FULL-CRY.

J.G.y fec.t

A scene from "John Jones" (or if you prefer it) Davy Jones, by John Doyle, 'HB', 1831. An example of the bland type of caricature which was fashionable in Leech's youth.

Taste was becoming more sophisticated, more refined and less dogmatically masculine. What was suitable for the club and the gaming den was not thought appropriate for the family. By 1830, the year in which that much caricatured monarch George IV died, Cruikshank had abandoned such prints and the new star of political satire, John Doyle, "HB" as he signed himself, was so muted as scarcely to be a caricaturist at all. Savage caricature, grotesque adumbrations of form, face and mien, disappeared for several generations. Fortunate for John Leech that it did, for he was not destined to be a strong portrait caricaturist and was not really a caricaturist of individuals or suited to the brutality that had sold the separate caricature print.

Leech began by offering separate drawings to the print-sellers. Encouraged by his sister Caroline, he had taken a sketch "of beggars going out in the morning and returning at night" to the great print shop of McLean in Haymarket. McLean paid a guinea for it,[6] but whether it was used or not appears to be unknown. No doubt Leech could see that the new taste demanded *books* of comicalities, landscape folios of illustrated humour like Alken's, plain or coloured but with little letter press. They were really the separate prints of yesterday, bound together with a conventional title, and Leech, very much a man of his time, decided to offer thereafter groups of caricature types executed in the new lithography. John Doyle, a miniaturist by profession, had taken up lithography as his medium for political prints, the caressing chalk lines softening his satire, so that his characters became more like portraits (see illustration left). The lithographic line spoke to the viewer like a page from the artist's sketch-book, it was as such the ideal vehicle for a gallimaufry of impressions, individual figures, scenes taken apparently at random. It was exactly this that Leech produced for a print-seller (possibly McLean)[7] in about 1835 in *Etchings and Sketchings by A. Pen Esq*, four pages of oddities of the London street scene, "clever sketches, slightly caricatured, of cabmen, policemen, street musicians, donkeys, broken-down hacks"[8] and many other thumbnail likenesses.

Robert Seymour was the artist who seemed to combine the humour of sport with the tradition of caricature most successfully. It was his great popularity that persuaded the publishers Chapman and Hall to employ a young journalist, Charles Dickens, to write a text to Seymour's illustrations. The book became *Pickwick Papers*. The partnership lasted for only two issues and on 20 April, 1836, Seymour committed suicide in London. There was almost a scramble among the illustrators to succeed to his place; Thackeray was an eager contender, Buss attempted to get it, "Phiz" hoped to aspire to it and the unknown Leech also called on Dickens.

Leech must have visited the novelist at Furnivals Inn in the middle of July 1836 at the suggestion of George Cruikshank who had given him an introduction. Dickens was evidently encouraging but told him that H.K. Browne, "Phiz", had already been appointed as Pickwick's illustrator. Nothing daunted, Leech asked if he might have a share in Chapman and Hall's Library of Fiction, with which

6. Leech albums, Bodleian Library, MSS Eng misc e 946/17.

7. Grolier Club bibliography lists copy with no date or publisher's name given.

8. Frith, op. cit., Vol. 1, p. 21.

"Mr. Pickwick and Sam in the Attorney's Office." Illustration for The Pickwick Papers by H.K. Browne.

9. House, M. and Storey, G., *The Letters of Charles Dickens Vol. 1 1820-1839,* Clarendon Press, 1965.

10. Leech albums, op. cit. Gerald S. Davies was a master at Charterhouse School and one of the most perceptive of Leech's earlier commentators. The entry in *Bryan's Dictionary* is by him.

11. *The Paris Sketch-Book,* 1840, p. 158.

Dickens was not connected. He then returned home and, unsolicited, worked on an illustration for The Bagman's Story in *Pickwick,* where Tom Smart is confronted by the mysterious chair. He returned this to Dickens on August 23rd, but the novelist was away. Dickens, somewhat cautiously sent the little watercolour on to the publishers with a covering note. "The chair's not bad," he wrote, "but his notion of the Bedroom is rather more derived, I should be disposed to think from his own fourth pair back, than my description of the old rambling house."[9] It was a bold move by the rather desperate young eighteen year old, a move that did not appear to have been fruitful; but it had been an important introduction, Dickens did not forget him.

* * * * *

Lithography was the up and coming medium of the 1830s and, as we have seen, it might predictably have superseded engraving, for it was easier to handle, and particularly adaptable for the amateur and the untrained artist, precisely from where the life blood of caricature had traditionally come. John Leech's lack of formal apprenticeship, his simply intuitive feelings for his subjects, made him an ideal candidate for lithographs; furthermore he may have appreciated their flexibility and popularity in France.

We know that Leech visited France, possibly in the last few months of 1836. There is an important, but hitherto overlooked reference to this visit, contained in Mr George Evans' albums at Oxford. There, in a paper by the Revd Gerald S. Davies, delivered in 1883, Mr Evans has copied: "In 1836 I know that he paid a visit to France and stayed a few weeks with friends at Versailles. I believe I am right in saying that he made the acquaintance of a French artist and saw him a little at work in his studio. He made here too his first studies of Frenchmen and indeed I imagine that the few weeks abroad had not a little bearing on his subsequent work."[10]

Paris was both the centre of lithography at this time and the very centre of caricature, with the works of Philipon, Daumier and others circulating freely, or sufficiently freely. After the punitive September laws of 1835, the King and Government could not be satirised and as Thackeray wrote in his essay of 1840, the caricaturists looked elsewhere: "But there is always food for satire; and the French caricaturists, being no longer allowed to hold up to ridicule and reprobation the King and deputies, have found no lack of subjects for the pencil in the ridicules and rascalities of common life."[11] The French men turned to the life of the bourgeoisie and the *comédie humaine,* Leech too turned his eyes in that direction, tinged as they already were by the British love of sport.

The fact that Leech had direct contact with French caricature at this impressionable age and may have studied under a French caricaturist is highly significant. He was certainly the only major British satirical artist to form such a link at a time when the old caricature styles were on the ebb and a new Continental approach was needed to fill the vacuum. Just how much he was influenced by his Versailles stay is shown in one surviving sketch of French men, both spirited and natural (see below).[12] More to the point however was his undoubted change of direction in several series of caricature folios published by W. Spooner and W. Soffe, both of the Strand. Although undated, these lithographs, coloured by hand, were drawn in 1837-38 as is proved by Spooner's Strand address appearing on many of them, the publisher not having moved there from Regent Street until 1837.[13] They are entitled *Droll Doings, Funny Characters,* an unnamed set and *The Human Face Divine and De Vino.* Crucially, they were done well after the French trip and more importantly still, after the great French caricaturist Honoré Daumier had produced some of his best middle class themes. His *Types Français,* 1835, *Gallerie Physionomique* and *Croquis d'Expressions,* 1838, were all appearing at this time, caricatures certainly, but also graphic Gallic insights into the world of bourgeois France, the tradesman, the petty official, the self-contained little family, the trials of parenthood, the struggles of conjugal bliss. Philipon's magazine *Charivari* had begun in 1832 and after 1835 was the main source of Parisian humour. It is evident from the lithographs that Leech knew the journal, but at least two specific references are made to *Charivari* in his later published work as well.[14]

12. Charterhouse School.

13. The date given in Grolier Club bibliography is incorrect.

14. *Punch,* Vol. 27, p. 100; *Punch,* Vol. 38, p. 248.

A group of foreigners probably sketched in 1838-39 and used for Leech's earliest Punch *illustration in 1841.*
Charterhouse School

31

PRETTY DEAR.

Illustration from The Comic Latin
Grammar, *1840.*

Inspired by the sporting humour of Alken, reacting strongly against the coarse jokes of Robert Seymour (Leech is recorded as having found nothing funny in them), Leech was the first artist to grasp the importance of the French caricature of types and situations on this side of the Channel. *Droll Doings* and *Funny Characters,* though far less assured in the drawing than French work, begin to investigate the inner world of the suburbs, its bewildered householders, pompous shopkeepers, raffish swells and precocious juveniles; Leech is still drawing caricatures, but the visual banana skins of Seymour are replaced by the verbal and situational banana skins of the comedy of manners in a purely English way.

Funny Characters is perhaps the earliest. It is a cruder collection than the others, more Seymouresque and shows a gradual mastery of the figure and the medium between early and later prints. No. 3, "Come Maria", shows a pair of hideous old maids imagining they are pursued by young men, but from No. 17, "Oh My How Sweetly Pretty", a circle of women admiring a child, the wit is in the ludicrous circumstance rather than in the ludicrous visage.

All of these are in the vignette style of contemporary French work and in No. 36, "Well! pray who are you?", one finds the central figure of a dandified shop assistant the closest yet to Parisian draughtsmanship (Colour Plate 2, page 37). This set also has one of his earliest equestrian works "Kicking up a dust" which is also his earliest reference to railways. *Droll Doings* has mostly domestic scenes. No. 14, "A Tender Question", is related to a Seymour subject,[15] but with all the venom extracted from it, the flirtatious lady in yellow and the simpering man in blue, echoed by a picture of nudging asses on the wall behind them (Colour Plate 3, page 37). The colour can be quite vivid and certainly helps along both the flat captions and the occasionally weak draughtsmanship.

The set undertaken for W. Soffe of 380 The Strand, were probably the latest. They include domestic incidents, confrontations between shopkeepers and urchins (a recurring Leech theme), old maids, dandies and hen-pecked husbands. It is this latter subject, a well-tried Daumier preoccupation, that comes closest of all to Daumier's style in execution. A pair of timid husbands consult one another on a wind lashed pavement as "Companions in Misfortune" (opposite). Cowed by the weather and their wives, they stand with slightly bent knees, facing each other, the left hand man framed in the curve of his open and dripping umbrella. Leech, like Daumier, has made great play with the diagonals of slanting rain, the clothing moulded by shading and following the natural circle of the vignette. Two "umbrella" subjects by Daumier appeared in 1835, "Le Tour du Parapluie" and "La Pluie Jour de Visites" in his series "Plaisirs de l'hiver", which Leech might have seen.

Leech seems to have kept abreast with Parisian work throughout the 1840s. In fact some of the most striking comparisons can be made in the middle of that decade. In the Spring of 1845, the artist was asked to illustrate some of "Mrs Caudle's Curtain Lectures" in

15. "Mr. Viggins..." in *Sketches by Seymour,* published by T. Fry, n.d.

COMPANIONS IN MISFORTUNE.
___ Peckover! my boy! why the duce dont you put up your Umbrella?
God bless you, Figgins! I'm going to fetch M.rs P. from Chapel; and if the
Umbrella got wet I should never hear the last of it.__ But where are you off to?
__Why, you see, I'm just taking a little walk, because M.rs F. has got company.

"Companions in Misfortune." Lithograph coloured by hand, one of the series of Soffe's humorous sketches by Leech, 1837-38. Signed with the wriggling line.

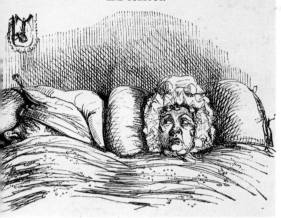

MRS. CAUDLE'S CURTAIN LECTURES.

LECTURE VIII.

CAUDLE HAS BEEN MADE A MASON.—MRS. CAUDLE INDIGNANT
AND CURIOUS.

"Mrs Caudle's Curtain Lectures."
Vignette illustration for Punch,
1845.

Punch, a suburban story by Douglas Jerrold, in which the misanthropic Mrs Caudle delivers nightly monologues to her hen-pecked husband. Ideal subjects for Leech's pencil, it was he who was responsible for the most famous of the narrative's scenes. The couple are shown in bed, Job Caudle turns away from his wife with his nose just over the sheet, while Mrs Caudle, wakeful and disgruntled, looks at us full face (left). This illustration was so popular that Leech turned it into a single lithograph, which with a pair, was sold for a shilling coloured (below). The origin of this design can be found in Daumier's "Les Moeurs Conjugales", No. 29, which had appeared in *Charivari* in November, 1840 (opposite). The French couple lie in much the same way as their English counterparts, the husband to the left, the wife to the right, their heads embosomed in the pillow in a similar fashion, the nose of the man a more visible version of the Leech nose. The very sketchiness achievable with the lithograph makes the point, but the prints are also alike in atmosphere. The

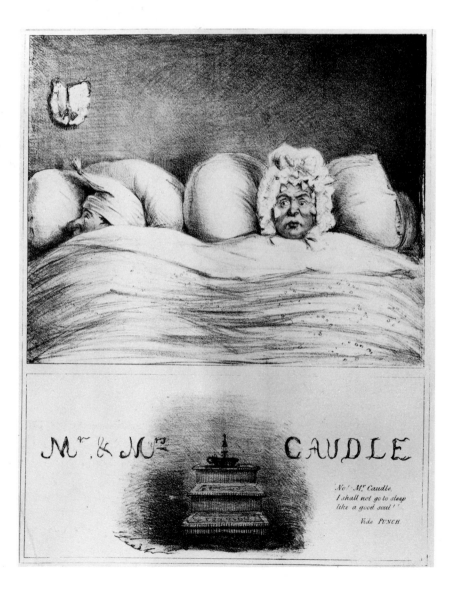

"Mr and Mrs Caudle". Separately issued lithograph coloured by hand, drawn to meet popular demand, 1845.

"Les Moeurs Conjugales", No. 29 by Honoré Daumier, 1808-1879. This caricature appeared in Charivari, *November 1840, and must have influenced Leech.*
Hammer Foundation

"Le Tailleur" by Honoré Daumier, 1808-1879. Daumier's satires of bourgeois life had a strong influence on Leech's style.

spontaneous and sketchy hand that Leech was developing was a direct inheritance from the French, where it reached its height in Daumier (above and left), Gavarni, Doré and Guys. Although English wood engravers tightened up Leech's free lines, they interpreted them closely enough in the backgrounds for this rapidity of observation to be communicated. The Victorians were always commenting on the naturalism in these backgrounds, a French feature unique to Leech. In 1848, we find the artist actually imitating Daumier in a free rendering of the French caricaturist's famous villain "Robert Macaire" (see illustration overleaf).

In the last of these caricature series, *The Human Face Divine and De Vino,* he has returned much more to the British caricature of contrasts. As it happens we know a lot about the circumstances in which these groups of prints were produced. In 1838, immediately after Leech's twenty-first birthday, he was induced, through his usual generosity, to accept an accommodation bill; the drawer being

RESIGNATION OF LOUIS-PHILIPPE.

"Ah! c'est ce bon tricolor! Tu ne vaux plus rien, mon ami, comme drapeau—N'importe! Tu ne me quitteras jamais—comme mouchoir."

An illustration of "Robert Macaire" by John Leech, which appeared in Punch *in 1848. "Macaire" was one of the supreme inventions of Daumier.*

"Constancy." Lithography by Lefevre, coloured by hand, one of the series of Soffe's humorous sketches by Leech, 1837-38. Signed with the wriggling line and "delt".

unable to pay, the young artist was promptly detained. He was placed in a sponging house in Newman Street kept by a Mr Levy, a sheriff's officer, and remained there a fortnight. Inside, he managed to support himself "by drawing cartoons and caricatures" according to Percival Leigh, designing them on stone for Spooner at a guinea each, "a friend having negotiated their sale".[16] The friend was certainly Leigh, the lithographer was almost certainly Lefevre of that same Newman Street, whose imprint appears on most of the early caricatures (see illustration below).

There is no hint in any of them of the artist being under pressure or hurried, indeed Leech recounted elsewhere that he spent part of his detention kissing pretty girls through a grille![17] But perhaps he already knew that an advance from the publisher Richard Bentley would be sufficient to liberate him.

The benevolent Dickens must have been working behind the scenes for the young artist. As Editor of *Bentley's Miscellany,* in which *Oliver Twist* was then appearing, he would have had considerable

CONSTANCY

Leave you dear girl !! never_ never ___ (while you have a shilling)

16. Frith, op. cit., Vol. 1, p. 92.

17. Henry Silver Diary, *Punch* Office, 1 February, 1860.

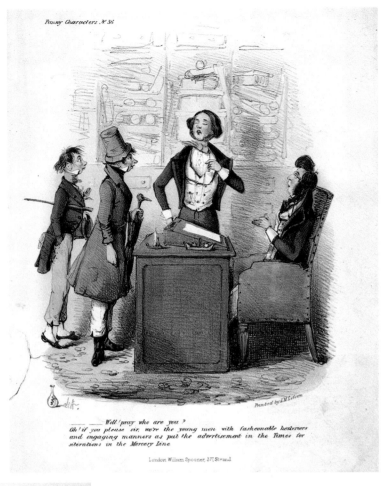

Colour Plate 2. "Well! pray who are you?" Lithograph coloured by hand, one of the series Funny Characters, *1837-38. It is signed by a leech in a bottle and shows the French influence in the artist's work.*

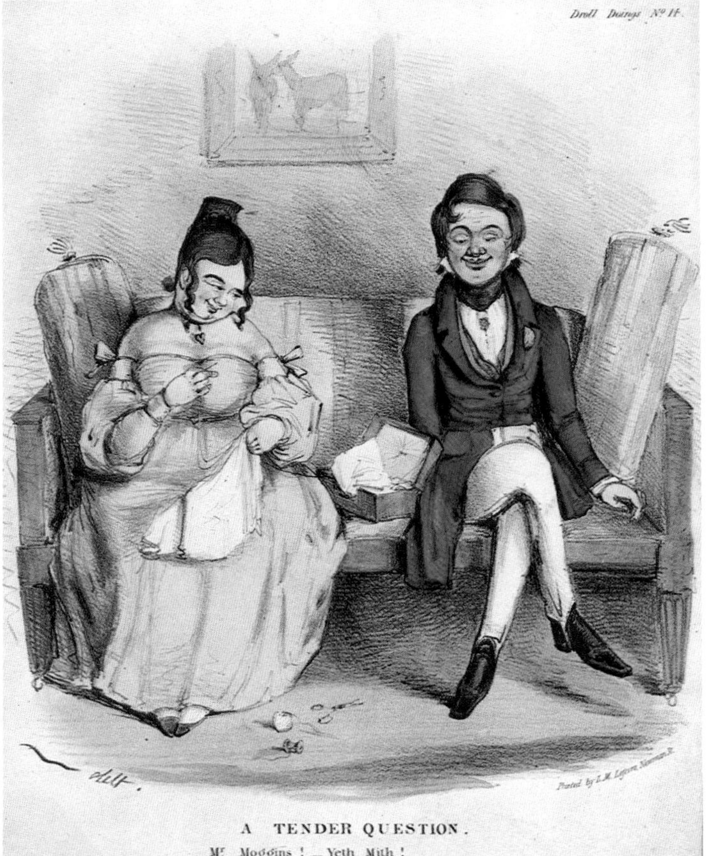

Funny Characters No 36
Well! pray who are you?
Oh! if you please sir, we're the young men with fasheenable hexteriors and engaging manners as put the advertisement in the Times for alterations in the Mercery Line
London William Spooner, 377, Strand

Droll Doings No 14
A TENDER QUESTION.
Mr Moggins! _ Yeth Mith!
Wos you hever in love, Mr Moggins?
London. W. Spooner, 377, Strand.

Colour Plate 3. "A Tender Question." Lithograph coloured by hand, one of the series Droll Doings, *1837-38. It is signed by the wriggling line, signifying a leech.*

18. Bentley Papers, British Museum, Add MSS 46613.
19. Barham, R.H., *Life of the Rev. R.H. Barham,* Vol. 2, p. 67.
20. *Illuminated Magazine,* Vol. 2, 1844.

influence with the publisher. In October 1837, Richard Bentley drew up a contract with Leech[18] for a work called "The Modern Rakes Progress" with a text by R.H. Barham. Leech gives no fixed address on this document (he was probably detained) but agreed to supply an etching on steel "in his best style" for five guineas with the promise of more illustrations at the same price. Barham describes Leech as "no more than a boy" but showing great talent, and adds that although the work was not published, the plates eventually came out elsewhere.[19] Leech must have regarded that first five guineas as a godsend to him.

A visual and verbal postscript to this nasty incident in the sponging-house can be found in the magazine story of six years later (see below).[20] Leech's drawing, so often autobiographical, shows a young man detained for debt as Mr Moses Levy of Newman Street steps into his bedroom. The text amply describes Leech's predicament — "Few birds liked a sponging-house for four months, and would come down handsomely to gat [*sic*] away; but if he stayed, no matter, the officer was sure of a good haul either way; three pence for a glass of water, sixpence for a sheet of paper, a shilling for porterage every letter we carried to the post, noble profits."

"The arrest of Peter Cockerell by Mr Levy." Illustration to The Illustrated Magazine, *1844.*

A fashion illustration by Gavarni.

Shortly afterwards there was a similar detention in Cursitor Street and Leigh adds: "From that period to the close of his life he remained subject to repeated demands for pecuniary assistance under continued pressure, which at the outset, he could not withstand."[21] Although there is no direct evidence for it, it seems likely that the bill was accepted on behalf of his *father* and that from this time onwards he was more or less maintaining the failed coffee-house keeper and his wife. He would certainly have had to support his brother and sisters, all younger than himself, and this coupled with the father's indigence, meant that Leech was burdened by others' debts and over-work from the very outset. These must be the "distressing family affairs" referred to darkly by Millais which worried the artist "beyond endurance".[22]

* * * * *

But fresh opportunities were opening up for him as a result of these lithographs. The one inheritance from the Regency which did survive the change in taste for more sober prints, was the burlesquing of new fashions in dress. Immediately after Waterloo, George Cruikshank had brilliantly satirised both male and female costume in his "Monstrosities" and Robert Cruikshank and William Heath had portrayed the age of the dandies with their absurdly high collars, tight coats, cauliflower frills and eye-glasses. Some of these exquisites, with their grotesque heads, emaciated bodies and bursting stays, were a little coarse for early Victorian England, but so many Victorians were Regency men at heart, that the genre was bound to survive and in Leech more than in most. The French fashion plates created the right spring-board for this satire; the French caricaturist Gavarni was a fashion illustrator for *Le Journal des Gens du Monde*, 1831, so that the humour and accuracy in costume caricature often went together. Leech was very quick to spot this and produced in 1840, a witty explosion of designs entitled *The Fiddle Faddle Fashion Book and Beau Monde A La Française* containing "numerous Highly-Coloured Figures of Lady-Like Gentlemen". The text was by his friend Leigh and the engraved plates showed a sort of unisex costume where dandies in ringlets and waisted coats actually appeared like women! (See illustration page 41.)

The engraved line was too harsh a medium for Leech's delicate art. *Fiddle Faddle* is actually less influenced by the new French style than the other works and the reason is not far to seek. After introducing the young man to Dickens, George Cruikshank gave him lessons in etching at about this time.[23] The results of this, more savage caricatures, are in the fashion book. Perhaps Leech felt that a mastery of etching on steel opened up greater opportunities among the publishers. His turning away from it to wood engraving may have prompted some unfriendly remarks about him by Cruikshank. "Yes, yes, very clever," he remarked to Frith, "The new school, you see. Public always taken with novelty."[24]

Daumier's gestural style was strongly influenced by the theatre and

21. Frith, op. cit., Vol. 1, p. 93.
22. Evans Letters, Houghton Library, Harvard, MS Eng 1028. Letter from Millais, 31 October, 1882.
23. Frith, op. cit., Vol. 1, p. 76.
24. Frith, op. cit., Vol. 1, p. 20.

Illustration from The Comic English Grammar, *1840.*

HELIOGABALUS.

Illustration from The Comic Latin Grammar, *1840.*

25. Charterhouse School.

26. *The Dickensian,* Vol. 34, 1937-38, p. 6.

27. Ray, Gordon, *The Letters & Private Papers of W.M. Thackeray,* Vol. 3, p. 363.

28. Barham, op. cit., Vol. 2, pp. 15-16.

Leech's work has a similar quality to it. An ardent theatre-goer all his life, one of the earliest of the artist's surviving drawings[25] is of J.P. Harley, the actor, in the leading part of Dickens' play *The Strange Gentleman,* 1836-37. This was issued as a single caricature print in coloured lithograph, receiving the comment from Dickens "I think he has not got the face well, or the hat," but "the general character is very good."[26] There seems little doubt that Leech was feeling his way through French caricatures, the fashion plate, the stage play, to where his own works would develop an easy composition and a coherent harmony. The single figure was too facile and the grotesque head too savage for his fastidious pencil and sensitive wit. In a letter of some years later, Thackeray explains to a correspondent that Leech "prefers a multitude of figures",[27] a fair enough comment on an artist mirroring society rather than individuals.

Probably among the last of this early series of lithographs was the print issued on 20 June, 1840. "The Regicide Pot Boy — The Patriotic Imitator of France" is a nationalistic lithograph that imitates French caricature but parodies French republicanism. After the attempt on the life of Queen Victoria on 10 June, 1840, the culprit is shown in all his gross imbecility, sporting revolutionary favours. Leech was intensely loyal and intensely monarchistic; this was to be only the first in a number of such outbursts of patriotic indignation.

The disappointing start to his association with Bentley had improved with the final appearance of Theodore Hook's *Jack Brag* in 1837, his first major book, but the author criticised the designs to Barham who wrote that "the figure of Jack was not at all what he [Hook] meant; he intended him to be a smart, dapper little fellow, and though imprudent and vulgar, not bad-looking."[28] An inability to stick close to other men's texts was to be a besetting sin of Leech's! A much greater opportunity came his way in 1840 however when he took his place beside George Cruikshank as second illustrator to him in *Bentley's Miscellany,* engraving his way through Barham's *Ingoldsby Legends, Richard Savage, Mr Ledbury* and the *Marchioness of Brinvilliers.* As literature they are apart from the first, totally unmemorable. Barham's whimsical legends could have been the ideal catalyst for Leech's humour, but the steel plate on which Bentley insisted was not, as already mentioned, his medium. Paid advances of £45 (£7 for square subjects and £6 for vignettes, and 25/- for woodblocks), Leech was earning good money. But the work looks backwards to George Cruikshank and in particular to books such as *Three Points of Humour,* 1823, or *Three Courses and A Dessert,* 1830.

More suitable to his pencil were the verbal explosions of his friend Percival Leigh, by now also a Bentley author. Leigh's humour which revolved round the pun, was very well adapted to the early Victorian taste for funny text books, the nineteenth century prelude to *1066 and All That.* The worse the puns the more the Victorians loved them and Leech's beautiful designs are really the only things in these volumes that excite one today. The first for Bentley was *The Comic*

An engraved plate from The Fiddle Faddle Fashion Book and Beau Monde A La Française, *1840. Steel engraving coloured by hand.*

"...the young gentleman who do the lovers at the wells."

English Grammar: A New and Facetious Introduction to the English Tongue, published 1840. Leech supplied fifty illustrations to this, the majority of them wood engravings and mostly taken from contemporary scenes which were his forte. There is a tremendous advance on the crude work for *Bell's Sporting Life* done a few years earlier, and one does not have to seek far for an explanation.

J. Orrin Smith, the wood engraver, had begun to give Leech instruction in about 1838-39. Smith was a friend of Kenny Meadows, a collaborator who paid him more than he did his illustrator! Leigh actually describes this tuition as going on for "a twelvemonth or thereabouts" with the cunning Smith getting free work out of his brilliant pupil.[29] The illustrations to *The Comic English Grammar* are clear and clean wood engravings. There is a delicacy of touch in the detail and hatching which is not lost and an excellent balance of light and shade. Some designs look back to the comic lithographs, the best look forward to *Punch* and contain that combination of humour and compassion which typifies mature Leech. Particularly good from this aspect are "Comical Conjunction", "Apple Sauce" and "the young gentleman who do the lovers at the Wells" (left).

The Comic Latin Grammar, also of 1840, was published by Charles Tilt, but is a slightly less appealing volume. There are eight Leech etchings, several very boldly handled in the Cruikshank manner, and a multitude of tiny vignettes, derived in spirit from *Hood's Comic Annual*. A note at the end lists twenty further titles to be issued from Leigh's unquenchable pen including "A Laughable System of Logic", "Jokes on Geology", "Optical Oddities" and "The Pneumatic Jest Book"; the delight of the Victorians in all this was apparently insatiable. *The Comic Latin Grammar* made a considerable impact. Leech's father was obviously impressed when he wrote to the artist's sister in Dublin on 11th December, 1839. "It has turned out a most decided Hit. A second edition is in print already. The first 2,000 copies sold immediately. Mr. P. Leigh and John are on a sudden become famous." (Letter in Reading University Collection.)

Another success and a much more publicised one was Leech's *Comic Envelope* of 1840. He was beginning to have the swift reactions of the illustrative humorist to current events, and the talk of that year was about Sir Rowland Hill's newly introduced Penny Post. William Mulready RA had been commissioned to design a sort of universal envelope with symbolic images of the peace, plenty and comunication which the new service would bring. The design was altogether too ponderous, a Britannia at the top signalling to east and west, angels flying and chinamen and redskins receiving their mail. Leech could hardly resist this and Fores published his version in which a bloated Britannia sat above a blindfold lion, top-hatted postmen hang in the sky, postboys beat their horses and a chinaman pulls a long nose across the page (see illustration opposite). London was amused, but not so Mulready, who thought the artist's sign-manual of a leech in a bottle, was a personal snub to himself; it was ten years before he was reconciled to Leech.

29. Frith, op. cit., Vol. 1, p. 76.

"Fores's Comic Envelopes No. 1.", 1840, a parody of the envelope designed by William Mulready RA for the General Post Office.

Another chance, even more in accord with his gentle style of satire came his way this year and was published the next, *The Children of the Mobility Drawn From Nature by J. Leech* (see illustrations on pages 44 and 45). Here the artist went back to lithography to produce for Richard Bentley a humorous look at street arabs under the guise of the peerage. London children are given mock coats of arms and invented pedigrees to parody the fashion for books on noble families, yet at the same time they are treated with sympathy and affection. In these illustrations, so strongly characterised that they recall the style of Gavarni, Leech shows the children of Irish immigrants, Italian instrumentalists and chimney-sweeps, forcing comparisons that Mayhew was to point out in the 'fifties. Leech's own life, the absence of ready money, the accommodation in garrets, left a lasting impression on him, even when his fortunes were changing.

The present was taking on a different complexion, he signed two favourable contracts with Bentley in the space of eighteen months, the one for *Bentley's Miscellany* bringing £95 in advances and the other for *The Wassail Bowl* with £31 10s in advances and £51 10s for 81 wood engravings.[30] Despite this, he was continuing to borrow

30. Bentley Papers, op. cit.

CHILDREN OF THE MOBILITY. PL. 5.

LONDON, PUBLISHED BY RICHARD BENTLEY, NEW BURLINGTON S^T FEBRUARY, 1, 1841

Children of the Mobility, *Plate 5. Leech produced this book for Bentley in 1841, satirising the annuals and drawing attention to the children of the London streets. Lithograph.*

CHILDREN OF THE MOBILITY. PL. 8.

LONDON, PUBLISHED BY RICHARD BENTLEY, NEW BURLINGTON S^T FEBRUARY. 1,1841.

Printed by J.R. Jobbins

Children of the Mobility, *Plate 8. Another street scene in the series. Leech like Thackeray takes the intimate view-point and observes compassionately. In this lithograph both a Punch and Judy show and an infant funeral take place together in the background.*

Two illustrations from The Comic Latin Grammar, *1840.*

HALF-AND-HALF.

31. Dimsdale Collection (see Note 1).
32. ibid.

from the publisher, could not gain independence from creditors and was locked into a circle of loans, rent arrears, more work and more loans.

His relaxation was to get away from London into the country and enjoy the company of young Charley Adams in a natter about horses. Adams, with an acute nose for business had decided to take up land surveying. He had gone down to Hertfordshire to play understudy to Anthony Jackson of Barkway near Royston, managing and advising the great estates in that area and dabbling in the latest profitable venture, acquisitions of land for the railway. The country life suited Adams very well; coincidentally Barkway was in the heart of the Puckeridge Hunt, a rolling wooded country, webbed by small lanes and with some very fine hedges. There were also romantic entanglements and Leech would not have been very surprised in August 1839 to learn that Charley had made a runaway marriage with a Miss Elizabeth Sibley, and now that her family were pacified, the couple were living happily together at Buntingford. In December 1841 Leech wrote to Charley from his lodgings in Judd Street, Brunswick Square, asking for £25 urgently. ''I don't want to lay myself (just now when I am getting independent of them) under obligation to Publishers, and therefore as I think you about the most likely man I know (having the power) to do a disinterested kindness I apply to you ...''[31] Charley could not help this time and Leech replied from temporary lodgings shared with Percival Leigh.[32]

13 Chapel Place
Cavendish Square

My dear Charley,

I have luckily obtained some 'filthy rooms' to go on with else I had been in a pretty fix — You can have no idea how I have been bothered the last few days moving — at the very last moment I found that the rooms I had engaged could not be got ready for me until next week thereby completely throwing me out, and obliging me to come here, where I am stopping with my friend Leigh, the illustrious author of 'The Comic Latin Grammar' — Believe me my dear Charley as regards the loan, I take your will for the deed — I know if it had been in your power you would have helped me — and that assurance prompts me to say that if you can *spare* ten pounds in a few days I should be glad if you would let me have it — for I should then be able with what I have to muddle on till the middle of next month, but don't worry yourself about the matter — Treat me as an old friend who will give you credit for the best feelings and intentions — Now mind that —

I most sincerely hope that your wife will get safely through her confinement and that the result will be satisfactory to you and your friends — Talking of confinements — I am thinking seriously of getting spliced myself — I begin to find single blessedness anything but agreeable —

indeed, witnessing your domestic felicity has set me about *bettering* myself — Heaven send us all good ending. I have often reproached myself for not having sent the Grammars & other works to you — you shall have them soon — I have lately got much promise for my part in Hood's Comic Annual, which perhaps you have seen advertised. I should like you to see it — I think it one of the best things I have done. . . . .

Yours Faithfully
John Leech

Adams happily obliged with the request and may have smiled over Leech's disenchantment with the bachelor life. Leigh was a brilliant man to collaborate with but not so congenial to live with if W.J. Linton's memories are to be believed. Linton, then approaching his heights as an engraver, was summoned from his bed in Judd Street in the early 'forties, to attend the local police station. There he found Leech, fairly sober, supporting Leigh, quite drunk, both detained for jostling a passer-by. The following day Linton helped to bail them out. At the court hearing a police sergeant, recognising the artist who looked a bit pale, shouted out "Like a leech sir?".[33]

One drab lodging after another did not appeal to the family instincts of John Leech, the success of the *Grammars* and the envelope made him more determined to settle. At twenty-four, his youthful skinniness had gone and he was extremely prepossessing to look at, tall, broad and with a Roman head of curly brown hair, side whiskers and bright blue eyes (left).[34] It was only a question of time before he met the right girl, typically for an artist who was ever observing and remembering, he met her face to face in the street. So fascinating was this young woman that John trailed her all the way to her door and then got an introduction.

Annie Viola Eaton, was an almost archetypal beauty of the 'forties. Dark-haired with a trim figure and big black eyes, she must have seemed to Leech the very original of the sibyls who stared out of the *Books of Beauty* and *Drawing-Room Scrapbooks*. Annie or Ann was a year or so younger than John, having been baptised on 10 December, 1818.[35] She was the only daughter and eldest child of Charles and Anne Eaton of Knutton near Wolstanton in Staffordshire, where her father had owned a farm. After becoming a widow before 1834, Mrs Anne Eaton had continued to live at Knutton and her daughter was probably visiting London friends when Leech saw her in late 1841. A whirlwind courtship resulted in Annie Eaton being brought to the altar in the month of May 1842 and the artist establishing himself in grander circumstances at 9 Powis Place, Queen Square.[36] What kind of wife was Miss Eaton to make for the big, gentle caricaturist whose heart she had captured? Her graceful body and fragile prettiness were to become Leech's *ne plus ultra* of the British girl, decorating a thousand of his engravings and delighting a whole generation from Frith and Millais to Dickens and Thackeray. She absolutely lionised her husband, making his life

A self-portrait in chalk, about 1838.
Garrick Club

33. Linton, W.J., *Memoirs*, 1895, pp. 59-60.

34. The reputed self-portrait at the Garrick Club shows him at this age.

35. Information from Staffordshire County Record Office.

36. Caroline Leech refers to the marriage as May 1843 which must be incorrect but adds that the new house was chosen by Mr. Leech. Leech albums, op. cit.

as comfortable and conformable as possible, but she was said to be silly and empty-headed, though Dickens and others tolerated her. Her presence in his work certainly does not diminish it and we have to be thankful for her benevolent influence.

Six months before he met Annie Eaton, another event occurred that was to equally change his destiny, a new magazine was born. In about 1839, a few gentlemen in the Orrin Smith circle including Douglas Jerrold, Thackeray and Leigh, had mooted a new satirical magazine to be called The London Charivari, based on the Parisian one to which the admired Daumier contributed. The artists were to be Kenny Meadows, Leech and possibly Alfred Crowquill. This idea got no further than discussion, but a year later the same plan was considered by Mark Lemon, Henry Mayhew, Joseph Last and Ebenezer Landells, the wood engraver. Their scheme came to fruition and the new journal appeared on 17 July, 1841. Leech was not among the artists, but Leigh was all ready to introduce him. On that first morning as the presses pounded away and Landells strolled up and down outside the Strand office, they learnt incredulously that ten thousand copies had been sold. *Punch* had arrived on the stage.

Chapter Three

PUNCH'S FAVOURITE MAN

eech's adoption by the young men of *Punch* was not a foregone conclusion in the summer of 1841; the writers were not prepared to accept the artists as their equals and Leech was merely the friend of Percival Leigh. Lemon and his friends (who were not known for their understanding of the visual arts) had enlisted a bevy of second rank artists for the magazine. There was A.S. Henning,[1] a rather weak draughtsman, Brine[2] who pretended to know about figure drawing and H.G. Hine[3] who was really a landscape painter. The only real humourist among them was William Newman who contributed tiny woodcuts called "blackies" for the page endings, and *he* was considered uncouth by the proprietors.

Leech was given his opportunity in the fourth issue of *Punch* on 7 August, 1841, to draw the main satirical page subject known as "Punch's Pencillings". These large scale caricatures were based on the French models, where one lithograph formed the hub of the magazine. For his debut Leech chose a page of jottings of foreign characters to be seen in the neighbourhood of Leicester Square, sallow artists with goatee beards, musicians with tousled hair and the like. The page entitled "Foreign Affairs" is not Leech at his best. In fact the original drawing (see illustration page 31) has faint similarities with the work of John Doyle, "HB".[4] Leech's famous sign-manual of a leech in a bottle, appears in a small scroll at the centre.[5]

"Foreign Affairs" was a failure, not because of the drawing, but due to the slapdash way in which Leech organised his time. Misjudging the amount of work involved, Leech sent his drawing on the wood block so late to the engravers, that it was impossible to engrave it to meet the publishing deadline. In consequence *Punch* did not appear on time, distribution failed and there was a serious fall in that week's circulation.[6] Leigh must have been furious, although it was impossible to be angry for long with the ingenuous and gentle artist. They were all to learn later on that although Leech worked best under pressure, he was always inclined to be unpunctual. Nevertheless the proprietors were not pleased and even less pleased when shortly afterwards he tried to get a higher price for his work. Consequently there was little *Punch* work in 1841; not a very encouraging start.

Between January 1842 and December 1843, that is throughout the four volumes following *Punch's* inauguration, Leech steadily re-

1. Archibald Samuel Henning (d. 1864) the brother-in-law of Kenny Meadows.

2. Studied with T. Woolner and A. Elmore.

3. Henry George Hine (1811-1895) RI 1864, and VPRI 1888-95.

4. Charterhouse School.

5. From 1837 Leech was using the signature of a leech in a bottle.

6. Frith, W.P., *John Leech His Life and Work,* 1891, Vol. 2, p. 3.

THE STARVED-OUT ALDERMEN.

DREADFUL CASE OF DESTITUTION.

instated himself with the editor and his fellows. In the summer of 1842 he was being given what he was best at, social satire, linked to a story or a paragraph. These included some "Social Miseries" on quack doctors, debt collectors and ghastly juveniles, the last of which was to establish itself as a recurring Leechian theme. The artist worked best in total independence or with a tale to which he felt sympathetic, so that late in 1842, Albert Smith's racy and piquant *Physiology of the London Idler* was a superb opportunity. Through eleven instalments the artist could depict the metropolitan characters he liked most, dilapidated dandies, coffee-house loungers, rustic and foreign visitors, cheeky urchins with their fingers to their noses. *Side Scenes* followed in 1843 with further witticisms from the epigrammatic Smith and loaded sketches of parvenus, servants and pretty society girls from Leech. The separate illustrated joke was only just appearing in 1842-3 (there are two or three by him in *Literary Chit-Chat* for example) but as yet there was no scope in genre illustration, where he was to become the master.

From December 1842 with the "French Fox" Leech was involved with the main political cuts in *Punch,* although it was July 1843 before he was regularly contributing to the most topical of Punch's Pencillings, beginning with "Rebecca and Her Daughters". This return coincided with an event which is quite important in the history of caricature and with which Leech is closely connected. In the July of 1843, the exhibition of "cartoons" for decorating the Houses of Parliament was held at Westminster Hall, and *Punch* celebrated this great jingoistic event by producing satirical "cartoons" of its own. This began on July 15th with "Substance and Shadow" by Leech, the hungry and indigent of London looking on at the exhibition designs. It is captioned "Cartoon No 1" and a further five of these "cartoons" follow. Until that moment, cartoon had meant a design for a large picture, now it *began* to mean a large political satire, the word tripped off the tongue more easily than "Punch's Pencillings". The new usage only came in slowly. In 1895, cartoon was described as "a large full-page or double-page block of a satirical nature, usually placed in the middle opening of the paper, and for the most part still dignified by being 'unbacked' by other printing".[7] Leech, the great innovator in visual terms, was also the instigator of a verbal change.

The reason that Leech's popularity still hung fire was partly due to the nature of *Punch* and the fact that his colleagues did not understand his genius. The "cartoons" were the joint decisions of the *Punch* table and came to be discussed over a weekly dinner on Saturdays when the magazine was made up. This consensus was more in the hands of Jerrold, Lemon and the Mayhews in the early days and between 1845 and 1847, Leech proposed only eleven subjects himself. He was far less fluent in this world of political satire, than in the unmasking of the comedy of manners and it is difficult to imagine that he was much in sympathy with Jerrold's radicalism or the Mayhews' appeal to the lower middle class.[8] But he was enough *their* man in 1845 to show The Queen and Prince Albert (whom he

7. Spielmann, M.H., *The History of "Punch",* 1895, p. 188.
8. Henry Silver Diary, *Punch* Office, 27 May, 1863. Silver actually records that there were "noisy Punch dinners" because of this.

"The Momentous Question." Punch cartoon, 1845, one of the rare occasions in which Leech satirised Queen Victoria and Prince Albert.

THE MOMENTOUS QUESTION.

"TELL ME, OH TELL ME, DEAREST ALBERT, HAVE *YOU* ANY RAILWAY SHARES?"

WHOLESOME PREJUDICE.

" RAILROADS, SIR ! I HATE RAILROADS, AND I SHALL BE VERY GLAD WHEN THEY'RE DONE AWAY WITH, AND WE'VE GOT THE COACHES AGAIN."

disliked) in unfavourable circumstances during the Railway Mania and its subsequent collapse (above). The continual caricatures of Lord Brougham with his "bottle-nose" are rather repetitive, but once the artist can set his scene in the domestic world, his territory, we begin to be amused.

In June 1843, *Punch* acquired what it had hitherto lacked, a writer of social satire equal to Leech's skill as a humorous draughtsman. W.M. Thackeray, versatile columnist and erstwhile illustrator, moved into the magazine's pages with "Miss Tickletoby's Lectures on English History". Thackeray remembered Leech from Charterhouse and a friendship was resumed. Thackeray's earliest efforts in the magazine were no more successful than the artist's had been, but once he had found his forte, social satirising, there was no holding him. Leech was to be strongly influenced by this writer, who had

Angelina. "WILL MY DARLING EDWIN GRANT HIS ANGELINA A BOON?"
Edwin. "IS THERE ANYTHING ON EARTH HER EDWIN WOULD NOT DO FOR HIS PET?—NAME THE BOON, OH, DEAREST—NAME IT!"
Angelina. "THEN, LOVE, AS WE DINE BY OURSELVES TO-MORROW, LET US, OH! LET US HAVE ROAST PORK, WITH PLENTY OF SAGE AND ONIONS!"

9. Forster Collection, Victoria and Albert Museum Library, Forster 354, 48 B 28 and 48 E 4. The sketch is reproduced by permission of the Victoria and Albert Museum.

such a developed visual sense. Thackeray, weak draughtsman that he was, nonetheless took on mannerisms of Leech.

One reason why John Leech's sketches began to hit the public's imagination was that he typified himself as the Victorian householder, the family man whose aspirations were precisely those of hundreds of the magazine's devotees. His manners and life style were always most engagingly unpretentious, his preferences were for solid and wholesome food, good wine, comfort rather than luxury and entertainment round his own hearth. Early in 1845, he and Annie had made a move from Bloomsbury to Hammersmith, a move into the rather sylvan atmosphere of a quiet suburb, the furthest distance from the West End that they were ever to go. They had almost certainly been encouraged to settle there by Mark Lemon, *Punch's* Editor, who had moved into a smug turretted villa at No 12, Brook Green in 1843. The Leechs moved in next door at No 10 and began a new life in what was then a middle class backwater. Leech was obviously enjoying the fresh sights and sounds, observing the niceties of Victorian bourgeois customs at first hand and transcribing them into his highly autobiographical weekly drawings. Lemon's house, which had a weather vane, was humorously christened "Palazzo della Pineapple", Leech's was given no name but he was clearly amused at being a "villa dweller" from the tone of a letter to John Forster.[9]

> Brook Green
> Hammersmith
> Friday.

My dear Forster,

I shall calculate upon the pleasure of your company to dinner on Monday next at five o'clock unless I hear from you to the contrary — Dickens I trust understood that he was expected — If you do not come with him you had better bear in mind that our house or rather box is "eligibly suitable" opposite some alms houses at the corner of Cornwall Road the Brook Green end. Our predecessor was pleased to call it Gelert House. — To prevent mistakes I subjoin a representation thereof.

[The sketch illustrated in the margin]

a. the grand entrance
b. palings
c. summer house
d. Brook Green

I hope nothing will prevent you coming until I see you, and afterwards.

> Believe me
> Yours Faithfully
> John Leech

It was no unfortunate accident that Douglas Jerrold's brilliant papers on "Mrs Caudle" began in the magazine at this time, nor that they became part of the popular mythology of London. Even after Jerrold and Leech had dropped her, Mrs Caudle was still being featured on the provincial stages of the theatre.

Leech's arrival in the suburbs had also coincided with Sir James Graham's order for calling out the Militia in early 1846. Leech joined and was able to have a wealth of fun at the expense of these over-domesticated, inept and under-courageous amateur soldiers in "The Brook Green Militia Man". This stunted little householder, with his musical comedy uniform, tries his prowess as a marksman in his backyard surrounded by geese, donkeys and screaming children. The text says "The gallant fellow of Brook Green, who has already voluntarily undergone the exertions of a review, and the honours of a bivouac, has been accustoming himself to a laceration of his feelings by rehearsing a parting from the wife of his bosom." Leech imagines him in every conceivable situation in his sleepy street, intoxicated but with bayonet fixed, doing double duty with his wife and baby beside him, and being presented with colours (an old shirt tied to a stick)! In the last Leech's trim villa is visible in the background (see illustration below). The Militia Man is never seen without his umbrella and pipe, even in the direst emergency, and through Leech becomes the stereo-type of all the cartoonists who have looked at the volunteers of Victorian times or the Home Guard in our own.

In 1848, still in Brook Green, Leech and Mark Lemon enlisted as Special Constables during the Chartist Rally of that year. Leech obviously entered into the spirit of the occasion, highly amused by the mobilisation of his clerkly neighbours and their stern claims of

PRESENTATION OF COLOURS TO THE BROOK GREEN VOLUNTEER.

THE GREAT TENTH OF APRIL, 1848.

Special Constable. "NOW MIND, YOU KNOW—IF I KILL YOU, IT'S NOTHING; BUT IF YOU KILL ME, BY JINGO, IT'S MURDER."

DOMESTIC BLISS.

Wife of your Bussum. "OH I DON'T WANT TO INTERRUPT YOU, DEAR. I ONLY WANT SOME MONEY FOR BABY'S SOCKS—AND TO KNOW WHETHER YOU WILL HAVE THE MUTTON COLD OR HASHED."

10. Dimsdale Collection, 17 April, 1848.

the Englishman's home being his castle. In one *Punch* engraving, he shows a diminutive "Special" waving a large baton at a huge specimen of working class manhood "Now mind, you know," he threatens, "if I kill you, its nothing; but if you kill me, by Jove! it's murder!" (left). Leech always aimed at fairness and probably had some sympathy with the protesters. In a letter to Charles Adams, he sets down his experiences: "Old Mark and I were Special Constables on Monday last — you would have laughed to see us on duty — trying the area gates, &c., &c. — Mark continually finding excuses to take a small glass of ale, or brandy and water — Policeman's duty tho is no joke, I had to patrol about from ten at night until one in the morning — and heartily sick of it I was! It was only my loyalty and extreme like of peace and order that made me stand it."[10]

That was exactly Leech's stance, patriotic, prepared to champion the under-dog on occasion or stand up for the commonsense view, but essentially apolitical. As Jerrold and Mayhew became lesser stars in the *Punch* galaxy and Thackeray gained the upper hand, Leech's sketches became more and more in accord with the readers; no longer radicals, but businessmen in the suburbs, lawyers, doctors and the inhabitants of vicarages and colleges. As a "family" paper, *Punch* was finding that its greatest asset was in having a family man as chief cartoonist. That solid and dependable readership wanted to see itself mirrored week by week; they wanted to absorb every detail of their own day to day lives and the humour that was in them. So Leech, immured in the centre of it all at Brook Green, drew their massive furniture, their Sunday dinners, their precocious youngsters, omnibus rides, their visits to shops, to the seaside, to the doctor, their dunning by unscrupulous tradesmen and their hoodwinking by artful urchins. Leech, the Brook Green ratepayer becomes the Everyman figure of this generation and though the guises may change from the Volunteer to the Special Constable, from the ardent young husband to the portly alderman, it is Leech within the clothes laughing at himself *and* his fellows.

The Brook Green household certainly produced that captivating series, "Domestic Bliss', which began in the summer of 1847. The cast consists of a harrassed bread-winner, an overworked wife and a surrounding retinue of clinging children and demanding domestics. In the first (left), the father figure, a touzle-headed young man in an untidy study, perhaps a writer or artist like Leech himself, tries to work against the mewing of cats, the beating of a toy drum and his helpmate's interjections. "I don't want to interrupt you, dear," says the wife of his Bussum, "I only want some money for Baby's socks and to know whether you will have the mutton cold or hashed." In a later episode a similar husband, "Edwin", tries to put on a shirt with no buttons and "Angelina" nursing the baby protests, "You can't expect me to do everything". The Brook Green families go on their summer holidays and use the bathing machine and when one of the more wealthy among them gives a dinner party, it is interrupted by a breathless servant shouting, "Gracious Goodness Master! There's the kitchen chimley a-fire — and two parish ingins knocking at the

DOMESTIC BLISS.

Servant (rushing in). "OH! GRACIOUS GOODNESS, MASTER! THERE'S THE KITCHEN CHIMLEY A-FIRE—AND THE TWO PARISH INGINS KNOCKING AT THE STREET DOOR."

SOMETHING THE MATTER WITH THE KITCHEN BOILER.

(Affectionately Dedicated to PATERFAMILIAS, whoever he might be.)

Colour Plate 4. "Hyde Park As It Will Be." Folding frontispiece to Punch's Pocket-Book for 1846. *Steel engraving coloured by hand.*

Colour Plate 5. "Preparatory School for Young Ladies." Folding frontispiece to Punch's Pocket-Book for 1851.

Affectionate Husband. "Come, Polly—if I *am a little irritable, it's over in a minute!!*"

street-door!" (top illustration page 55). The actual studied expressions of the appalled hostess and the servant scarcely able to contain herself, are superb. Leech was clearly in his element in this little suburban community where everyone knew each other's business and each gossip provided him with fresh illustrations for *Punch*.

The Victorians found endless amusement in servants; they had a lot of them and, like Swift a century earlier, found them a useful vehicle for satirising their betters. Already in 1841, Thackeray had created a character called "Jeames" in *The Britannia*, the complete gentleman's gentleman, full of snobbery, prejudice and ignorance. Another personage of similar type-casting was Jerrold's "Jenkins", the toadying journalist who had always been depicted in *Punch* pages during 1843 as a pampered and powdered footman. The two came together in 1845 when Thackeray created his immortal "Jeames Plush of Buckley Square" which was illustrated by Leech with all his power at depicting the breed, cockaded hats, knee breeches and well developed calves. Thackeray portrayed his outrageous flunkey in epistolary style, making the grotesque Jeames write letters to *Punch* in his atrocious orthography. "I elude, Sir, to the unjustafiable use which has been made of my name in your Journal, where both my muccantile speclations and the *hinmost pashns of my art* have been brought forrards in a ridicklus way for the public emusemint." It was a pity that Leech did not continue his illustrations of Jeames. Thackeray soon afterwards supplied his own sketches, but the seeds were carefully sown in Leech's mind.

Lady. "You wish to leave—really it's very inconvenient. Pray—Have you any reason to be dissatisfied with your Place?"
Flunkey. "Oh, dear no, Ma'am—not dissatisfied exactly; but—a—the fact is, Ma'am, you don't keep no wehicle, and I find I miss my Carriage exercise."

Leech's fun-making of servants was not always of the subtlest, but he used the writers of *Punch,* Gilbert à Beckett with his "Guide to Servants", Jerrold with his "Jenkins" and Thackeray with "Jeames" to create a whole family of terrible retainers, footmen who fancied themselves lords, maids with airs and graces, hall-boys with incredible swagger and impudence. The earliest flunkey subject is in the middle of 1843, some follow in 1844 and 1845 but the bulk of them appear in the wake of the writers. Leech (who never had a flunkey) takes the absurd speech of Thackeray, the toadyism of Jerrold and the scenery of à Beckett's Below Stairs to create a believable creature who struts and squawks for us. Flunkeiana, the visual chronicling by John Leech of John Thomas, the archetypal London footman, decorative and always useless, begins in earnest in mid-1848, continuing for the rest of his life. Leech was doing what Rowlandson did with Dr. Syntax, introducing a lively and laughable butt, episode after episode, but with John Thomas it was someone that everybody knew, part of that vast phenomenon — middle class life.

In the middle of 1845, Leech gives his readers a foretaste of what is to come; "Humility" depicts a cockaded footman with his stave, carrying a ceremonious cover from which a roast piglet facetiously protrudes. "Jeames's Diary" follows in the autumn with Thackeray's drawings following very much the humorous line of Leech. In the summer of 1846 "Thomas" appears again, exquisite,

DIFFERENT PEOPLE HAVE DIFFERENT OPINIONS.

Flunkey. "APOLLO? HAH! I DESSAY IT'S VERY CHEAP, BUT IT AIN'T
MY IDEER OF A GOOD FIGGER!"

indolent and abominably cheeked by a cockney — a favourite Leech combination. At the end of 1847 in the *Punch Almanack for 1848* (for which Leech did a tremendous amount of work), the footman appears once more in "The Close of the Season — The London Footman 'used up'." In this delightful parody John Thomas lies exhausted on a couch, ministered to with smelling-salts by a host of chamber-maids while the cook appears with nourishment. From then onwards he features as a frequent performer in Leech's cast of characters.

The series Flunkeiana begins properly in July 1848 and goes on with slight intermissions until 1864. In the earliest of these a bewildered lady of the house is confronted by a magnificent specimen of the race wishing to give notice; Leech has got his stance and well-developed calves to perfection. "Not Dissatisfied exactly", explains the exquisite footman, "But the fact is Ma'am, You don't keep no vehicle, and I find I miss my carriage exercise." (See illustration opposite.) A couple of issues later John Thomas has migrated to the country house and lies indolently in a chair while the harvesters are glimpsed busily at work through the window. Others follow, a fat flunkey is given notice by the Marchioness "Because I don't match Joseph" and a trio of back stairs peacocks complain of their fare of roast beef as "ver coarse — very coarse indeed sir!" One of the most delightful, one suspects Leech may have overheard it, shows John Thomas at the seaside in a tam o'shanter, questioned whether he enjoys it by a pretty French maid. "Par Bokhoo Mamzelle" he answers, from a deliciously posed attitude, "Par Bokhoo, I've been so accustomed to gaiety in town, that I'm awmost killed with Arnwee down here!" In 1852, he has the same recognisable features on a Belgravia doorstep refusing the cheap-jack wares of an image-seller. "Apollo", says John Thomas disdainfully, "I daresay its very cheap, but it ain't *my* ideer of a good figger!" (See illustration left.)

Leech is basically a compassionate illustrator, but he hits out most severely at pretension and the snobbery that Thackeray finds so absurd, and for which the description "snob" had only recently been coined. This is peculiarly Victorian where John Thomas puts over his "side" on the country footman in autumn 1852, describing the champagne he has received at Bury St Edmunds as "All Gewsberry"! More preposterous but nearer the truth is the flunkey out of place exclaiming "There's just one question I would like to ask your lady-ship — Ham I engaged for work, or Ham I engaged for Ornament?" The pretty boudoir sketched in as background to this incident, the Trollopian figure of the mistress and the mincing servant are obviously observed from life. In October 1857 John Thomas, hat in hand, explains to Mary the kitchen-maid "There's too much red in the livery — and that don't suit my complexion — never did!" In January 1864 he is again protesting at his diet "Mutton and Legs of Pork, I think its 'igh time some new Hanimal was inwented!" This drawing with its superbly characterised expressions of kitchen-maids, cook and housekeeper, gives a charming and surely rare glimpse of the Victorian Servants' Hall.

SERVANTGALISM;

OR, WHAT'S TO BECOME OF THE MISSUSES?

Servant Gal. (who has quarrelled with her bread-and-butter.) "IF YOU PLEASE, MA'AM, I FIND THERE'S COLD MEAT FOR DINNER IN THE KITCHEN. DID YOU EXPECT ME TO EAT IT?"

Lady. "OF COURSE, I EXPECT YOU TO EAT IT, AND AN EXCELLENT DINNER, TOO."

Servant. "OH, THEN, IF YOU PLEASE 'M, I SHOULD LIKE TO LEAVE THIS DAY MONTH." [*Exit Idiot.*

11. National Census, 1851, Public Records Office.

John Thomas's under-study is the hall-boy, a well-padded little brute, bursting out of his brass buttons and heaving with self-importance. He is often in the back of the John Thomas sketches but has a few of his own, notably "Unfeeling Observation" of December 1847 where a cockney urchin remarks "Oh Look Here Bill, Here's a poor Boy been and had the hinfluenza and now he's broke out all over buttons and red stripes!" Leech seems to like the cockney who, however poor, is not actually subservient. In 1849 the hall-boy is answering no bells but stuffing his mouth with green peas and apple tart. In June 1850, he is exercising his mistress's hideous dog (Leech hated pet dogs!). Probably the most uproarious incident is one of December 1857 where a shabby genteel lady has put a rustic boy into page's uniform. "Samuel" who has come recently out of a straw yard is instructed to wait at table but asks "Pleaz M', Be oi to wear My Breeches?"

The *dramatis personae* of Leech's underworld would not be complete without the pretty servant maids. The first one appears in late 1846 helping her employer to her bath. Afterwards Leech seems to have taken courage and regarded the whole genus as fair game. Mary is the aider, abettor and admirer of John Thomas, but she is also the admirer of others. In 1849 Leech has her letting in a "nice gentleman" because of his "moustaches" who secretly makes off with the hall furnishings! However she really comes into her own in *Punch's* Volume 24 of 1853, where Leech begins his brilliant antidote to Flunkeiana — Servantgalism. In this new departure the artist's free drawing captures illuminating moments in the servant's life. A splendid cockney gal with a turned up nose toasts a large foot by the fire and observes "I tell you what, Cook, With my Beauty and Figger, I ain't a going to stop in sarvice no longer, I shall be orf to Horsetraylier." About six of these drawings follow in quick succession, one senses that Leech knew that he was on to a good thing and couldn't stop himself, the evident enjoyment coming through the line. Leech creates a magnificent bundle of pride, a maid who won't work without "a footman" and another scullion ordering "sating shoes" and a "lady's fan". Later in 1853, we have one of the irrepressible housemaids leaving her card on another and a heavily laced servant, bursting into her mistress's bedroom with the desire to leave as "the hother servants, is so 'orrid and vulgar, and hignorant, and speaks so hungrammatical"! The setting for this, the middle class bedroom with its heavy half-tester and attendant solid furniture is too close to be anything other than the real thing (see illustration opposite).

The artist's increasing popularity and indispensibility to *Punch* resulted in a modicum of prosperity and in early 1848, he was able to move from the suburban Brook Green to the more substantial middle class affluence of 31 Notting Hill Terrace, Kensington. This is certainly reflected in the drawings and in the bigger establishment that he was maintaining. In April 1851, he had two living-in servants, Elizabeth Drew, a thirty-two year old Somersetshire cook and her younger sister Sarah to act as maid.[11] These two must have acted as a

SERVANTGALISM ; OR, WHAT'S TO BECOME OF THE MISSUSES ?—No. 9.

Lady. "WISH TO LEAVE! WHY I THOUGHT, THOMPSON, YOU WERE VERY COMFORTABLE WITH ME!"

Thompson (who is extremely refined). "HOH YES, MAM! I DON'T FIND NO FAULT WITH YOU, MAM—NOR YET WITH MASTER—BUT THE TRUTH HIS, MAM—THE HOTHER SERVANTS IS SO 'ORRID VULGAR, AND HIGNORANT, AND SPEAKS SO HUNGRAMMATICAL, THAT I REELY CANNOT LIVE IN THE SAME 'OUSE WITH 'EM—AND I SHOULD LIKE TO GO THIS DAY MONTH, IF SO BE HAS IT WON'T ILLCONVENIENCE YOU!"

stimulant to the drawings even if they were not actually portraits. One suspects that new issues of *Punch* were received with great hilarity in the Leech family's kitchen. In 1857, Leech takes us into the nursery where the nurse-maids are unable to write their love letters "for the rackett". An equally hooped and bonneted nurse-maid of 1863 crows that her last family considered she "hadn't ought to be anythink but a Nursery Guvness!" But it is not always the domestic alone that comes under his scrutiny; "Servantgalism" and "Fine Ladyism" of 10 July, 1858, has two socialite mothers complaining of neglectful nurse-maids while resting in indolence in a lush and stuffy drawing-room. Leech, like his namesake, had a way of penetrating every chink and crevice of the Victorian home and of opening out the complacent bourgeoisie for themselves.

Much of this humour surrounds the pretensions of shabby genteel families or more opulent ones that are run on a knife edge. The façade of prosperity in rather cramped surroundings is a recurring theme and the essence of his wit and humour here; it cannot have been far from Leech's situation most of the time, but unlike his neighbours he could always see the funny side of it.

* * * * *

Over the years the Leech repertoire built up to cover a great cross-

PUTTING HIS FOOT IN IT.

Little Hairdresser (mildly). "YER 'AIR'S VERY THIN ON THE TOP, SIR!"

Gentleman (of ungovernable temper). "MY HAIR THIN ON THE TOP, SIR! AND WHAT IF IT IS! CONFOUND YOU, YOU PUPPY, DO YOU THINK I CAME HERE TO BE INSULTED AND TOLD OF MY PERSONAL DEFECTS? I'LL THIN YOUR TOP!!"

NEW CRICKETING DRESSES TO PROTECT ALL ENGLAND AGAINST THE PRESENT SWIFT BOWLING.

A LITTLE BIT OF HUMBUG

Shoemaker. "I THINK, MUM, WE HAD BETTER MAKE YOU A PAIR. YOU SEE, MUM, YOURS IS SUCH A REMARKABLE LONG AND NARRER FOOT!"

section of Victorian society. To look through his pages in *Punch* is to view the Mid-Nineteenth Century Cake with one slice removed, revealing the follies and fashions of his society and its innermost feelings. Thackeray had urged in the *Paris Sketch-Book* that British caricaturists should look to France for inspiration, so that their work might be an index of the times. Then generations to come would "have the advantage of knowing, intimately, exactly, the manners of life and being of their grandsires, and calling up when they so choose it, our ghosts from the grave to live, quarrel, swindle, suffer and struggle on blindly as of yore."[12] As the 1850s unfolded, Leech had achieved this. In his multitude of drawings we find every walk of life. There is one school-mistress, a host of ingratiating drapers' assistants, apothecaries, cabbies, lodging-house ladies, ruffians, railway officials, costermongers, soldiers and sailors. We are introduced to places where the camera was never to stray, the interior of fish-shops, hairdressers (see illustration opposite above), shoemakers (above), we see early bookstalls on railway stations, street acrobats, cheap eating-houses, minstrels, skating parties, crossing-sweepers (page 64), cricket matches (opposite below), oyster-sellers, billiards in one place and archery in another. He presents us with brief encounters on the street corner, the interiors of undergraduate digs at Oxford (page 64) and the tobacco wreathed rooms of bachelor swells in Piccadilly (page 65).

It would be useless with the Victorians to have had a humorous drawing without an amusing text, their humour, puns and *double entendre* relying so much upon the written word. Leech proves himself time and time again to have his ear as closely attuned to

12. *The Paris Sketch-book,* p. 173.

ARITHMETIC IN THE UNIVERSITY.

SIGNS OF THE COMMISSION.

"I SAY, FRANK, MY BOY—IF TROUNCER'S AT 5 TO 2, AND NUTSHELL AT 3 TO 1, WHAT'S THE BETTING AGAINST THE PAIR OF THEM?"
"I'M SURE I DONT KNOW—TAKE YOU 6 TO 1."

GOOD SECURITY.

Boy. "PLEASE, SIR, GIVE ME A BROWN?"
Swell. "SIXPENCE IS THE SMALLEST MONEY I HAVE, MY LITTLE LAD."
Boy. "VEL, SIR, I'LL GET YER CHANGE; AND IF YER DOUBTS MY HONOUR. HOLD MY BROOM!"

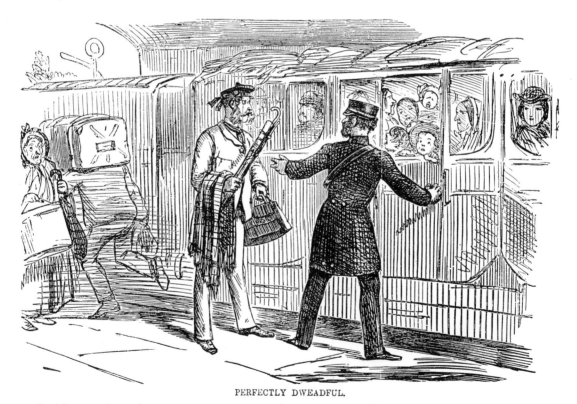

PERFECTLY DWEADFUL.

Guard. "NOW, SIR! IF YOU'RE GOING ON BY THE EXPRESS. HERE'S JUST ROOM FOR ONE!"
Tourist. "WHA-T! GET IN WITH HAWWID OLD WOMEN, AND SQUEEMING CHILDREN! BY JOVE! YOU KNOW! I SAY! IT'S IMPAWSIBLE, YOU KNOW!"

First Heavy Swell (lately absent). "Well, 'Gus, my boy—How did you keep it up here on Christmas Day?"

Second Do. "Oh! It was terribly slow—for all the World like a Sunday without 'Bell's Life!'"

mannerisms of speech and dialect as his eye was to the eccentricities of form. His cockneys talk authentically, so do his rustics and his preposterous army officers lisp and lose their "r's" as perfectly as any of Lord Cardigan's best men (see illustration opposite below). He is also immensely quick to capitalise on verbal fashions, the most ephemeral fashions of all. In 1847 he adopts the latest phraseology for a swell or a dandy as "a Fast Man" and in 1848 it is "stunner" applied to girls, horses, pictures and clothes, Leech has one swell admiring another's "stunning great-coat", the other replies "I flatter myself it's rather 'down the road' ". The free use of the current slang shows how much Leech was in touch with the conversation of this modern world, as much in touch as his unceasing pencil.

This strong oral memory often runs together with strong imitative powers and the capacity to mimic. We do know from his *Punch* contemporaries that the quiet Leech was nevertheless a brilliant story

THE RISING GENERATION.

Old Gentleman. "Bless my heart! this vibration of the carriage is very unusual! Pray, my little man, have you any apprehension of accidents on railways?"

Juvenile. "Oh, none in the least; and especially with such a fat old buffer as you to be shot against."

13. Silver, op. cit., 2 July, 1862.

14. ibid., 20 November, 1861.

15. Evans Letters, Harvard University MS Eng 1028, letter from A.A. Hare, 14 March, 1886.

16. *The Rising Generation*, A Series of Twelve Drawings on Stone, 1848.

teller and an excellent hand at mimicry. Henry Silver records in his diary "J.L." imitating "Douglas Jerrold at Rose Cottage throwing hair back and sprinkling salt with gusto over goose-berry tart!"[13] and again he notes down Leech's doing an excellent impersonation of the stage character "Lord Dundreary".[14] An equally telling remark is made by Leech's friend A.A. Hare, who saw everything from mimicry to wood engraving: "The public have had the results — we had the rehearsals. I cannot remember anything more exquisitely comic than Leech's account of some of the Bathing at Biarritz. He would make himself look like a fat Frenchmen or great French lady about to tempt the waves — with a twinkle of fun in his clear blue eye which was perfectly irresistible."[15] Leech may have had this gift as an aid to his illustrative work, being able to enter the characters as well as depict the appearances of those he portrayed. There is also much in Leech's dialogue and the visual presentation that reminds one at once of the contemporary novelists, and not the episodic novelists of the early century but the new social school.

The crazes and obsessions of the Victorians passed through his pages too, as they came and went. There is the polka-mania (1845), the clamour over Jenny Lind's singing (1847), the new cab regulations (1851), the Census (1851), the Great Exhibition (1851) (illustrated opposite below), poultry-mania (1852), table-rapping in the same year, battledore and shuttlecock (1856), carpet-croquet (1863) and the waltz (illustrated page 69). Leech laughed long and often at Victorian gadgetry, the steam engine of course, but also electro-magnetism (1852), and mechanical brushes (1863), a contribution was a parody of Darwinism (1863).

Leech was not alone among the Victorians in liking juvenile subjects, the Academy exhibitions were full of them and simpering "tots" featured in endless stories and magazine columns. But his coy young misses and wilful, precocious little men remain amusing in the drawing if not in what they say. Leech's juvenile work begins in the early lithographs of the late 1830s and continues through *Punch* in the 1840s culminating in the highly successful "The Rising Generation" series of 1846 to 1847 which were also published as a book.[16] The scenario is very often the same, a confrontation between a cheeky little boy and an easily shockable uncle or grandfather, what we now call the generation gap. An early one of this genre shows a miniature gent in frock coat and waistcoat warming his buttocks by a roaring fire and saying "You can't expect a young feller to be always at home; and if you don't like the way I go on, why I must have chambers, and so much a-week!" Later on, tiny sprats of ten eye a handsome woman in lace and velvet and remark "Jeuced Fine Gurl ... I should like to catch her under the mistletoe!" The best is a railway carriage where a languid youth tells an elderly passenger that he is not frightened of accidents "especially with such a fat old buffer as you to be shot against" (see illustration left). When the juveniles were not the sons of friends in Brook Green or Notting Hill Terrace, they were London urchins, ancestors of a whole range of *Punch* street boys.

SINGULAR BUT RATHER ALARMING EFFECT PRODUCED BY IMPRUDENTLY TRYING THE HAT AND TABLE MOVING EXPERIMENT.

A DELICATE ATTENTION.

AN OLD GENTLEMAN, ANXIOUS THAT HIS WIFE SHOULD POSSESS SOME TRIFLE FROM THE GREAT EXHIBITION OF 1851, PURCHASES (AMONGST OTHER THINGS) THE STUFFED ELEPHANT, AND THE MODEL OF THE DODO.

DOMESTIC ECONOMY.—HOME BREWING.

As the typical paterfamilias and householder, Leech lived very much in the dimension of his cartooning and much of it is autobiographical. In 1842 for example, soon after their marriage, the Leeches decided that they would like to experiment with different beers. John wrote to Charley Adams in the country as the most likely authority.[17]

"While I am writing to you I will touch upon the subject of beer! My wife is extremely fond of that beverage — she is looking over my shoulder, and says it is not so and that it is very unkind of me to say so — but that's all Humbug — We have been trying all sorts of ale but somehow it turns sour — now I want you to send me a barrel of beer made from malt, and hops — you know where it is to be got I dare say — will you do this old fellow!"

The beer was delivered with fairly disastrous results as described in another letter to Adams:[18]

"... as touching the beer, I made a bad mess of it — the shaking it had on the road put it into a state of efferveeseence ... I can't spell it — so I'll say phizzling — the consequence was that when I took the bung out it nearly blew the roof of the house off and covered me all over with malt and hops."

Predictably enough, a similar subject was drawn out by him in the end of 1843 to appear as "Home Brewing" in *Punch's Almanack* for 1844 (above). The Almanacks had been introduced at Mayhew's suggestion in 1842 to boost the magazine's circulation from six thousand to ten thousand, at which point it would break even.[19] The almanack contained elaborate headings and borders and Leech's support, enlisted for 1843, became so indispensible after 1852, that he was practically designing the whole twelve pages. The detailed small scale drawings of London life, hunting, dandies, fishing

17. Dimsdale Collection, 18 July, 1842.
18. ibid., n.d.
19. Spielmann, op. cit., pp. 31-33.

expedities, are often among the best works, but the preparation of so much material at the end of a year in winter time proved very exhausting. The *Punch* table used to cheer him into his dinner place when the work was finished![20] "Hip! Hip! Hurrah!" he writes to Charley Adams in December 1852, "The Almanac is finished, and now for a day with the Puckeridge."[21]

Some time about 1847, Mr Punch, urbane, civilised and metropolitan, discovered the country. It was an important discovery because it recognised the needs of the new readership who lived in the shires, indulged in country sports and needed to see something more familiar than the "Brook Green Volunteer" or "Domestic Bliss". The fact that Mark Lemon was a sporting man and that Leech was always running down to the Adamses in the hunting season, was a great help; it was also to reveal Leech as one of the great hunting illustrators of all time. In the autumn of 1845 there is a telling sign of

20. Silver, op. cit., 15 December, 1858.
21. Dimsdale Collection, 14 December, 1852.

Original pencil drawing of waltzers, about 1845.   Charterhouse School the times in "Anti-Railway Meeting of Fox-Hunters", a doubty horseman being chased down a track by a winged locomotive, a theme that Leech returns to. In the *Almanack* for 1846 for instance "Meeting with Something Like a Check" [22] shows the whole field of a smart hunt stopped by an on-coming express train, hunting becomes a permanent *Almanack* feature hereafter. Leech's own experiences or inexperiences in hiring horses figure in 1847; in the first half of the year he has a novice swell hiring a "werry fresh" horse and another city gentleman facing a high hedge, being assured by a baleful rustic "there ain't no other gate ou o' this vield". The cockney sportsman, so much the staple diet of Seymour, becomes a favourite Leech character; he is confronted by ditches and turns back, goes right through a five-bar gate to the astonishment of a cow and tells his mare not to attempt a spiked gate because he's "Father of a Family". In December 1848, a cockney swell tells a friend "I see the 'ounds several times and none of yer nasty 'edges an' ditches!"

For a lover of the noble science like Leech, there needed to be something a little more tangible in these hunting sketches than even his acute observation was capable of — a personality. The scraggy youths from Hoxton or Bow with their scraggier horses were amusing enough, but the series needed a more substantial figure with an independent life whom the parodyist could build round. With John Thomas strutting among the flunkeys and Edwin and Angelina

22. Original drawing in the Ray Collection. See Ray, Gordon N., *The Illustrator and The Book in England 1790 to 1914,* Morgan Library, New York, 1976, p. 85, illus.

A CAREFUL RIDER.

"A STILE, EH? AHEM! THAT'S A SORT OF THING THAT REQUIRES A GOOD DEAL OF JUDGMENT."

simpering among the tea-kettles of "Domestic Bliss", Leech introduced a winner in 1849, Mr Briggs and his "Pleasures of House-keeping". Briggs is a solid Victorian householder, who like the Brook Green Volunteer is attached to his snug suburban home but is catastrophically accident prone. One loose slate requires an army of Irish navvies to attend to it, the builders occupy the sitting-room and arrive with a score of absurd chimney-pots (below). (Leech had moved to and renovated 31 Notting Hill Terrace the previous year.) Exhausted by the workmen, Briggs goes in search of horse exercise, buying a hack which is frolicsome and mounts the pavement whenever it meets an omnibus. Leech must have recognised early on that Briggs in a scrape had the same potential as a Pickwick. Briggs in a scrape with a horse had a huge appeal to readers up and down the social scale. "The Pleasures of House-keeping" became "The Pleasures of Horse-keeping" (see illustration page 72). Briggs' dogged Britishness was enormously heartening. Whatever he did wrong, he was always prepared to try again, no more unsuitable horseman could ever be more intrepid. So successful had the series become in September that *Punch* appends a note to Mr Briggs' bathing mishap: "We understand he has accepted an invitation to spend a few days with a friend of his during the Hunting Season — No doubt we shall be enabled to depict some of his performances."

PLEASURES OF HOUSEKEEPING.

SOMEHOW OR OTHER, EVER SINCE THE ALTERATIONS, THE CHIMNEYS HAVE TAKEN TO SMOKE INTOLERABLY. THE BUILDER IS ASSURING MR. BRIGGS THAT BY SOME VERY SIMPLE CONTRIVANCES THEY CAN BE EFFECTUALLY CURED.

PLEASURES OF HORSEKEEPING.

MR. BRIGGS, PERSUADED THAT "A GOOD HORSE CAN'T BE A BAD COLOUR," HAS PURCHASED A SPOTTED AND HIGHLY-TRAINED STEED FROM A CIRCUS; BUT THE WORST OF HIM IS THAT AMONGST OTHER THINGS HE HAS BEEN TRAINED TO SIT DOWN ON HIS HAUNCHES WHEN HE HEARS A BAND PLAY, AND YOU MAY IMAGINE HOW DISCONCERTED POOR OLD BRIGGS WAS THE FIRST TIME HE DID SO.

MR. BRIGGS GOES OUT FOR A DAY'S HUNTING, AND HAS A GLORIOUS RUN OVER A SPLENDID COUNTRY.

Hunting fever develops in Briggs despite fierce opposition from Mrs Briggs, first to his shiny tops and then to his cap which she consigns to the fire. He presents himself for the Metropolitan Steeple Chase, changes his horse at a reputable dealer and finds him undeniably frisky after a frost. When he finally gets to the hunt, Mr Briggs has a great trouble in shutting the gates, a tremendous test of arm and crop in a superbly depicted winter landscape. Later in the season he comes up against a "protectionist" who forbids him to use his gaps (below) and in the early summer the resolute rider puts his hunter in harness to drive "a few friends quietly down to the Derby" with terrible results. During the early 'fifties "Our Friend Briggs" as he becomes popularly called is sent on fishing expeditions (illustration on page 74), rabbit-shooting parties and ventures on to grouse moors, all in the steps of Leech who tried each pastime in turn. After 1852 he bows on less often; by that time the artist was working with new inventions but the immortal Briggs had made his

MR. BRIGGS HAS ANOTHER DAY WITH THE HOUNDS.

MR. BRIGGS CAN'T BEAR FLYING LEAPS, SO HE MAKES FOR A GAP—WHICH IS IMMEDIATELY FILLED BY A FRANTIC PROTECTIONIST, WHO IS VOWING THAT HE WILL PITCHFORK MR. B. IF HE COMES "GALLOPERRAVERING" OVER HIS FENCES—DANGED IF HE DOANT!

TRIUMPHANT SUCCESS OF MR. BRIGGS.

SOMEHOW OR OTHER (ASSISTED BY HIS LITTLE BOY WALTER), HE CATCHES A JACK, WHICH, TO USE MR. B.'S OWN WORDS,
FLIES AT HIM, AND BARKS LIKE A DOG!

mark. "Tom Noddy", the inveterate little horseman based on
Leech's friend Mike Halliday comes to the fore in these years, but
even he, never quite surpasses Mr B.

With such an extraordinary cast of characters, figments of his vivid
imagination and yet instantly recognisable as types, Leech had
become famous. *Punch* and Leech were household names for healthy
fun, acceptable satire, something that would amuse Queen Victoria,[23]
in fact something that had the same sort of dependable permanence
as the monarchy. Richard Doyle, a more fanciful and decorative
illustrator than Leech, had been his companion on *Punch* for the first
ten years. Very often Leech's middle class genre subjects needed the
counterbalance of fairies and monsters and spookiness which Doyle's
art provided. Even Doyle's genre subjects are other-worldly whereas
Leech's are straighter than anything the public had ever known.
Doyle left in 1852, to be replaced by John Tenniel, the only other
strong illustrator to work during the great Leech era. Tenniel's
superb animals and sturdy cartoons certainly helped Leech to
concentrate on what he most excelled in, modern episodes and
country life. *Punch* also provided some opportunities outside black
and white work; the frontispieces to the *Punch Pocket-Books,* which
he drew for twenty years, are a nice mix of fantasy and realism and

23. An album of Leech pencil drawings
is in the Royal Library, Windsor.

demonstrate what a superb watercolourist Leech could be (Colour Plates 4 and 5, page 56).

It is small wonder that when Thackeray was asked to write on Leech in 1854 for *The Quarterly Review,* he should single out his friend as *Punch's* favourite man with the public. "Fancy a number of *Punch* without Leech's pictures! What would you give for it? The learned gentlemen who write the work must feel that, without him, it were as well left alone."[24] Though generous and probably true, it caused great trouble at *Punch* when published, and must have caused Leech great embarrassment. "I ought *never* to have said that Punch might as well be left unwritten but for Leech," Thackeray wrote to Percival Leigh, "It was more than my meaning, which is certainly that the drawing is 100 times more popular than the writing — but I had no business to write any such thing."[25] But Thackeray left *Punch* in 1855, though stressing that this was not the reason. His best summing up of their dual partnership in the paper shows how much their two arts did for the outlook of the 1850s. "We cannot afford to lose Satyr with his pipe and dances and gambols. But we have washed, combed and taught the rogue good manners."[26]

24. *Quarterly Review,* December 1854, pp. 75-86.

25. Ray, Gordon, *The Letters & Private Papers of W.M. Thackeray,* Vol. 3, p. 418.

26. Thackeray, W.M., Works, XIII, p. 484.

MR. BRIGGS, STIMULATED BY THE ACCOUNTS IN THE NEWSPAPERS OF THE DARING FEAT OF HORSEMANSHIP AT AYLESBURY, AND EXCITED BY MR. HAYCOCK'S CLARET, TRIES WHETHER HE ALSO CAN RIDE OVER A DINING-ROOM TABLE.

Chapter Four

LEECH AND DICKENS

B y the mid-1840s, Leech, still only twenty-six or twenty-seven, was in touch with many of the greatest writers of his age. *Punch* had done it; it had re-opened that acquaintance with Thackeray begun at Charterhouse, it had put him on terms with Thomas Hood, R.H. Barham, Douglas Jerrold and the Mayhews and must surely have kept him under the eyes of Charles Dickens. One of the puzzles for the admirer of Leech is why such a close friendship between the artist and the two greatest novelists of the Victorian period, Thackeray and Dickens, was not more fruitful? In the case of Thackeray it must be that the author preferred to be his own illustrator during Leech's most productive period. The artist had to be content at that time with lesser names, the rollicking novels of W.H. Maxwell and the travelogue novels of Mrs Fanny Trollope. Dickens was clearly keen to use Leech's work at the beginning of their friendship; the fact that he did so decreasingly through the 1840s tells us much about Leech himself.

The abortive attempt to illustrate *Pickwick* in 1836 did not deter Leech from trying again in November 1842 when Dickens' new title of *Martin Chuzzlewit* was announced. Dickens replied promptly on November 5th in a very warm letter which reveals how much the novelist knew of Leech's steady progress and of how much he himself had helped behind the scenes. "... I have never forgotten the having seen you some years ago," he writes, "or ceased to watch your progress with much interest and satisfaction. I congratulate you heartily on your success; and myself on having had my eye upon the means by which you have obtained it."[1] Dickens hopes to be able "to avail myself of your genius" in *Chuzzlewit,* but everything depended on the attitude of H.K. Browne, "Phiz", who was doing the majority of Dickens' illustrations.[2]

Browne was intractable and Dickens was obviously disappointed when he replied, as he had hoped in the first letter "to approve your acquaintance, and not to lose sight of you any more".[3] Happily the outcome of all this was an invitation. "But", wrote the novelist on November 7th, "as I desire, notwithstanding, to lay a small quantity of salt on the tail of your private and personal coat, will you give me the means of doing so, by joining our family dinner table next Sunday at half past five?"[4]

This was the beginning of a productive friendship, "the Sparkler" as Dickens liked to call himself was five years Leech's senior and

1. *The Letters of Charles Dickens,* edit. House, Storey and Tillotson, 1974, Vol. 3, p. 359.

2. Hablot Knight Browne, 1815-1892, Dickens' chief illustrator from 1836-57.

3. *The Letters of C.D.,* op. cit., Vol. 3, p. 359.

4. ibid., p. 361.

Scrooge's Third Visitor.

Illustration from A Christmas Carol.

5. Frith, W.P., *John Leech His Life and Work,* 1891, Vol. 2, p. 4.

6. Hole, Reynolds, *The Memories of ...,* 1892, p. 17.

7. Forster, John, *Life of Charles Dickens,* 1928, p. 299.

altogether more astute, mature and worldly. Leech was shy, retiring and reticent in everything except his brilliant drawings; Dickens was confident as novelist, essayist and columnist, as actor, agitator and reformer, as gregarious literary man and inquisitive investigator. The attraction of these two very different men for one another must have been their opposite personalities, often the foundation for the best sort of friendship. W.P. Frith, who met Dickens' new friend at about this time, described him as "a tall, thin and remarkably handsome young man" (see Colour Plate 20, page 131).[5] A few years later he was described as "tall, but slight in figure, with a high broad forehead, large blue-grey Irish eyes, and a face full of expression. When he saw anything that he disliked, when he was bored or vexed, there was 'a lurking trouble of the nether lip', but the sunniest of smiles when he was enjoying the ridiculous, or giving pleasure to his friends. He was modest in his demeanour, and silent as a rule, as one who, though he was not working, was constrained to think about his work."[6] Modest, thoughtful but with a sense of the ridiculous, these are characteristics that would have commended him to Dickens; he soon became a constant companion of the writer and within the year they were planning a book together.

Dickens had decided to write a Christmas story alongside *Chuzzlewit* and in the autumn of 1843 he was busy on *A Christmas Carol* creating the unforgettable shapes of Scrooge, Bob Cratchit and Tiny Tim. As he said himself, he "wept and laughed and wept again" as he wrote it.[7] *A Christmas Carol,* with its sense of mystery and wonder, its humour and pathos and its Dickensian message of charity, was exactly the right blend for Leech's pencil. Although it is probably not his greatest work, it is probably the one he is best recalled by, certainly the only one that has remained a household name. Even those who hardly know the name of Leech, at once have a visual image of his work when *A Christmas Carol* is mentioned.

Leech would have been working on these at his usual feverish pitch in October and November 1843. There were to be four illustrations etched on steel and coloured by hand and four text wood engravings. Dickens probably chose the subjects, and there is every indication that he wanted the *Carol* to be a special book. The etched plates, done in vignette, were in Leech's most accomplished style, and the most sensitive drawing is the frontispiece of "Mr Fezziwig's Ball" with warmth and gaiety bursting out of the page (Frontispiece). Scrooge is treated with brilliant austerity in "Marley's Ghost" (Colour Plate 6, page 81), his spare figure hunched over a mean fire, "Scrooge's third visitor" has an almost baroque flamboyance about it (margin illustration) and "The Last of the Spirits" tremendous dramatic effect (Colour Plate 7, page 81). The wood engravings were interpreted by W.J. Linton with astonishing accuracy, the detail being finer than in any other of Leech's published works. When the first page proofs were sent to 9, Powis Place, in early December, Leech began to fret. Dickens reassured him by letter on the 14th. "I do not doubt, in my own mind, that you unconsciously exaggerate the evil done by the colourers," he writes, "You can't think how

The Dance at Trotty Veck's.

An illustration from The Chimes.

8. *The Letters of C.D.,* op. cit., Vol. 3, p. 608.

9. ibid.

10. Patten, Robert L., *Charles Dickens and His Publishers,* 1978, pp. 144-150.

11. Frith, op. cit., Vol. 1, p. 103.

12. *The Letters of C.D.,* op. cit., Vol. 4, p. 233.

much better they will look in a neat book, than you suppose."[8] Perhaps Leech was satisfied for the book's appearance was greeted enthusiastically and immediately reprinted, the only dissenting voice being Maclise who called it "the very climax of vulgarity in its *mise en planches*".[9] To our eyes the colours are mute and pleasant, particularly showing that Leech, though principally a black and white artist, was a superb colourist too.

The tremendous success with the public of *A Christmas Carol* was not matched by a financial success for Dickens. It proved a disaster. Dickens had arranged to publish the book on commission, the publication expenses to be born by him and the publishers to have a commission on sales. But the cost of producing such a delightful little quality book far outweighed its retail price. The accounts show that the cost of colouring Leech's plates was excessive, far outstripping the payment to the artist.[10] It does not appear that Leech was particularly anxious for the colour work; it was Dickens' decision alone. Leech's part had been highly successful and at least one contemporary thought it far surpassed the work of Dickens' regular artist, H.K. Browne. Frith considers that Leech should have gone on to illustrate the major Dickens works — "There was no doubt a disposition on the part of 'Phiz' to exaggeration in his illustration of Dickens characters," he writes, "sometimes to the verge of caricature, and even beyond it; this fault Leech would have avoided, as his exquisite etchings in Dickens' Christmas books fully prove."[11] The reason why Leech, in spite of being a more "modern" illustrator than "Phiz", did not get the jobs is probably contained in a sequel to *A Christmas Carol.*

In 1844 Dickens began on a fresh Christmas tale, *The Chimes, A Goblin Story.* The appearance of the book was to be less lavish and Leech was to share the honours of illustrating with Doyle, Maclise and Stanfield. Leech had five wood engravings here, all figure subjects and all admirably engraved by his old neighbour W.J. Linton. It was the fashion at this time to have gift books illustrated by several hands, but the end result is far less harmonious than the *Carol.* It was a smooth run for Leech except that Dickens wanted some alterations to the vignette page of Richard returning home in an unkempt state. Leech met him at the Piazza Coffee House, Covent Garden, and altered the block within a day. Dickens was able to reply on the 3rd, "The alteration in respect of the figure of Richard will be quite sufficient; and I assure you that your cheerful readiness to give yourself trouble on my account gratifies me exceedingly. It is a real pleasure to me to say so, and to work with you. I have the greatest diffidence in suggesting any change, however slight, in what you do — you are so ready to make it."[12] *The Chimes* was a resounding success, far more profitable than the *Carol* and so Dickens was encouraged to plan three further Christmas stories involving Leech.

The books were *The Cricket on the Hearth,* for Christmas 1845/46, *The Battle of Life,* for Christmas 1846 and *The Haunted Man* for Christmas 1847/48, but none of them were to have quite the acclaim of the *Carol.* Dickens must have consorted considerably with

The Song of the Kettle.

An illustration from The Cricket on the Hearth.

13. The Letters of C.D., op. cit., Vol. 4, p. 395.

14. ibid., p. 442.

15. Forster, op. cit., pp. 439-440.

16. Forster Collection, Victoria and Albert Museum Library 48 B 28 and 48 E 4.

17. ibid. (Forster 227).

Leech; he writes to him on 2 October, 1845, about *The Cricket,* "I am now settling myself to work: and hope in ten days time or so, to be in a condition to wind you up and set you going. If you are in the mood, therefore, to illustrate my poor fancies, we will hold discourse together on the subject, in about that time."[13] Leech was to do more work on this book, seven subjects, than on the other later publications, all full of variety; there among them was a fireside with a cat, a fireside with a nursing mother, a peasant girl and a rustic jig. Edwin Landseer had been asked to contribute a dog illustration and as the same hound appeared in Leech's design, Landseer had to send the block along to insure a family resemblance! (See illustration left.) There were no hitches except that Dickens considered at the end of November, when everything was ready, that "the Carrier is hardly handsome enough".[14]

The 1846 volume, *The Battle of Life,* was probably the most unfortunate book Leech ever illustrated. Dickens had only approached him to do three subjects, Maclise was doing four and Doyle contributing three, besides this there were three Stansfield landscapes. It has already been touched on in connection with *Punch* that Leech was extremely unpunctual and constitutionally unsuited to working to deadlines; on *The Battle of Life* he proved to be both more careless and more sensitive than he could afford to be.

The problems began with his first design for the book "The Parting Breakfast", a lovely and fresh vignette subject of figures and a mail coach, integrated most successfully with the text. By the late autumn, Leech was almost certainly working on the *Almanack* for *Punch* and would, therefore, have been late with Dickens' work. John Forster, who had collected the illustrations together for Dickens, actually says that the publication had "been delayed expressly for these drawings to the utmost limit".[15] Before Friday, 13 November 1846, ominous date, Forster wrote to Leech on Dickens' behalf expressing misgivings about the illustrations of Michael Warden waiting in the lawyer's office. Leech replied, "in very great haste", that, "If you think the face of Warden too old, I can alter it in ten minutes if you would let me have the block back — and I would rather do so than leave it to the engraver."[16] Over the weekend there seems to have been further discussion as to how many illustrations Leech was to do and probably by Sunday 15 November, Dickens was looking again at the block of "The Parting Breakfast" (see illustration page 80) which did not please him. Forster, acting as intermediary tried to straighten out the situation and explained that the Clemency Newcome drawn by Leech for the "Breakfast" was too ugly for the novelist. Dickens' text describes her as she "hovered galvanically about the table as waitress" and there she is on page 28. Leech, under great pressure and with his part not distinctly explained, was clearly upset and wrote to say as much on Monday, 16 November:[17]

My dear Forster,

I really cannot say off hand how many illustrations I can make within the week, indeed, I assure you I feel so

plied the Doctor (he seemed to know that nobody else

wanted anything to eat), he

"The Parting Breakfast" from The Battle of Life.

embarrassed by the conditions under which I am to make my share of the drawings that I hardly know what to do at all. *Conscientiously* I could not make Clemency Newcome particularly beautiful — if you will read a little beyond the words 'plump and cheerful' — you will find the following — 'But the extraordinary homeliness of her gait and manner would have superseded any face in the world' — 'To say that she had two left legs and somebody else's arms and that all four limbs seemed to be out of joint and to start from perfectly wrong places' &c &c — again she is described as 'having a prodiguous pair of self-willed shoes' — The impression made upon me by such a description as I have quoted certainly is that the character so described is both awkward and comic — Of course I may be wrong in my conception of what Dickens intended but *I* imagin'd the lady in question to be a sort of clean 'Slowboy' — The blessed public (if they consider the matter at all) will hold me responsible for what appears with my name, they will know nothing about my being obliged to conform to Mr Maclise's idea. I cannot tell you how loathe I should be to cause any delay or difficulty in the production of the book or what pain it would give me to cause either Dickens or yourself any annoyance — I must confess I am a little out of heart.

Believe me ever
Yours Faithfully
John Leech

This letter did not suit Dickens and John Forster was again writing to Leech on the receipt of it. Leech's reply was much more conciliatory but also more specific about his own feelings.[18]

Brook Green
November 18th 1846

My dear Forster,

Perhaps I was wrong in using the word 'conditions' in my note to you — I should have said 'circumstances' and by being 'embarrassed' by them I meant that I found it very harrassing to do work (that I am for several reasons anxious to do well) under the constant feeling that I have too little time to do it in, and also I meant to convey to you that the necessity (which I certainly supposed to exist) of presenting a sort of resemblance to the characters as conceived by Mr Maclise, made it a rather nervous undertaking to me — It seems I expressed myself clumsily as the tone of my note appeared to you anything but what I intended it to be — any suggestion from you I should always consider most valuable. I send you one drawing — completed this morning at four o'clock, and I assure you I would spare [no] time nor any personal comfort to shew my personal regard for both yourself and Dickens.

18. Forster Collection, op. cit. (Forster 231).

Colour Plate 6. "Marley's Ghost", illustration for A Christmas Carol *by Charles Dickens, 1843.*

Marley's Ghost.

The Last of the Spirits.

Colour Plate 7. "The Last of the Spirits", illustration for A Christmas Carol *by Charles Dickens, 1843.*

Hot and breathless as the Doctor was, it only made

him the more
impatient
for Alfred's
coming.

"Michael Warden" from The Battle
of Life.

I should not like to promise more than two other
drawings, if Saturday is positively the last day — I might
be able to do more than two other drawings but I should
not like to promise and fail. Pray overlook my glaring
defects in the block I send and

Believe me ever Yours Faithfully
John Leech

PS   I should like if there is no objection, that Linton
should engrave for me.

In this climate of confusion, the seeds of Leech's gravest mistake
were probably sown. Hassled by Forster, and with the feeling that he
must complement if not compete with Maclise, the artist misread the
text in Part Two and sent an erroneous design to the engraver. Somehow Dickens and Forster missed it; Marian was shown eloping *with*
Michael Warden, when Warden was not intended to be there in the
story (left).

"When I first saw it," Dickens wrote to Forster, "it was with a
horror and agony not to be expressed. Of course I need not tell *you,*
my dear fellow, Warden has no business in the elopement scene. *He*
was never there! In the first hot sweat of this surprise and novelty, I
was going to implore the printing of that sheet to be stopped, and the
figure taken out of the block. But when I thought of the pain this
might give our kind-hearted Leech; and that what is such a
monstrous enormity to me, as never having entered my brain, may
not so present itself to others, I became more composed; though the
fact is wonderful to me. No doubt a great number of copies will be
printed by the time this reaches you, and therefore I shall take it for
granted that it stands as it is. Leech, otherwise is very good, and the
illustrations altogether are by far the best that have been done for any
of the Christmas books."[19]

Dickens' real warmth towards the artist is shown by the fact that
Leech was back again in the next Christmas book for 1848, *The
Haunted Man And The Ghost's Bargain.* In one place, Leech had to
nearly reproduce the design in Tenniel's frontispiece, but perhaps his
Punch colleague John Tenniel was an easier person to work alongside
than Maclise R.A.! The five contributions are broadly domestic,
superbly rounded figures sometimes leaning to the humorous, sometimes to pathos, but all boldly conceived. The fact remains however
that this was the last work to come directly from Dickens although
the writer so obviously admired Leech's satirical sketches, perhaps he
found him too unreliable to work with, perhaps he valued his friendship too highly to wish to put it once again to the test.

Dickens' enthusiasm for his friend's work was unabated when he
wrote a most glowing review of *The Rising Generation* in 1848.
Twelve of the famous *Punch* series of precocious youths had been
transferred to lithograph, coloured by hand, and published at the
Punch office in stiff yellow paper wrappers with a vignette by Leech.
Dickens, like so many of his contemporaries, recognises the
originality in Leech, appreciates the modernity of his subjects, their

19. Forster, op. cit., pp. 439-440.

A FRESH MORNING.

voice being the accurate voice of the period and the statement of it in fresh and palatable terms — something entirely new.

"In all his designs," writes Dickens, "whatever Mr Leech desires to do he does. His drawing seems to us charming, and the expression, indicated by the simplest means, is exactly the natural expression, and is recognised as such at once. Some forms of our existing life will never have a better chronicler. His wit is good-natured, and always the wit of a gentleman. He has a becoming sense of responsibility and restraint; he delights in agreeable things, and he imparts some pleasant air of his own to things not pleasant in themselves; he is suggestive and full of matter, and he is always improving. Into the tone as well as into the execution of what he does, he has brought a certain elegance which is altogether new, without involving any compromise of what is true. Popular art in England has not had so rich an acquisition."[20] Only a dozen or so years later, Charles Baudelaire was saying similar things about the French artist Constantin Guys, the preoccupation with "modern life" was in the wind and contagious for both writers and illustrators.

By the end of the 1840s John Leech and his wife were part of the Dickens' circle. The great "Boz" not only dined with the Leeches, he made up touring parties of his friends and included John Leech in them. At the beginning of April 1848, Dickens took Forster, Lemon and Leech to stay at the White Hart, Salisbury, from where they travelled around to Winterslow, Stonehenge and explored the city. Leech was a keen walker and according to Henry Silver "walked at a good pace, for he was fond of real exercise, and hated lazy lounging".[21] Perhaps it was on this occasion that Leech gave his friend the walking-stick, inscribed "C.D. from J.L." which the novelist often carried with him.[22] In late December 1848, he joined Dickens and Lemon again for a trip to Norwich, in which the three friends explored Stansfield Hall, scene of a famous murder, and then put up at the Royal Hotel, Yarmouth, for the first days of January 1849. The following month he was with his wife and the Dickenses at his favourite resort, Brighton, first staying in lodgings and then at the Bedford Hotel. He was in Paris with Dickens in February 1850[23] and in 1853 joined the novelist at his rented home, the Chateau des Moulineaux, Rue Beaurepaire, Boulogne. It was the often repeated September holidays that Dickens remembered most vividly: "For several years we always went to the seaside together in the autumn, and lived, through the autumn months, in constant daily association."[24]

Probably the closest intimacy developed between the two families on a memorable visit to the Isle of Wight between July and September 1849. Dickens rented an attractive villa called Winterbourne at Bonchurch. There were magnificent views across the downs and there was a waterfall nearby that Dickens turned into a perpetual shower-bath. The Leeches took a neighbouring house

20. Frith, op. cit., Vol. 2, pp. 66-67.

21. Silver, Henry, "The Home Life of John Leech", *Magazine of Art,* Vol. 16, p. 119.

22. Yates, Edmund, *Recollections,* 1884, Vol. 2, p. 151.

23. Johnson, E., *Charles Dickens,* 1953, Vol. 2, p. 728.

24. Hole, op. cit., p. 87.

Awful Appearance of a "Wopps" at a Pic-nic.

called Nile Cottage and were joined there by Dicky Doyle on 23
August. The Dickens' party included the novelist's wife, Miss
Hogarth, numerous children and Mark Lemon, Augustus Egg,
Douglas Jerrold and "Phiz". The holiday began enormously
cheerfully, Dickens organised his friends into a club called the Sea
Serpents and under a serpent banner, took them on picnics to Cook's
Castle where they boiled potatoes and ran races with the corpulent
Mark Lemon. Despite the coolness of the island they were disturbed
on at least one picnic by that summer pest — wasps, and Leech had
great joy in setting it down for *Punch* as "Awful Appearance of a
'Wopps' at a Pic-nic"[25] (above) which appeared in 1849.

By the beginning of September, despite frequent dining between
the houses, lots of games and forfeits, neither Dickens nor the
Leeches were feeling particularly well, the air was so enervating. On
about 22 September, disaster struck in the form of a bathing accident
to the luckless Leech. Dickens takes up the story in a letter to Forster:

"And now for my less pleasing piece of news. The sea has been
running very high, and Leech, while bathing, was knocked over by a
bad blow from a great wave on the forehead. He is in bed, and had
twenty of his namesakes on his temples this morning. When I heard
of him just now, he was asleep — which he had not been at night!"
The following day he added less favourable news, "Leech has been
very ill with congestion of the brain ever since I wrote, and being still
in excessive pain has had ice to his head continuously, and been bled
in the arm besides. Beard and I sat up there all night." On the 26th he
could add surprising developments. "My plans are all unsettled by
Leech's illness; as of course I do not like to leave this place while I
can be of any service to him and his good little wife. But all visitors
are gone today, and Winterbourne once more left to the engaging

25. *Punch,* Vol. 17, p. 76.

THE EFFECTS OF TIGHT LACING ON THE OLD LADY
OF THREADNEEDLE STREET.

26. Forster, op. cit., pp. 503-4.

27. Evans Letters, Harvard University MS Eng 1028, letter from T. Armstrong.

28. Layard, G.S., *Shirley Brooks — A Great Punch Editor,* p. 165.

29. Cuthbert Bede, *nom de plume* of the Revd Edward Bradley (1827-1889).

30. Evans Letters, op. cit., letter from Cuthbert Bede, 14 August, 1884.

family of the inimitable B. Ever since I wrote to you Leech has been seriously worse, and again very heavily bled. The night before last he was in such an alarming state of restlessness, which nothing could relieve, that I proposed to Mrs Leech to try magnetism. Accordingly in the middle of the night I fell to; and, after a very fatiguing bout of it, put him to sleep for an hour and thirty-five minutes. A change came on in the sleep, and he is decidedly better. I talked to the astounded little Mrs Leech cross him, when he was asleep, as if he had been a truss of hay ... What do you think of my setting up in the magnetic line with a large brass plate? 'Terms, twenty-five guineas per nap'." [26] Dickens did everything that a friend could do, sleeping on a sofa at Nile Cottage for several nights after Leech's recovery. But the concussion, for that is what it undoubtedly was, may well have contributed to his later nervous illnesses.

One criticism that might be levelled at the gentle Leech is that despite enormous powers as a draughtsman, he preferred to keep off the great issues of the day, to confine himself to the satire of the middle classes at home and abroad, the absurdities of the fox-hunter, the suburban householder, the pretentious tradesman or lackey. This seems an undeniably safe standpoint amid the great social and political convulsions of his time, Chartism, revolutions, exploitation and incredible railway frauds and bank swindles. As *Punch* became progressively less radical, there was less need for it to dwell on these follies. As chief cartoonist, the apolitical Leech was happy to go along with the decisions of the *Punch* table, concerning the "big cut".

Part of Leech's trouble was that he was far happier in sketching from memory where the subject had filtered through his note-books and then his mind, than in direct portraiture. The Victorian caricaturist was becoming *more* of a portraitist and the public wanted stronger resemblances. He had trained himself in the early days by going night after night to the lobbies in order to get parliamentary portraits, trying "to draw not only the face of a man but his whole body, his gait and his general appearance ...". [27]

Although not attuned to this political work and often hurried by some of the suggestions of the *Punch* table, he could work swiftly and deftly if gripped by enthusiasm for his project. Shirley Brooks remembered the decision, commission and completion of the French Emperor cartoon in February 1859, executed with surprising speed. "Sure of hand, he drew the figure on the wood-block, without making any sketch of it, as he had before done Mr Punch's Fancy Ball, which was far more elaborate, but the dozen or so figures were drawn within three hours." [28] This was all right if the likenesses were correct, but Leech had difficulty with them. Cuthbert Bede, [29] an early *Punch* contributor, recalled that the artist needed encouragement with these caricature portraits. "I remember Leech bringing in his sketch of Bp Wilberforce, 'Soapy Sam' saying 'What we want is more Bishops' and expressing himself very dissatisfied with the likeness. I suggested a slight difference in the mouth — and he altered it to his satisfaction — & was highly pleased... It seemed to distress and perplex him, when he could not *at once* hit off the likeness!" [30]

Later on, Leech refused to follow celebrities around and decided to rely entirely on *carte de visite* photographs, a perfectly respectable solution to his dilemma. It was the job of Mark Lemon to procure these and when he didn't there were difficulties. One such outburst in February 1859 is interesting because it reveals Leech's attitude to the political "cuts" in particular and politics in general. "Spar ... between JL and ML," records Henry Silver, "J saying he wants portraits, has only 7, M thinks he might look out for them himself. J. says he hasn't time, hates politics and never thinks of them when walking out. Detests big cutting." [31] It is not surprising to discover therefore that though Leech was responsible for 223 large political cartoons out of 314 in the magazine's first five years, he proposed only eleven subjects himself! [32]

Despite this he did produce over the years some very remarkable political works, some no doubt suggested by Mayhew and Jerrold but others from his own closely held convictions. In a number of these he

31. Silver diary, op. cit., 17 February, 1859.

32. Spielman, M.H., *The History of "Punch"*, 1895, p. 170.

"General Fevrier" Turned Traitor — Leech's most famous political cartoon which appeared in Punch *in February 1855.*

'GENERAL FEVRIER" TURNED TRAITOR.

shows a great mastery in tragic subjects, an unexpected mastery to anyone unfamiliar with his reflective, often melancholy, nature. Among the most compelling and chilling images are "The Poor Man's Friend" of 1845, in which Death, a terrible spectre, comes as a welcome relief to a pauper, desolate and miserable. A similar scene that became etched on the nation's memory ten years later was "General Février turned Traitor", a highly charged cartoon in the middle of the Crimean War. The Tsar commenting on the Allied Armies in the Crimea had said "Russia has two generals in whom she can confide — Generals Janvier and Février." But February carried off the Tsar himself in 1855 and Leech depicts a gaunt skeletal soldier placing a cold hand on the prostrate Emperor (illustration opposite).

Leech's delicate, chiding art was not the mark of a major political caricaturist, but as Frith says, "as personality was the essence of the political cartoons, the use of it was unavoidable; but Leech managed to be personal without being offensive to the chief actor, unless, as in

"The Fagin of France After Condemnation", a satire on George Cruikshank's illustration to Dickens' Oliver Twist. Punch, *1848.*

THE FAGIN OF FRANCE AFTER CONDEMNATION.

(*Slightly altered from "*OLIVER TWIST*.*")

" GOOD BOY, D'ASSIS ; WELL DONE," HE MUMBLED. " MONTPENSIER, TOO ; HA ! HA ! HA ! MONTPENSIER, TOO ; QUITE THE GENTLEMAN NOW—" * * " AN OLD MAN, MY LORD ; A VERY OLD, OLD MAN ! "

Colour Plate 8. "John Leech as Master Matthew", a self-portrait in watercolour, showing the artist in his costume for Dickens' production of Every Man In His Humour, 1845. Charterhouse School

Colour Plate 9. "Charles Dickens as Captain Bobadil", a watercolour of the author by John Leech, done during the same production of Every Man In His Humour, 1845. Charterhouse School

the case of Louis Philippe and a few others, he considered that their escapades deserved severe castigation.''[33] (See illustration on page 87.) The artist's most savage attacks were reserved for the proprietors of the sweat shops, those cruel exploiters of the poor seamstresses and dressmakers who toiled in appalling conditions, for a pittance, in order to produce clothes for vain society ladies. In *Punch's Almanack* for 1845, he illustrates the making of cheap clothing in a powerful and terrible drawing of cross-legged skeletons, stitching away, watched over by a prosperous and callous Jew (illustration below). This certainly shows Leech's anti-semitism (due to his sponging house experiences) but also his great humanity which was, in visual terms, the outcome of his friendship with Dickens.

That Dickens should have had a powerful influence on Leech's opinions is not so very surprising; two incidents in their friendship stand out in this respect. The great *cause célèbre* of 1849 was the trial and execution of the murderers, Mr and Mrs Manning. The crime aroused great public interest because it was committed by a married couple, and Mrs Manning was a foreigner who had once worked for the aristocracy. The gutter press dwelt at length on every gruesome detail. On 13 November, 1849, the Mannings were executed in public outside Horsemonger Lane Gaol, in the midst of a large and ghoulish crowd. Dickens and Forster attended this revolting spectacle as observers and Leech joined them, presumably at Dickens' suggestion. The novelist wrote two letters to *The Times* in which he voiced his disgust at the scene "the wickedness and levity of the immense crowd", "thieves, low prostitutes, ruffians and vagabonds" showing no pity when "the two miserable creatures who

33. Frith, op. cit., Vol. 2, p. 24.

THE CHEAP TAILOR AND HIS WORKMEN.

FROM THE MINING DISTRICTS.

AN ATTEMPT AT CONVERTING THE NATIVES.

Assiduous Young Curate. "WELL, THEN, I DO HOPE I SHALL HAVE THE PLEASURE OF SEEING BOTH OF YOU NEXT SUNDAY!"

Miner. "OI! THEE MAY'ST COAM IF 'E WULL. WE FOIGHT ON THE CROFT, AND OLD JOE TANNER BRINGS TH' BEER."

attracted all this ghastly sight about them were turned quivering into the air".[34] Leech produced at once his "The Great Moral Lesson of Horsemonger Lane" for *Punch,* an eye-witness report of the scene, showing the bestial and carnival atmosphere of the crowds with children playing tipcat at the gaol gates. It was not Leech's usual vein but the drawings were the underlining of Dickens' letters, the two men were working in consort.

In 1855 Lord Robert Grosvenor tried to introduce a Sunday Closing Bill which would shut the club houses, public houses and beer shops and encourage people to go to church. This sincere measure, introduced by the evangelical Grosvenor, had the effect of inflaming working-class opinion, because it made no allowance for their limited leisure time. A demonstration was organised in Hyde Park on 2 July, 1855, to protest about the Bill, an astonishing crowd of 150,000 turned up, including women and children and some very inflamatory speeches were made. Leech, out for a Sunday stroll, was also present and was alarmed by the number of police on duty and the way in which an orderly demonstration was generated into a riot of sizeable proportions. It seemed to him that the part the police had played was definitely provocative and he voiced his fears to his friend and fellow artist, Augustus Egg. Dickens wrote to him two days later:[35]

> Tavistock House
> 4th July 1855
>
> My dear Leech — I saw Egg yesterday, and he told me what you have told him you saw of the Police in Hyde Park. I cannot rest — I really cannot — without urging you in the strongest manner, to write a letter to The Times today with your name and address, stating the plain fact. It is what a public and known man is bound to do.

Leech responded with a letter to *The Times* on the 7th:[36]

> Sir, Although I was one of the quiet spectators in the Park last Sunday, I should not have troubled you with my testimony as to the Violent conduct of the police but for the complacency with which the Home Secretary (as I read in your Parliamentary report of this day) dwells on the ease of identifying individual policemen by letter and number. I saw myself a policeman, when ordered to drive back the people who were leaning over the railings of the drive, strike without any preliminary warning, the feet and ankles of a lad, who was positively doing nothing, in such a manner as to cause him the most acute pain, and I shall not soon forget his look of agony and astonishment. Now, I beg to assure you, as one pretty well acquainted with London and its people, and tolerably well used to crowds, that although I was very anxious to take this man's number, with a view to bringing him to the punishment he deserved, I found it, in the confusion, and in the necessity I was under of preserving my own skull, absolutely

34. *The Times,* 14 November, 1849.

35 *Nonsuch Dickens,* Vol. 2, p. 676.

36. *The Times,* 7 July, 1855.

impossible to do so.

I feel it right to state that, although I witnessed a good deal of unnecessary violence on the part of some of the police, others of the men behaved with great tolerance and good temper under much provocation. This, however, is only an additional reason why those who so grossly misconducted themselves should be followed up, when possible, and dismissed from situations for which they are so manifestly unfit —

I am, sir, your obedient servant,
John Leech

On 14th July Leech's first comment on the incident appears in the pages of *Punch*. In an unusually elaborate wood engraving the "Battle of the Hyde Park", the "Gallant and Daring Act of Private Lobbs" is depicted (below); Lobbs, a corpulent police constable is

BATTLE OF THE HYDE PARK.

GALLANT AND DARING ACT OF PRIVATE LOBBS (OF THE CRUSHERS), WHO, BY HIMSELF,
STORMED AN OLD TREE, AND VERY NEARLY CAPTURED THREE SMALL BOYS.

seen, baton at the ready, trying to reach three very small urchins in an old oak tree. Similar charges of by-standers go on in the background. The following week, 21st July, Leech evens out the odds against the police with his innate sense of fairness. Two ruffians are shown in conversation, one saying to the other, "I tell yer what, Bill, I think the Police are a Bad Lot — And I wish they was done away with altogether."

Dickens could also have been behind Leech's most controversial drawing published in *Punch* on 12 September, 1857. It is likely because *Punch* had ceased to be a radical paper and the Manning execution and the Hyde Park Riots were excellent precedents. In "The Great Social Evil" (below), Leech shows two prostitutes in the

THE GREAT SOCIAL EVIL.

Time :—Midnight. A Sketch not a Hundred Miles from the Haymarket.

Bella. "Ah ! Fanny ! how long have you been *Gay* !"

"WELL, JACK! HERE'S GOOD NEWS FROM HOME. WE'RE TO HAVE A MEDAL."
"THAT'S VERY KIND. MAYBE ONE OF THESE DAYS WE'LL HAVE A COAT TO STICK IT ON?"

"Well Jack, Here's good news from Home ...", Punch, 1855. Leech was a strong critic of inefficiency in the Crimean War.

neighbourhood of the Haymarket, the one leaning languidly, the other holding up her skirts from the rainy pavement, they are pretty, but weary and haunted. "Ah Fanny," says one to the other, "How long have you been *gay*?" Leech had captured a sombre moment in Victorian London, the drawing is vibrant, the subject compassionate yet objective. At such times Leech equals his greatest French contemporary Constantin Guys. "In many a scene," writes Frith, "Leech becomes a warm sympathiser with unmerited distress, and constantly his honest heart is stirred into indignation at some instance of injustice, then we find that the pencil which can deal so gently with childhood and woman can also, in indelible lines, stigmatise the stony-hearted oppressor."[37]

Although no longer depicting the sovereign, as he had in the 1840s, Leech could still be very scathing about government where it ignored the ordinary man and his needs. There is no better example of this than in his devastatingly terse comment on the neglect of the army during the Crimean War. The cartoon (shown above) appeared in

37. Frith, op. cit., Vol. 2, p. 242.

A GAY YOUNG FELLOW.

Young Rapid. "YOU ARE QUITE SURE THIS IS THE CORRECT
DRESS FOR A YOUNG FELLOW OF THAT PERIOD, EH?"
Mr. Noses. "OH, PERFECTLY CORRECT, SIR; AND REALLY LOOKS
SPLENDID ON YER!"

38. Frith, op. cit., Vol. 2, p. 63.

39. "Dickens as J.T. Danson knew
    him", Fielding, K.J., *The
    Dickensian,* Vol. 68, 1971-72, p.
    154.

40. *The Dickensian,* Vol. 34, 1938, p.
    10.

Punch in 1855. The patriotic fervour which had despatched the troops in 1854 was gradually being replaced by the growing realisation, chiefly due to the reports of "Russell of the Times", that the commanding officers were incompetent, the army ill equipped and that disease was claiming as many lives as Russian bullets. Leech had originally shared the illusions of his fellow citizens and had produced a cartoon showing a sturdy and jovial sailor speaking to his officer entitled "Jack's Holiday — A Scene off Balaclava".

A further sidelight on this friendship, which Frith describes as so "especially attractive to Dickens",[38] is revealed by a member of Dickens' staff on one of his journalistic ventures. Throughout the 1840s Leech had continuing money difficulties and the board of his father and unmarried sisters was a continual burden to him. He had somehow obtained Old Leech a printing job and pleaded with Bradbury to make use of him. Dickens was no stranger to importunate fathers and did his friend an act of kindness by finding the sad old man work. J.T. Danson worked on Dickens' *Daily News* in 1845-46 and leaves a painterly description of the chief skeleton in Leech's cupboard.

"I had two rooms allotted to me", he writes, "one for the Parliamentary Papers, & similar documents coming in daily. I asked for a Clerk to look to the due receipt, and arrangement, and custody of these: I agreeing to act as a sort of Librarian, and general Referee. I received one, in the person of a decayed elderly gentleman, who proved to be the father of Mr John Leech, already a prominent member of the Staff of 'Punch'. He had formerly kept a large Hotel (inherited, I think, from *his* father; and called, if I remember aright, the 'London Coffee House') at the corner of Newgate Street and Ludgate Hill. He was most willing, and most anxious to earn all his salary of 30/− a week; but I must confess he was of very little use."[39]

*   *   *   *   *

But perhaps the occasions when Dickens and Leech got to know each other best, and were most frank with one another, was over the amateur theatricals on which they both worked. Dickens was a most accomplished actor, Mark Lemon also had some talent and very soon the novelist gathered round him a cast of distinguished amateurs who gave performances for charity and special benefit nights. Leech's first involvement with this was in the summer of 1845 when he was invited to join the troop for Jonson's *Every Man In His Humour,* taking place at two London theatres in the autumn. Leech was given the part of "Master Matthew the towne gull", not a particularly taxing part but with some fairly long appearances. He was rehearsing from July and in August had to attend at Dickens' house to be fitted by the English Opera House tailor with a costume from a picture "the very thing for your dress".[40] (Colour Plate 8, page 88.)

The performance at Miss Kelly's Theatre, Dean Street, Soho, was one of the events of the London scene that September. *The Times,* which did not normally notice an amateur cast, went out of its way to

Manager. "LADIES AND GENTLEMEN—A—I MEAN RESPECTED INDIVIDUAL,—IN CONSEQUENCE OF THE GREAT ATTRACTION OF THE EXHIBITION OR CRYSTAL PALACE, I BEG TO ANNOUNCE TO YOU THAT THIS RIDICULOUS FARCE OF OPENING MY THEATRE WILL NOT BE REPEATED; AND YOUR ORDER WILL BE RETURNED TO YOU ON APPLICATION AT THE BOX-OFFICE."

describe the evening and the list of celebrities, Henry Mayhew, Frank Stone, John Forster, Mark Lemon and John Leech as "a complete curiosity". "Amateur performances", wrote the paper, "always go off well in a certain sense, because the privilege of expressing disapprobation is not allowed. But the triumph achieved on Saturday was far beyond the negative kind of success. Not only did the audience applaud with the utmost zeal, and call for all the actors, but their conversation among each other showed how sincerely they approved what they had witnessed."[41] Dickens had emerged as a very talented amateur and received plaudits of praise (Colour Plate 9, page 88), but *The Times* also noted that "he was excellently supported by Mr Leech as the empty, frivolous and foppish Master Matthew".

By popular demand the play was put on again at the St James's Theatre on Saturday, 15 November, 1845, the same cast taking part, but the audience including all the great names of the day. Prince Albert was there, so were the Duke of Devonshire, Lord Melbourne, Caroline Norton and the Carlyles, who strongly disapproved. It was thought to have been a better showing than its predecessor and *The Times* specially mentions "the mild homage of Master Matthew, paid with such quiet unobtrusive humour by Mr Leech".[42] One can imagine shy and pretty Annie Leech sitting in this galaxy of the famous and hoping that John would give a creditable performance. Her brother, Charles Eaton, had been brought in to play "William".

Once begun, the theatricals were infectious and further events were planned for 1846, a benefit performance at Miss Kelly's on 3rd January of Fletcher's *The Elder Brother* and a farce *Comfortable Lodgings*. Leech played Brisac in the first and Bombardier Babillard in the second. He also played The Marquis in *Animal Magnetism* at the end of the year. In 1847 there were highly successful tours of

Invitation card to the amateur performance at Miss Kelly's Theatre, September 20th 1845, in which Leech took part.

41. *The Times*, 23 September, 1845.
42. ibid., 17 November, 1845.

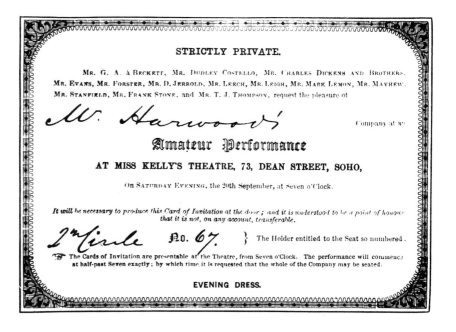

STRICTLY PRIVATE.

MR. G. A. à BECKETT, MR. DUDLEY COSTELLO, MR. CHARLES DICKENS AND BROTHERS, MR. EVANS, MR. FORSTER, MR. D. JERROLD, MR. LEECH, MR. LEIGH, MR. MARK LEMON, MR. MAYHEW, MR. STANFIELD, MR. FRANK STONE, and MR. T. J. THOMPSON, request the pleasure of

Mr. Harwood's   Company at an

Amateur Performance

AT MISS KELLY'S THEATRE, 73, DEAN STREET, SOHO,

On SATURDAY EVENING, the 20th September, at Seven o'Clock.

It will be necessary to produce this Card of Invitation at the door; and it is understood to be a point of honour that it is not, on any account, transferable.

2nd Circle No. 67.   } The Holder entitled to the Seat so numbered.

☞ The Cards of Invitation are presentable at the Theatre, from Seven o'Clock. The performance will commence at half-past Seven exactly; by which time it is requested that the whole of the Company may be seated.

EVENING DRESS.

THE PRIVATE THEATRICALS.

Every Man and *Turning the Tables* at Manchester and Liverpool, but it was in 1848 that the company reached its zenith with a performance in front of the Queen. This took place at the Haymarket Theatre on 17th May, a performance of *The Merry Wives of Windsor* had preceded on 15th May at the same theatre. It must have been in this latter play that Frith saw Leech take part and commented rather tartly on the artist's efforts as "Slender". "It is only in that character that I can remember him, though I must have seen him in others. The tone in which he said 'Oh, sweet Anne Page!' can I ever forget? There was a ring of impatience in his performance, a kind of 'Oh, I wish this was all over!' that was plainly perceptible to those who knew him intimately. Leech's tall figure and handsome face told well upon the stage, but with those his attractions as an actor ceased."[43] It was during the rehearsals for the farce *Animal Magnetism* at this time that Dickens became exasperated with Leech's shaky words. Referring to the tour of the *Merry Wives* to Birmingham the following June, Dickens wrote irritatedly to Lemon "we cannot drivel about Leech, but must either have him in or leave him out".[44]

His last appearance on the boards seems to have been at Knebworth House on 30 October, 1850, when *Every Man* was put on

43. Frith, op. cit., Vol. 2, p. 65.
44. Dexter, *Letters to Mark Lemon*, 1927, p. 73.

in aid of Bulwer Lytton's Guild of Literature and Art. He has left a delightful memory of this in "Private Theatricals", an illustration (shown opposite) that found its way into *Punch's Almanack* for 1851 on which he was then working. The scene is set in the saloon of a large Jacobean country house, everyone is gathered in costume for an amateur performance of *The Merry Wives* and busily learning their lines. Despite the change of play, the rich interior is a loose rendering of Knebworth with the introduction of the carved mantelpiece from the Queen's Bedroom. In the centre is the gross figure of Falstaff, easily identifiable as Mark Lemon. "The great Tudor Hall made a capital theatre, and the dresses in the old 'withdrawing-room' formed quite a pretty picture. All the neighbourhood was there: and the play would have gone off capitally, notwithstanding the melancholy sedateness of Mrs Page." It was a charming epitaph to Leech the actor.

PRIVATE THEATRICALS.

DISMAY OF MR. JAMES JESSAMY ON BEING TOLD THAT HE WILL SPOIL THE WHOLE THING IF HE DOESN'T SHAVE OFF HIS WHISKERS.

Mr Sponge is introduced to "Ercles."

Colour Plate 10. *"Mr Sponge is Introduced to 'Ercles' ", from* Mr Sponge's Sporting Tour, *1852.*

Colour Plate 11. *"A Day with Puffington's Hounds", from* Mr Sponge's Sporting Tour, *1852.*

A Day with Puffington's Hounds.

Chapter Five

LEECH IN THE SHIRES
WITH MR JORROCKS

I f Dickens' friendship with Leech had, with the exception of the Christmas books, been more influential than practical, his contact with the other great literary lion of the Victorian salons, W.M. Thackeray, was also of enormous importance. After that brief acquaintance at Charterhouse between senior and junior, Thackeray had re-established the friendship in about 1843 after meeting the artist at the *Punch* table. Leech dined fairly regularly at Thackeray's house in the 1840s[1] and was obviously regarded as part of the family circle, he went on riding expeditions with the novelist, met his English and French friends and shared his humour. Thackeray was close enough and perceptive enough too in recognising the artist's depressive and melancholy side, that obverse side to the sunny humorist of *Punch*. On his part, Leech followed Thackeray's work with interest and attended all of the novelist's famous lectures on "The Four Georges".[2]

Ironically it was the metropolitan, clubable and unsporting Thackeray who was to introduce Leech to his most famous collaborators, Mr Jorrocks and Robert Smith Surtees. Surtees was a sporting novelist in a Regency, not to say a Georgian mould. A member of the Whig gentry of Durham, R.S. Surtees took his sport and his prejudices seriously, he had the squire's traditional dislike of lords, upstarts, self-made men and adventuresses, all of whom feature in his books. His virtues were the virtues of the countryside, an undying respect for the chase, the gun and the rod, an infectious hospitality, a loyalty to one's neighbours if one could hunt across their land and *they* did not abuse *your* riparian rights. His world was more that of Rowlandson and Smollett than that of Leech and Thackeray, let alone that of Dickens.

Surtees had attained a steady success from 1831 when he had become Editor of *The New Sporting Magazine.* His rather pungent style of writing and his brilliant observations on horses and riders were well-timed to bring artistic and literary talent to the journal in the sporting atmosphere of the 'thirties. Surtees successfully lured Abraham Cooper, J.F. Herring, H.B. Chalon, Edwin Landseer and Francis Grant from other magazines, but none of these were literary illustrators or the counterparts to Surtees' brisk, pithy writing. Surtees' strong talent for characterisation led him naturally into the novel. *Jorrocks* first appeared as a serial in *The New Sporting*

1. Brookfield, C. and F., *Mrs Brookfield and Her Circle,* 1905, pp. 187 and 256.

2. Frith Correspondence, Victoria and Albert Museum Library, 12 January, 1857.

Magazine, 1831-34, and then in volume form in 1838 with twelve un-coloured illustrations by H.K. Browne, "Phiz". The third edition of 1843 had fifteen coloured plates by Henry Alken and *Handley Cross,* a continuation of the Jorrocks character, appeared the same year. Neither "Phiz" nor Alken were the ideal artists for the humorous and yet clearly modern life subjects of Surtees. Despite his heavy caricature, Surtees was a keen observer of changing country life, the advent of the railways, the emergence of the nouveaux riches, the growth of subscription hunts in the Shires. Phiz's small scale figures and Henry Alken's Regency gloss were not suitable for the mid-century even with a traditionalist author.

As far back as 1843, when *Handley Cross* was being completed, Surtees' publishers, Colburn, had suggested Leech as a possible illustrator. It was an interesting choice; Leech had as yet undertaken no sporting subjects in *Punch,* but Colburn must have known his contributions to *Bell's Life in London and Sporting Chronicle.* In the

"Don't check her, Jack; give her her head."

"Don't check her, Jack; Give her her head." An early hunting subject, Punch *1849.*

event, Leech's charge of six guineas an illustration was considered too much, and although Tattersall and Standfast were considered, the book appeared unillustrated. When *Hillingdon Hall* was appearing in *The New Sporting Magazine* in 1844, Tattersall this time tried to persuade Leech to draw for it, but again without any success.[3] The artist, whose price for square subjects had been £7 in 1842 was not going to lower his charge to £5, despite being pressed for money and continually having to borrow small sums from Charley Adams.

Surtees, who had as wide a choice of artists as any author, seems to have been searching for a new man to realise his books in the late 1840s. Still relying on "Phiz" and Alken, he does not seem to have thought of Leech whose hunting subjects had begun to be popular in *Punch* from the middle of 1847 (see illustration page 100). In May 1849, Surtees, on the crest of another success in *Mr Sponge's Sporting Tour,* began once more to seek out the perfect illustrator. Surprisingly his choice fell on Thackeray. Thackeray's charming and modest reply with its warmth towards his friend, was received by Surtees on 30 May, 1849.[4]

> 13 Young Street
> Kensington
>
> My Dear Sir, — I was very much flattered by your proposal to illustrate your tale, but I only draw for my own books, and indeed am not strong enough as an artist to make designs for anybody else's stories. You would find my pictures anything but comical, and I have not the slightest idea how to draw a horse, a dog, or a sporting scene of any sort. My friend Leech, I should think, would be your man — he is of a sporting turn, and to my mind draws a horse excellently.
>
> Thank you very much for the proposal and for your good opinion of my book. Are you the Charterhouse Surtees? Legends are current to that effect.
>
> Mr Jorrocks has long been a dear and intimate friend of mine. I stole from him years ago, having to describe a hunting scene with which I was quite unfamiliar, and I lived in Great Coram Street once too —
>
> Very faithfully yours, my dear sir,
> W.M. Thackeray.

Leech and Surtees must have met before 1851 when the true partnership begins, so how were they matched, the leading sporting writer of the day and the foremost sporting illustrator? The sporting squire from the North-East had the self-assurance of the gentleman; well provided for in money, land and homes, he had no need to justify himself or fight for a position in society. Leech on the other hand was unsure of himself, ashamed of his shifting fortunes, all the time aspiring (if unconsciously) to upper-middle class security, and the class that Surtees represented. Surtees was an instinctive

3. Cuming, E.D., *Robert Smith Surtees (Creator of 'Jorrocks') 1804-1864,* 1924, p. 222.

4. ibid., pp. 245-6.

horseman, an MFH and very much a leader in hunting etiquette and lore; Leech was a timorous rider, an inconspicuous member of the field who preferred a good steady mount to the drama of a lively horse. What they shared deeply was a love of the saddle; with Surtees this was combined with a great critical knowledge of horse-flesh, with Leech it was combined with acute observation of rider and mount, in every light, every weather, every situation.

Surtees' novels were based on the quick observation of his hunting friends much as Leech's sketches were, but imagination was not his strong point, he reported rather than invented, caricatured rather than developed his most brilliant personalities. But he was certainly aware of the strong creative gifts in others and in Leech particularly, where the "story line" of the artist's characters *did* progress naturally and where the short snatches of dialogue under the *Punch* pictures were often more realistic than those of the novelist's own text. This is nowhere more obvious than in Surtees' early recognition of Leech's "Mr Briggs" as a creation of genius, Briggs who had arrived at Bouverie Street in 1849 and was as intrepid as Mr Jorrocks without half that amiable cockney's measure of success. Surtees almost at once proposes a closer association with Mr Briggs for himself, as soon as *Sponge* has been considered by the publishers Bradbury and Evans, he writes to Mark Lemon to suggest Mr Briggs entrance into the new novel as one of its characters. Leech, less than enthusiastic, replied from Baslow in the autumn of 1851.[5]

"I have not had an opportunity of seeing Lemon on the subject of a former note of yours *in re* Briggs. The matter seems to me very funny, but upon consideration I should like to keep Mr Briggs separate, as he is exceedingly useful to me when I am in the country and hard up for a subject (which is sometimes I assure you). I think of doing him for instance, grouse shooting next week if anything ridiculous turns up on Tuesday, when I make my debut on the moors here: but there is no reason why your matter should not be used, only with another name for the hero . . .

You will at once see what I mean, I hope. If I *fixed* anything upon Briggs, I should not be able to make him jump about from hunting to fly-fishing and from fly-fishing to grouse shooting, and so on, which I can do at present without much difficulty."

Surtees with his respect for such a superb model did not let the matter rest there; shortly afterwards he approached Mark Lemon about contributing a *Punch* column featuring a Briggs-type character. Fortunately the suggestion was turned down and these two very different but very compatible Victorian stars were left to develop their own skills without conscious borrowings. When the negotiations were under way for the publication of *Sponge's Sporting Tour* in the summer of 1851, Surtees stressed in a letter to Bradbury and Evans how equal that partnership would be. "It required considerable pruning and trimming," Surtees had written of the book, "but there is the substance for a good sporting tale, which

5. Cuming, op. cit., p. 250.

Mr Sponge declares himself

Colour Plate 12. "Mr Sponge declares himself", from Mr Sponge's Sporting Tour, *1852.*

Colour Plate 13. "Mr Jogglebury Crowdey with his dog and his gun", from Mr Sponge's Sporting Tour, *1852.*

Mr Jogglebury Crowdey with his dog and his gun.

MR. PUFFINGTON, FROM THE ORIGINAL PICTURE.

Illustrations from Mr Sponge's Sporting Tour, *1852.*

6. Cuming, op. cit., p. 248.

7. Brookfield, op. cit., p. 187.

8. Cuming, op. cit., p. 252.

9. ibid., p. 253.

Mr Leech's illustrations will, I think, make sell. It should be ready about the middle of October or so."[6]

Leech's fame, by the late 'forties equal to the fame of *Punch,* could carry along with it authors far less distinguished than Surtees and that writer already had his following. While Mrs Brookfield of the Thackeray circle could refer to "Leech who does the large pictures in Punch" meaning the political sketches,[7] the majority of the readers would have thought his name synonymous with social cuts and Mr Briggs. Briggs, part self-portrait, part everyman figure, had a history going well back into the eighteenth century as the cockney sportsman on vacation; Dighton had used it, so had Seymour, and it would be an interesting speculation as to whether Leech had read *Jorrocks* previous to the appearance of his celebrated suburban horseman.

But the first piece of collaboration was to be with *Mr Sponge,* not the solid and dependable Jorrocks or Briggs, but an equestrian confidence trickster and limpet, as his name implies. "Soapy Sponge" is very much a Surtees creation, as one thinks of the Leech repertoire one realises that there are no cads in it (dandies, snobs, ruffians ocasionally but no cads), so Leech works closely with the text. *Sponge* had only completed its unillustrated run in the *New Monthly* a few months when Surtees began sending revised texts to Leech in late July 1851. He included a list of "scenes that I think will do for the illustrations" although he never expected the artist to follow it slavishly. Much of the business was done in their correspondence although the Leeches were fairly frequent visitors to Hamsterley Hall, Durham, as the two men had an instant liking for each other.

The Surtees novels and *Mr Sponge* in particular give us a day by day account of Leech working with an author of his own stature and his own inclinations. The earliest proposal seems to have been to issue it as a volume, but Bradbury and Evans were uncertain although Leech had committed himself to producing "twelve 'Sponge' illustrations on wood, the size of the Briggs cuts in 'Punch'."[8] Evans had proposed that the novel should be issued in twelve monthly parts at a shilling each, a more profitable and sure way of publishing and one with which Leech was delighted and was "sure we shall make a hit" as Surtees put it. Leech at once took command of the colour plates, that were to form the main attraction of each part and wrote to Surtees:[9]

"Mr Evans has just written to me about the newly proposed form of 'Mr Sponge' which I think excellent and admirably adapted to the work. I presume he will commence with the New Year, and as there are to be twelve coloured illustrations and *red* is a very taking colour with our craft, I write this to say that I think it will be well to have as many hunting ones in the twelve as we can, leaving non-hunting subjects for the wood-cuts. I will therefore go through my proposed list of illustrations again, and amend to this form for your approbation, and also make out a list for wood-cuts.

I think No 1 will still have to be Mr Sponge at the horse-dealer's

Illustrations from Mr Sponge's Sporting Tour, *1852.*

10. Surtees, R.S., *Mr Sponge's Sporting Tour,* 1852, p. 15.

11. Cuming, op. cit., p. 250.

12. ibid., pp. 261-2.

choosing his nags: at all events, that we cannot get him into scarlet at starting, if my recollection of matters is right.''

This easy relationship and natural understanding of roles, so different from Dickens and Forster acting as a middle man, must have helped Leech immensely. Surtees introduced his illustrator to his readers continually, not only in a reference to Mr Briggs but more overtly in the first number — ''We trust our opening chapters, aided by our friend Leech's pencil, will have enabled our readers to embody such a Sponge in their minds eye as will assist them in following us through the course of his peregrinations.''[10]

Leech's Sponge is neither too old nor too young. He is the least caricatured of the artist's anti-heroes, but every physical inch shows him to be on the make and his clothes, stance and easy familiarity reveal an ungentlemanly mien and cunning. Even in the judging of that great black horse ''Ercles'', the first coloured steel engraving of the series (Colour Plate 10, page 98), Sponge's swagger is too affected and even the groom and stable lad seem to be ''in the know''. Once in his hunting coat, Sponge seems to be transformed, he rides as part of the field but also as part of the landscape, he seems surer, defter and more at home than in the country houses or inns smoking other men's cigars and plundering their cellars. In almost all the big steel engravings Sponge alone is impassive, unanimated, wearing the trickster's inscrutability (Colour Plate 11, page 98). Only with the arrival of Lucy Glitters towards the end of the work is Sponge's emotion joyously visible in Leech's drawing (Colour Plate 12, page 103). Some of the situations seem perfectly set for Leech, particularly ''Hercules takes a Draper's Shop'' in which the artist's bêtes noires, the drapers' assistants, can be shown alongside a huntsman! Surtees obviously made the first choice but one letter shows Leech's preference coming through as he links the absurd to a specially good illustrative subject.

''There is one subject in particular which I must do,'' he writes to Surtees from Baslow in about July 1851, ''I had promised it to myself when I first read the story — I mean the Dandy Huntsman having his portrait taken in the harness-room mounted on the saddle-tree, or whatever it is called.''[11] The result is the extremely happy composition of ''Mr Bragg's Equestrian Portrait'' which satirises Cooper, Herring and Alken, all the earlier illustrators of Surtees' magazine and corresponds to his *Punch* studio subjects.

The success of these plates lay partly in the faithfulness to Leech's original drawing and the accuracy with which his hand-colouring instructions were followed. In point of washes, Leech used subtle watercolour shades, charming and ethereal in the way Rowlandson's had been for *Dr Syntax*. Because of this he was always in dire trouble with his colourers, whether *A Christmas Carol* or *Sponge*. Leech writes desperately to Surtees in August 1852:[12]

''That our friend S[ponge] has lost the hair from the top of his head is no fault of mine. It ought to have been coloured like the rest, and was in my pattern. But I assure you the colourers are troublesome

Mr. Jorrocks has a Bye Day

Colour Plate 14. *"Mr Jorrocks has a Bye Day", from* Handley Cross, *1853.*

Colour Plate 15. *"Mr. Jorrocks's Lecture on 'Unting' ", from* Handley Cross, *1853.*

Mr. Jorrocks's Lecture on "Unting".

Initial letter from Mr. Sponge's Sporting Tour, *1852.*

customers — a green horse or a blue man would not at all shock them if they imagined that there ought to be, for the sake of variety, those colours in the picture. For S's tops I laid on the darkest mahogany colour, and not only that, but made a marginal note that they were to be kept *very* brown throughout. But they don't care . . .''

The artist was also well aware that he was an amateur in the saddle compared to Surtees and must be advised on hunt practice and tradition. He writes in November 1851, ''If anything in the way of *detail* presents itself to you that I might leave out with my imperfect hunting knowledge, I shall feel greatly obliged by your putting me up to it. It won't do to make any glaring blunders.''[13] Leech was also able to report that he had seen an excellent coloured paper for the cover of the monthly numbers, ''a good scarlet — it will be quite new, and away from all other periodicals''.[14]

The smaller woodcuts, though less eye-catching than the page plates, are none the less a vital and integral part of the book. Each number had a decorated cover, one colour plate and seven or eight wood engravings including the spirited little initial letter. These have almost the function of a resumé at the beginning of each new chapter, reminding the reader of a character or a setting, very necessary when the serial parts begin in mid-sentence. Illustrator works closely with author in these tiny masterpieces. They are absolutely free and yet so balanced on the page, full of inventive detail, movement and authentic landscape scenery. A good example of this meeting of minds is the initial at the top of Chapter XLII of *Sponge,* a diminutive huntsman riding a quill pen with legs towards the spine of an opened book (margin illustration). This links up superbly with Surtees' dissertation on pens when Mr Sponge tries to write his hunting report, the pens become steeds. ''There *were* pens, indeed — there almost always are — but they were miserable apologies of things; some were mere crow-quills — sort of cover-hacks of pens, while others were great, clumsy, heavy-heeled, cart-horse sort of things, clothed up to the hocks with ink, or split all the way through — vexatious apologies, that throw a person over just at the critical moment, when he has got his sheet prepared and his ideas all ready to pour upon paper; then splut — splut — splutter goes the pen, and away goes the train of thought.''[15]

If this sort of thing endeared him to Leech, the novelist seems to have been prepared at this stage to ignore the oversights. Leech had lapses and as everyone who knew and loved him realised they were simply part of his character. For instance in Chapter XXIV, Leech has not followed the text carefully enough; the amusing wood engraving of ''His Lordship and Jack'' lounging by the fire, shows Jack still wearing the spectacles that he has broken a few pages before. The illustration of these twin hunting men, mirror images of each other, is very humorous, but it is not accurate and Leech had already drawn the fire of Dickens over similar errors. But with the realisation of the main characters Surtees was more than happy, especially so with that irritating sportsman ''Mr Jogglebury Crowdey

13. Cuming, op. cit., p. 250.
14. ibid., p. 256.
15. *Sponge,* op. cit., p. 231.

IN A HURRY.

Boy. "NOW THEN, SIR!—THE MORE YOU LOOK THE LESS YOU'LL LOIKE IT!—GET OVER, OR ELSE LET US COME!"

Gent. on Horseback. "GET OUT OF THE WAY, BOY!—GET OUT OF THE WAY!—MY HORSE DON'T LIKE DONKEYS!"

Boy. "DOAN'T HE!—THEN, WHY DOAN'T HE KICK THEE ORF?"

Initial letter from Handley Cross, *1853.*

of Puddingpote Bower". "Jog and Lord Brougham admirable," he wrote to Leech after the September 1852 part came out, "also Jog and the phaeton. He is quite the Jog of my mind."[16] (Colour Plate 13, page 103.)

Sponge seems to have been a considerable success with the sporting fraternity. The appearance of such personalities as Mr Jawleyford, Lord Scamperdale, "Jack", the Jogs and Lucy Glitters, in quick succession, aided and abetted by Leech's designs, made Surtees anxious to do more, and he wrote in July 1852, before Sponge had ended:[17]

> My dear Sir,
> As we clearly have the ball at our feet, it may be well to consider the best way of playing it. My idea is that a little exertion will give us a monopoly of illustrated sporting literature, and it would be well if you could get Messrs Bradbury & Evans to forward matters so as to do full justice to your capital sketches.
>
> ... I have my doubts whether the benefits do not counteract the disadvantages of straining a work through a high-priced periodical like the 'New Monthly' first. It certainly hasn't damaged 'Sponge', and it enables one to revise to great advantage. The sporting world is altogether different from the general world of literature, a book serving many sportsmen a long time. Some indeed get on capitally without any.
>
> I think, then if we could get Bradbury & Evans to put on a little more steam, we might as well hunt together, and confine ourselves entirely to their works, as it will give a higher tone to our performances. We have already hit the nail on the head, and we may as well drive it right home.

Both author and artist had scented success with *Mr Sponge's Sporting Tour,* the logical next step was to publish a new edition of *Handley Cross.* This had been in Surtees' mind for some time. In July 1852 he had written to Leech saying that he hoped to get a half share in the book out of the hands of Colburn and into the hands of his new publisher; he estimated that it would make fourteen or fifteen parts.[18] *Handley Cross,* already well-known and much illustrated, had the same chance in Leech's hands as *Pickwick* had had in the "Phiz" illustrations, the fat grocer of Coram Street being nearly as popular as the fat clubman of Goswell Street. As already mentioned, the general public had formed its own idea of Mr Jorrocks' physical peculiarities from Surtees' pungent narrative, at the same time the most renowned comic sportsman of the 'fifties was Mr Briggs! To some degree therefore the two coalesced as plans for the illustrated *Handley Cross* progressed. Despite his girth, red face and "vig", Mr Jorrocks in Leech's view is more nineteenth century than eighteenth century, more a character to identify with sympathetically than to guffaw at. The early Briggs illustration (*Punch,* Vol. 18, 1850, p. 64), "Mr Briggs, not being good at his 'Fences' goes

16. Cuming, op. cit., p. 262.
17. ibid., pp. 273-5.
18. ibid., p. 273.

MR. BRIGGS, NOT BEING GOOD AT HIS "FENCES," GOES THROUGH THE PERFORMANCE OF OPENING A GATE.

through the performance of opening a gate'', is already in the Jorrocks mould, with the careful observation of the horse, the strained but hardly exaggerated gesture of the rider, and the extraordinary detail of the winter woods and haycocks (illustration above). In the same year but a little later on, we have ''Mr Briggs has Another Day with the Hounds'' (*Punch*, Vol. 18, 1850, p. 34), providing a further Jorrocks type situation, infuriated farmer, angry rider and amused yokels in smocks. Again the background can be stared into like a piece of early morning landscape, the church tower, the gnarled trees and the cut and laid hedge, not to mention the different styles of horsemanship represented by other members of the hunt!

The next Briggs adventure ''Another Glorious Day'' has certain similarities in composition to ''The Kill on The Cat & Custard Pot Day'' of *Handley Cross,* particularly to the position of the hound on the left-hand side. Generally however, Leech seems to have devised new situations for his drawings, only using a familiar theme if it had seemed particularly successful. A case in point is the extremely humorous little woodcut in the early part of *Sponge* showing ''Lord Bullfrog formerly owner of 'Hercules' ''. The intrepid peer is dismounted and struggling with his steed in a field of unremitting clay.

Mr Jorrocks wants twenty

Colour Plate 16. *"Mr Jorrocks wants twenty", from* Handley Cross, *1853.*

Colour Plate 17. *"Fresh as a four year old Went off like a shot", from* Mr Facey Romford's Hounds, *1864.*

"Fresh as a four year old Went off like a shot

Illustration from Handley Cross, *1853.*

Leech must have felt this little design lost in a page of text, for it becomes in *Handley Cross* one of the most famous of the Jorrocks' images "Come hup! I say — You Ugly Beast", the brilliant colour plate of Chapter XIV.

Surtees' assumption, before *Handley Cross* was started, that "we already have the ball at our feet" was one of those optimistic pronouncements that bedevil the history of the illustrated book. The fact that *Handley Cross* was already well-known and that Surtees and Leech were so perfectly matched, counted for nothing in the face of publishing difficulties and ill health, most of it on the artist's side, and in the difficult political climate. Matters began promisingly in 1852. Leech bolstered his liking for the Squire of Hamsterley by sporting visits and Mrs Leech and Mrs Surtees were introduced. In August 1852, Leech was sufficiently in the saddle to suggest alterations to the novelist in the name of the new work: "It has just occurred to me that a second title to 'Handley Cross' would be advisable — getting in the name of Mr Jorrocks somehow, but of that you will be the best judge. It is a good taking title though I think."[19] The suggestion was readily accepted and the first number of the series in March 1853 bears the new title of *Handley Cross or Mr Jorrock's Hunt,* but before that the exact appearance of the hunting hero had to be decided upon.

As already mentioned Briggs and Jorrocks have some slight relationship to each other and it was up to the artist to work upon this; both characters are middle-aged, corpulent, courageous and irrepressible, but there are further similarities obvious from Surtees' description.

"Mr Jorrocks was a great city grocer of the old school, one who was neither ashamed of his trade, nor of carrying it on in a dingy warehouse that would shock the managers of the fine mahogany-countered, gilt-canistered, puffing, poet-keeping establishments of modern times. He had been in business long enough to remember each succeeding lord mayor before he was anybody — 'reg'lar little tuppences in fact,' as he used to say. Not that Mr Jorrocks decried the dignity of civic honour, but his ambition took a different turn. He was for the field, not the forum."[20]

A description of Briggs by Leech's contemporary Frith reinforces this amusing comparison:

"Leech gives us no hint by which we might guess in what condition of life the immortal Briggs made the fortune that enabled him to retire to his comfortable home in Bayswater; whatever his pursuit may have been, the taste for sport of every kind must have possessed the prosperous gentleman, to be indulged to the full — happily for us — when he had achieved his independence."[21]

John Jorrocks of course was more metropolitan than merely suburban; he was more brash, outspoken and extrovert than Leech's man, neither did he share Briggs' love of all sports, considering coursing and much else as a waste of time by comparison with the noble art of 'unting — "the image of war without its guilt, and only five and twenty per cent of its danger!"[22] But the two characters are

19. Cuming, op. cit., p. 275.
20. Surtees, R.S., *Handley Cross,* 1854, p. 56.
21. Frith, W.P. *John Leech His Life and Work,* 1891, Vol. 2, p. 171.
22. *Handley Cross,* op. cit., p. 130.

TRULY DELIGHTFUL!

GALLOPING DOWN THE SIDE OF A FIELD COVERED WITH MOLE-HILLS, ON A WEAK-NECKED HORSE, WITH A SNAFFLE BRIDLE, ONE FOOT OUT OF YOUR STIRRUP, AND A BIT OF MUD IN YOUR EYE!

"WELL, THEY MAY CALL THIS A HEALTH-GIVING PURSUIT IF THEY LIKE; BUT GIVE ME ROACH-FISHING IN A PUNT."

A Lee-tle Contre-temps—Jack Rogers and the Glove.

Colour Plate 18. "A Lee-tle Contre-temps — Jack Rogers and the Glove", from Ask Mama, 1858.

Colour Plate 19. "The Two Strings", from Ask Mama, 1858.

The Two Strings.

TESTIMONIAL TO JOHN JORROCKS, ESQ.

Illustrations from Handley Cross, *1853.*

23. Cuming, op. cit., p. 278.
24. ibid., p. 278.
25. Dimsdale Collection, 28 February, 1852.

out of the same mould, Surtees' more truly Georgian, Leech's definitely of the Victorian age, but both originating in the bucolic episodes of Smollett and Goldsmith or the hilarious scenes of Coombe's *Syntax*. It is difficult to believe that a hunting man like Leech had not read *Handley Cross* as we have said previously, but a letter of 5 January, 1853, to Surtees suggests not.

"I am now going to devote some attention to our (at least my) new friend Jorrocks. I have been reading the book, and like it much. It is a pity the fat hero does not appear a little earlier. In the three volumes it is of no great consequence, but in the monthly form it is rather a long wait between the numbers — However, the opening is so good, in my humble opinion, and smells so of the fresh country air, that I have no doubt His Majesty the Public will be content with it as it is."[23]

The appearance of the "fat hero" had to be decided upon at once as he and his niece Belinda were to feature in an imaginary scene for the paper cover of the serial parts. Leech therefore announced at once that he was going out into the shires to search for a subject — "If I can, I shall run down to Leamington and get some materials."[24] But the inspiration for John Jorrocks, MFH of the Handley Cross Hunt, was to come from a quite different part of the country.

Leech's chief recreation throughout the 'forties and 'fifties was to get down to Hertfordshire and stay with Charley Adams. Charley was now the complete country gentleman, or aspiring to be the complete country gentleman, living in some comfort at Barkway, on good if not equal terms with the local gentry. His railway work and his land agent's work had made him prosperous, he acted for Baron Dimsdale and other Hertfordshire magnates, he kept a goodish stable and indulged in picture collecting. The Red House, Barkway, still stands in the main street of the village (see illustrations on page 116), a very handsome, red-brick structure of 1760, with a grand entrance door and sash windows above, the whole place speaking of tranquility, solidity and money earned from the rich arable soil of North Hertfordshire. It was this life, a mixture of convivial neighbourliness, sport, robust masculinity, leisure and good breeding that had become Leech's fantasy world. The man who in town could never shake off the incubus of being a bankrupt's son, the former inmate of a debtor's prison, the constant and unwilling recipient of bills drawn on him by his sponging relations, fancied himself free and easy and accepted in Charley Adams' house. There were other country houses to visit but only Charley could be confided in, only Charley was "good for a touch".

"I propose now to come down tomorrow morning," Leech wrote to him of an impending visit in February 1852, "so, if you can get me a rocking horse, or a clothes-horse, or any horse excessively quiet and accommodating I will go out with you on Monday with 'her Majesty' or somebody, will come on Tuesday — to hunt on Wednesday — and back again on Thursday morning."[25]

The over-burdening weight of work and his ill-judged time limits made visits to Barkway act like a pressure valve. "Hip! Hip! Hurrah!

*The Red House, Barkway, Hertfordshire, in about 1860. Leech was a frequent visitor during Charles Adams'
residence there.*
Dimsdale Collection

The dining-room of Barkway House, about 1890, showing Charles Adams' collection of pictures.

Illustration from Handley Cross, *1853.*

The Almanack is finished," he announces joyously in December 1852, "and now for a day with the Puckeridge."[26]

It may in fact have been on this very visit that he caught sight of the villager who was to be the germ of Mr Jorrocks. In very early 1853 he was looking for the type of figure to introduce on the cover and according to Frith he found him at Barkway.

"Leech's old friend Mr Adams, tells me that a man named Nicholls, Lady Louisa Clinton's coachman, was the model for Mr Jorrocks. Leech never went anywhere, not even to church, without his little sketch-book; and on a special Sunday at Barkway Church, where Lady Clinton had her pew, she was followed by a little man who, after handing her ladyship her books of devotion, took his seat outside the pew, and became an unconscious study for Leech; who in a few minutes transferred an exact likeness to the sketch-book, which was afterwards as exactly reproduced in the 'hunting lecture'."[27]

Adams' descendants, however, think the original for Mr Jorrocks was one Beecroft, a coachman at nearby Newsells Park, who lived in one of Charley Adams' cottages and was more likely to have been known to Leech.[28] Unless photographs are shown to exist of these mid-Victorian worthies, it is doubtful if we shall ever know the truth, but it was certainly this pretty Hertfordshire village that gave Jorrocks his visual birth in all its glorious rotundity. Jorrocks' girth, almost as broad as he is long, his paunchiness, his excessively short legs and those jowels that disappear into the collar of his hunting coat are endemic to a peculiarly English sort of traditionalism. Whether Beecroft or Nicholls were the model, Jorrocks' spiritual antecedents are obviously to be found in Georgian literature, particularly in the prints and drawings of the sporting squire, W.H. Bunbury. (See Colour Plates 14 and 15, page 106.)

Handley Cross was itself preventing Leech hunting in the early part of 1853. "I should have written before," he told Charley Adams on 26 January, "but I have been hampered with work beyond measure and as it is The First Number of Handley Cross, cannot come out until March. It will be better that it should be so — for I shall then be enabled to get two parts completed before commencing publication by which means I shall have a little leisure — Mind you have the mare well worked there's a good fellow as I dont want like our friend Briggs to find her disagreeably fresh."[29]

Both author and artist were undertaking the work with unusual enthusiasm, Surtees revising passages to suit the parts and such was the freedom between them that Leech felt enabled to add textual suggestions. "On reading the book over carefully," he wrote to Surtees in February 1853, "I see towards the end of the story a good deal of space is occupied by legal proceedings. How shall we get in red coats in a court? I merely mention this as you write of adding and altering; a little dovetailing about that part would help me much... While you are about it I think I would get old Jorrocks into a good deal more fun before making him a victim. This would make more numbers, to be sure, but if he succeeds in a serial form (of which I have no doubt whatever), why, the more the merrier!"[30] The first ten

26. Dimsdale Collection, 14 December, 1852.

27. Frith, op. cit., Vol. 2, p. 153.

28. Robert Beecroft (1809-1891). Information kindly given me by Mr Robert Dimsdale.

29. Dimsdale Collection, 26 January, 1853.

30. Cuming, op. cit., p. 280.

Handley Cross *in original parts,*
March to June 1853.

issues appeared between March and December 1853 in their orange
covers (left), each with a resplendent hand-coloured Jorrocks plate.
The public got re-acquainted with the stout grocer and his supporting
cast of Pigg, Binjimin, Captain Doleful and Mr Muleygrub.

Surprisingly the book did not prove a success for Bradbury and
Evans. By the end of the year the public was obsessed by the political
situation in the Crimea and sales fell away. Leech's optimism about
keeping abreast of the work did not stand the test of time, by
December he had retired to Brighton feeling unwell, and even the
small wood engravings were not being completed. Bradbury and
Evans tried to put pressure on Leech through Surtees to finish his
work on the May 1854 part by the end of April and then conclude the
book at Part 15. Referring to Leech's lateness and ill health they did
add, "It is a great pity that he has not managed to get a little in
advance, so as to be prepared for a contingency like this. But so it is
when we have to do with great men."[31]

The publishers were so eager to conclude the unprofitable venture,
that the June part of the work was sent to Leech "made up" before
he had finished two of his little woodcuts and the July part excluded
some of his late designs. Understandably furious, he wrote to Surtees
on 31st July, "I received the number of 'Handley Cross' this
morning, and to my surprise and astonishment found it almost
barren of wood-cuts. I sent four drawings (besides the two introduced) on *Sunday week* last to Whitefriars, and tolerably good ones
too, I think — namely, 'Pigg being Examined in Court', 'Binjamin
and his Friend Exercising Mr Jorrocks' Hunters', 'Portraits of the
Plaintiff's and Defendant's Witnesses', and 'Pigg's Exultation at the
End of the Trial', none of which are in... I am very vexed at the
omission of the drawings, and I trust you will acquit me of any
neglect."[32]

But the friendship endured all this and Bradbury's continued as
publishers of *Handley Cross* in book form, where the "missing"
woodcuts duly appeared. On the proof title page of this book,
Surtees gave the credit to his artist collaborator in a way that seemed
fitting, referring to him as the Illustrious Leech. Leech's natural
shyness brought this immediate rejoinder, "The '*illustrious*' is a
leetle too strong! I feel that my modesty will not allow it to go out. It
looked as if you attributed J's longevity to the illustrations, which I
for one cannot on any account admit. You will excuse the very slight
alteration in the wording which I have taken upon myself to make...
Here's success to the volume and to our early meeting under the
scarlet cover again."[33] (Colour Plate 16, page 111.)

The two men were also closely involved together in the early
numbers of the new country magazine, *The Field*. In fact Leech
joined Surtees at Melton Mowbray in 1855 and 1856 when he was
acting as the paper's correspondent. They were also to collaborate
again "under the scarlet cover" in Surtees' serialised novel *Ask
Mama* in 1858 (see Colour Plates 18 and 19, page 114, and opposite)
and again in 1860 with *Plain or Ringlets,* Leech once more proving a
very poor time keeper on the latter book. His designs for both were

31. Cuming, op. cit., p. 282.
32. ibid., p. 283.
33. ibid., p. 284.

lively and continued to highlight changing fashions most faithfully, a subject to be developed in a later chapter. By the time that *Mr Facey Romford's Hounds* came out in 1864, both the writer and the illustrator were dead. Despite the vigour of the work in these later novels (Colour Plate 17, page 111) and the plethora of delightful woodcuts, the artist was not so truly at home as he had been with *Mr Sponge's Sporting Tour* and *Handley Cross*. There he had created something that became a legend and was to have its influence on all sporting illustrations for nearly a hundred years. In a last letter to Surtees, written on 13 January, 1864, Leech says "I . . . long to put on the red coat with you."[34] It was a most fortunate and happy co-operation, and with the exception of Millais, there was no other creator with whom Leech had such a satisfactory relationship. The fruits of it on the printed page endure as one of the greatest of author and artist partnerships.

34. Cuming, op. cit., p. 320.

"Imperial John's attempt to show the way", from Ask Mamma, *1858.*

Chapter Six

LEECH AND THE ARTISTS

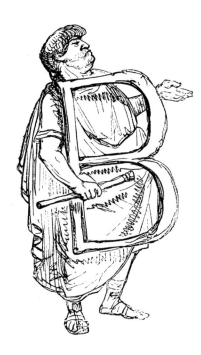

y the early 1850s John Leech was probably more widely known than any British artist with the exception of Edwin Landseer and a handful of Royal Academicians whose works were distributed in steel engravings. *Punch* and its weekly cast of Leech characters penetrated the most remote parts of the country and circulated in households that would never have bought a painting or could have possibly been termed artistic. At the same time his draughtsmanship was fresh, powerful, modern and totally in tune with its age, so that unconsciously a middle class audience of magazine readers was being schooled about new trends in art. Similarly, the artists were afforded a good deal more than amusement by the Leech illustrations as they came out in their tens week by week, and their hundreds year by year; they too assimilated the ideas and the standpoint of the best man on *Punch*. Mr Punch himself was a first class Philistine in the visual arts, both Pre-Raphaelitism and later Aestheticism were mercilessly ridiculed, but Leech, even if he remained silent in the paper, obviously had a wide circle of friends among London's artists.

Ruskin's enthusiasm for Leech seems to have come rather late in the day (much of it was actually posthumous) but it does give some indication of the interest felt for the cartoonist in serious artistic circles. "John Leech", Ruskin wrote, "was an absolute master of the elements of character — but not by any means of those of *chiaroscuro,* and the admirableness of his work diminished as it became elaborate. The first few lines in which he sets down his purpose are invariably of all drawing that I know the most wonderful in their accurate felicity and prosperous haste." He continues, "... of all rapid and condensed realisation ever accomplished by the pencil, John Leech's is the most dainty, and the least fallible, in the subjects of which he was cognizant. Not merely right in the traits which he seizes, but refined in the sacrifice of what he refuses."[1] The educated Victorian's view of Leech was first an enthusiasm for the wood engravings, then for his oil sketches in the 1860s and finally acclaim for the drawings sparked off by Ruskin's eulogies.

It is astonishing that Ruskin and other figures from the academic hierarchy should have been so moved by an artist who had received no formal training, had attended no school, and was in a branch of art scarcely recognised by the profession. It was all symptomatic of a great change of attitude in the 1850s, a great breaking out from the

1. Ruskin, John, *Catalogue of Leech exhibition,* 1872.

straight-jacket of historical painting towards greater naturalism and a new seriousness about social and political themes. Leech had also been adept at fitting into the new role of the artist as a society figure and in mixing with brothers of the brush who had already arrived in Society. "I met ... John Leech," Frederick Leighton wrote to his mother, "the man who does all those admirable caricatures in *Punch* — he is a very pleasant and gentleman-like person!"[2] It was a view by a fellow artist that Leech would have approved.

Leech's somewhat desultory training as an artist had included a period with a painter and this brought him into contact with one leading artist, which was to have far-reaching consequences. Mrs Fanny McIan was an historical painter, married to the actor turned painter Ronald Robert McIan A.R.S.A. and they practised at several addresses in the Bloomsbury area between 1838 and 1845. In 1840 they were living at 82, Newman Street, that ill-fated thoroughfare that Leech knew so well; later they were close to the Leech's early married home in Brunswick Square, at 9, Coram Street. They may have met as neighbours or as mutual friends of Charles Dickens who seems to have benefited from McIan's theatrical background. It is strange to think of the young Leech in 1842-43, standing alongside the forthright and Jacobite Mrs McIan, experimenting in oils with such subjects as "The Escape of Alaster Macdonald" or "A Buccaneer's Daughter", both of which she had recently exhibited. It was in this way that William Powell Frith first encountered Leech resolutely copying a still-life. Frith recalled:

"A Scottish painter ... named McIan ... lived with his wife, an accomplished artist, somewhere in the neighbourhood of Gordon Square. Calling one morning to see Mrs McIan, I found her in the studio, not, as usual, hard at work at her own easel, but superintending the labours of a pupil, who was ... hard at work at another; and the pupil, a tall, slim, and remarkably handsome young man, was John Leech."[3]

Leech's disaffection with his early *Punch* years, before he got into the stride of his social cuts, is manifest in what he then told Frith. "I like painting much better than what I have to grind at day after day, if I could only do it, but its so confoundedly difficult, you know, and requires such a lot of patience."[4] His desire to be taken seriously and therefore to be taken as a serious painter was a recurring theme for the rest of his life and Mrs McIan held out great hopes. Frith recalled that "that lady seemed convinced that he had but to persevere and the difficulties would fall before him, as, to use her own figure, the walls of Jericho fell before the sound of the trumpet."[5]

The friendship with Frith became a close one, the two men dined frequently at each other's houses and went on holiday together, Leech's growing reputation as an illustrator of the social scene exactly paralleling Frith's widening public and his entry into the Royal Academy. Much more importantly, Leech's subjects, the metropolitan, the domestic and the resort, began to influence Frith's own work. Leech excelled in figure groups, Frith likewise extended *his* range. By 1851, when Frith and Leech visited Ramsgate together,

2. Barrington-Ward, Mrs, *Life of Lord Leighton,* 1906, Vol. 2, p. 68.

3. Frith, W.P., *John Leech His Life and Work,* 1891, Vol. 2, p. 4.

4. ibid., p. 5.

5. ibid.

STARTLING EFFECT OF THE "GOLD DIGGINGS."

Reduced Goldsmith (loq.). "NOW THEN, HERE YOU ARE!—A HANDSOME GOLD SNUFF-BOX AND A HA'PORTH OF SNUFF FOR A PENNY!"

the illustrator's infectious and very spontaneous approach to the contemporary scene, an inspiration caught, a sketch dashed off and the result in print soon after, was affecting the painter's vision. He began to tire of costume subjects and fanciful pictures to explore the drama of modern life.

"About the year 1852," Frith writes, "I began the first of a series of pictures from modern life, then quite a novelty in the hands of anyone who could paint tolerably. When the picture which was called 'Many Happy Returns of the Day' was finished, Leech came to see it, and expressed his satisfaction on finding an artist who could leave what he called 'mouldy costumes' for the habits and manners of everyday life."[6] Frith's picture was actually not conceived until a couple of years later, but the gist of the story, Frith's gradual change of emphasis and Leech's feelings are correctly expressed. Was Frith also unconsciously acknowledging a debt to Leech in "Many Happy Returns", because Leech had made a reputation in juvenile subjects in the late 'forties?

The scene in Frith's studio, when a couple of traditionalist costume painters examine "Many Happy Returns" appeared in *Punch* in April 1856 entitled "Scene in a Modern Studio" (opposite). The caption digs gently at the traditionalists' inability to come to terms with modern life subjects.

Leech's thrust towards the modern subject and Frith's success with it are closely linked, most of all by that new appreciation of modern moral subjects in the novels of the 'fifties. The comparison is surprisingly apt for we know that Trollope was met with the reaction, "No historical novels please", when he visited a publishers about 1858.[7] Thackeray's short stories and occasional papers too were predominantly about the people around him, the citizens with whom he rubbed shoulders. Often Leech's drawings seem to be the visual counterparts of Thackeray's essays, particularly such books as *Our Street,* 1848, for just as in the novel one is introduced to an alley, a courtyard and an incident, the remainder of the world sketched in loosely, so it is with Leech, the main characters being in crisp focus, the background fading into the rumble and hubbub indicated with a few lines (margin illustration). As W.L. Burn has said, "It was the present that the mid-Victorians were interested in; it was their own faces that they were never tired of looking at in the mirror."[8]

The Pre-Raphaelites, with their love of truth to nature, were regarded askance by Frith, but Leech had many friends among them, particularly John Everett Millais and Holman Hunt. Leech would have agreed wholeheartedly with these young painters' attempts to relegate costume pieces to the past and to paint the world around them, but he would have had strong divergences of opinion over technique, as will emerge.

All the *Punch* cartoons concerning artists which decorate his pages in the 1850s have this one concern of Leech's at their heart; the artificiality of the studio, the absurdity of the lay figure, the posed and tendentious use of the professional model, when flesh and blood people were walking the streets. Of the seven illustrations con-

6. Frith, op. cit., Vol. 2, p. 15.

7. Sadleir, Michael, *Trollope: A Commentary,* 1933, pp. 141 and 173.

8. Burn, W.L., *The Age of Equipoise,* 1964, p. 80.

tributed, one "The Artist gives the Finishing Touch to his picture" has Bohemianism as its butt, three deal with testy and Philistine clients, the remainder are gentle assaults on costume painting (see illustration on page 125). In "A Visit to the Studio", 1859, the painter protests loudly to his friend that he may knock his lay figure over "and spoil all her folds", but in fairness to Leech, "Our Artist Enjoying Himself in the Highlands", 1852, shows the hardships of following nature *too* closely! But Leech's general tenor in these delightful illustrations is an impatience and irritation with subject painting. A number of artists and engravers watched John Leech at work and their accounts leave no doubt why he had little sympathy with punctilious and fussy brushmanship.

Leech usually carried a small notebook with him wherever he went, and several friends mention this as the source of his inspiration, particularly Frith and his engraver Joseph Swain, but it was for notes rather than composition.

"He never had any models," Swain recalls, "and rarely ever made any sketches. He showed me a little note-book once with a few thumbnail sketches of bits of background, but he seemed never to

SCENE IN A MODERN STUDIO.

JACK ARMSTRONG HAS PAINTED A MODERN SUBJECT, FROM REAL LIFE, AND PAINTED IT UNCOMMONLY WELL.—STRANGE TO SAY, HE HAS SOLD HIS PICTURE.

MESSRS. FEEBLE AND POTTER (*very high-art men, who can't get on without mediæval costume, and all the rest of it*) THINK IT A MISTAKE.—CURIOUSLY ENOUGH, *THEIR* PICTURES ARE UNSOLD.

MR. B. AS HE APPEARED FROM SIX IN THE MORNING UNTIL THREE IN
THE AFTERNOON, WHEN—

forget anything he saw, and could always go back in his memory for any little bit of country, street, he might want for background, etc."[9]

Frith corroborates this: "I am sure that Leech never used a model in the sense that the model is commonly used by artists, for the thousands of human beings made immortal by his genius; but that he made numberless sketches for backgrounds, detail of dresses, landscapes, foregrounds, and bits of character caught from unconscious sitters, there can be no doubt. How wonderful was the memory, how sensitive the mental organisation, that could retain and reproduce every variety of type, every variety of beauty and character."[10]

He was certainly using a notebook when he immortalised the Hertfordshire coachman in Barkway Church and he was also replenishing his stock of characters in an anecdote recounted by one of his friends.

"On one occasion he and I were riding to town together in an omnibus, when an elderly gentleman in a very peculiar dress, and with very marked features, stepped into the vehicle, and sat down immediately in front of us. We were the only inside passengers. For whom or for what he took, or probably mistook, us, I know not, but he stared so hard, and made such faces at us, that I could hardly refrain from laughter. My discomfiture was almost completed when Leech suddenly exclaimed, 'By the way, did Prendergast ever show you that extraordinary account that has been recently forwarded to him?' and, showing me his note-book, added, 'Just run your eye up that column, and tell me what you can make of it.' Instead of a column, the features of the old gentleman were reflected upon the page with life-like fidelity."[11]

Reynolds Hole, who was a very close friend at the end of Leech's life remembered many such instances of setting down information in a kind of shorthand: "He gathered welcome material in fields fresh and pastures new. Sometimes he would say, 'I must make a memorandum', and would trace a few mysterious lines in his sketchbook to be developed hereafter; and sometimes he would ask, with the meekest diffidence, if he were told an anecdote worthy of illustration, 'May I use that?' as though you were conferring a priceless obligation, instead of receiving a privilege, in playing jackal to such a lion."[12] Leech's attempts to draw from the life were unsuccessful. He spent the best part of a day in drawing Hole's wife at Caunton Manor and in the end had to destroy it as a failure.[13]

Many of his friends, particularly the sporting ones, refer to his accuracy as a sketcher of landscapes, the fences, trees, moors and rivers that have the real scent of the country about them. Frith was particularly enthusiastic about his Scottish scenery: "No praise can be too extravagant for all the backgrounds that form so perfect a setting for the gem-like figures of Mr Briggs."[14] (See margin illustration.)

Reynolds Hole found him in a similar state of ecstasy with pure landscape when he took him on a trip to Sherwood Forest. He had been staying with Hole at Caunton Manor, and his parson friend had expected him to be bored with the countryside and its absence of

9. Frith, op. cit., Vol. 2, p. 51.

10. ibid., p. 14.

11. ibid., p. 238.

12. Hole, Reynolds, *The Memories of ...*, 1892, p. 26.

13. ibid.

14. Frith, op. cit., Vol. 2, p. 175.

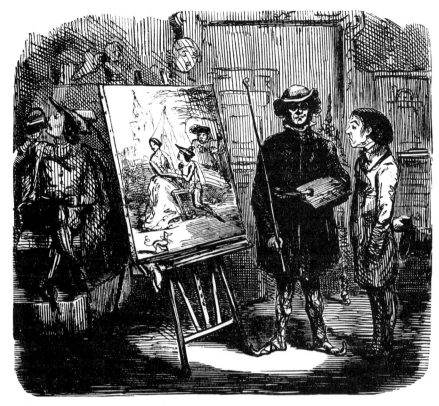

PERFECT SINCERITY, OR THINKINGS ALOUD. No. 4.

Artist, No. 1. "THERE, MASTER OKER, I FLATTER MYSELF THAT WILL TAKE THE SHINE OUT OF YOUR PRECIOUS PRODUCTION, ALTHOUGH YOU DO THINK NOBODY CAN PAINT BUT YOURSELF."
Artist, No. 2. "HEY! DEAR, DEAR, DEAR! THAT'S VERY BAD. BY JOVE, MY BOY, IT'S A DREADFUL FALLING OFF FROM LAST YEAR. IF I WERE YOU, I SHOULD THINK TWICE BEFORE I SENT IT IN."
Artist, No. 1. "MERE ENVY.—ILLIBERAL HUMBUG."

people. "But when, having left our carriage, we wandered among the grand old oaks and the golden bracken, he closed his sketch-book, almost as soon as he had opened it, and murmuring, 'This is too delicious,' sat down in the sunshine."[15]

Hole's sylvan description of the forest, the languid artist reclining against the tree bole and the carriage waiting is almost one of Leech's own illustrations or if not one of Frith's new modern life subjects. The connection between these two is intricate and has to be pieced together as the friendship grew.

Frith as he says, was experimenting with modern subjects from 1854, the first, suggested by a holiday at Ramsgate and to be called "Ramsgate Sands", was in preparation in the Spring of 1852, although not exhibited until two years later. Frith returned to Ramsgate in the summer of 1852 and took his friend Leech with him, the result being two very amusing seaside illustrations in *Punch* in October of that year, one "A Sketch at Ramsgate" (page 126) being almost from the beachside vantage point of Frith's picture. Leech had already prophesied that the new "picture would be a great hit" so his presence must have been very encouraging to Frith as he worked in a different genre.

15. Hole, *Memories*, op. cit., p. 19.

A SKETCH AT RAMSGATE.

Ellen (who loves a joke at AUNT FIDGET'S *expense).* "GOOD GRACIOUS, AUNT! THERE ARE TWO OFFICERS!"

Aunt Fidget (a short-sighted lady). "BLESS ME, SO THERE ARE! WELL; THEY MAY BE OFFICERS, BUT THEY ARE NOT *GENTLEMEN*, I'M SURE, OR THEY WOULDN'T STAND LOOKING AT US IN THAT IMPUDENT MANNER."

The overwhelming success of "Ramsgate Sands" at the Royal Academy of 1854 ushered in a new era of modern life subjects, crowded, concentrated and with at least some moral content. The fact that the viewer was offered a series of life in groups, was very like Leech's pictures, the slight humour of them making the similarity striking, the Hogarthian stage set placing them strongly within the English tradition. There was a revival of interest in Hogarth's works. Frith himself was to work on a Rake's Progress and Hogarth's claim to be an illustrator of real life rather than a caricaturist also fitted Leech.

From the period of his life on *Bell's,* John Leech had been interested in the race course and had contributed some sketches to *Punch,* notably in 1846 and then in 1850 to 1853. The men of *Punch* habitually went to the Derby together in a break and it was this social side of the race meeting that Leech depicted, the mixture of the rich, the poor, the indigent, the reckless and the easily duped. He placed the multi-coloured life of the course under his magnifying-glass, not without harsh comments, for Leech was not a great supporter of betting. The three most significant sketches appeared in June 1851, and the same month of the two following years. The first "Not

WHEN IT IS DELIGHTFUL TO LOSE A BET.

Grace. "*Teddington* First?—Then that will make four dozen and a half. Remember, Sixes! Two dozen White, and the rest Pale Drab and Lavender."

THE YOUNG GENT WHO IS GOING TO MAKE A RAPID
FORTUNE BY BETTING.

16. Frith, W.P., *The Memoirs ... A Victorian Canvas,* 1957, ed. Nevile Wallis, p. 88.

Difficult to Foretell'' shows an open landau containing a wealthy couple, in the foreground a footman is busy drawing bottles from a hamper, to the right a gypsy woman is attempting to read the fortunes of the carriage occupants. In a very similar composition of the following year ''Miss Violet & Her Offers'' Leech illustrates a narrative with a dark-eyed beauty in the carriage being flattered by a race-going beau. The footman is there once more, so is the gypsy, but the scene is more comprehensive, other people sit in the landau and a top-hatted man watches a race through a telescope from a nearby coach. The illustration of June 1853 ''When It is Delightful to Lose a Bet'' (above), has the same scene greatly extended, the whole of the carriage is included now as a focal point, two admirers look into it and the beauty leans forward. Leech has created a slice of the fashionable world that could only be Epsom, the footman has disappeared into the background, but other groups capture our interest, swells sharing a bottle in the distance, a woman turning to listen to her husband and a masterly representation of a man trying to eat with knife and fork on his knee! The germ of the 1851 idea had burgeoned and was about to develop into something big. Frith must have seen this brilliant image unfold and grabbed it for his ''Derby Day''.

Frith did not visit the Epsom race course until May 1856 and was deeply impressed by ''the abundant material'' which he found in the race-goers. ''The more I considered the kaleidoscopic aspect of the crowd on Epsom Downs, the more firm became my resolve to attempt to reproduce it.''[16] The artist began making drawings and collecting models together that summer and the completed painting was shown as ''Derby Day'' at the Royal Academy of 1858 and

"The Race Meeting". Pen and ink drawing by J.E. Millais, 1853. Ashmolean Museum.

SKETCH OF A "LORD OF THE CREATION" ON HIS RETURN FROM THE DERBY.

17. Ruskin, John, *R.A. Notes*, 1858.

18. In the Ashmolean Museum, Oxford.

19. Typescripts of letters originally in the possession of Sanders of Oxford, 1969.

visited by the Queen. A rail was placed in front of the six foot long masterpiece and the crowds surged about behind it, ravenously devouring the minutiae of the painting. Ruskin, the most percipient of critics, had the following to say about it in his Academy notes.

"It is a kind of cross between John Leech and Wilkie, with a touch of daguerrotype here and there, and some pretty seasoning with Dickens sentiment."[17]

Frith had unofficially used a contemporary photograph of the race course to help him with the picture, Ruskin had associated the picture with the sweep of the camera, but also with Leech's illustrations. How apt that he should have linked those carriage groups, those circles of figures on the ground, the individualised figures of gamester and gypsy with Leech and then mentioned Dickens, whom Leech had illustrated.

Leech's *Punch* subjects on Derby themes had also struck a chord in a much younger, prodigious artist, whose controversial work was just being acclaimed by Ruskin. John Everett Millais, a founder member of the Pre-Raphaelite Brotherhood, had recently embarked on a series of drawings of modern life subjects based on social and moral questions. Although treating the subject with a great deal more tension and pathos, his pen and ink drawing "The Race Meeting"[18] is clearly inspired by the sort of commentary undertaken by Leech, especially that influential engraving of *Punch* in June 1852 (see illustration left). The meticulous pen line and heightened reality of gesture is more akin to Doyle in the Millais drawing, but the setting is inescapably Leech's.

Leech had met Millais in about 1853 and there was at once a strong mutual attraction. Twelve years Leech's junior, but with a similar sort of athletic build, striking good looks and natural exuberance, the two artists were very soon treating each other as equals. Millais' stylishness and good manners would have appealed to Leech; Millais must have appreciated the close friendship of a man known the length and breadth of the country. That summer of 1853, they had dined together at the Garrick, where Leech had been a member since 1849, and discovered their joint love of country sports. Millais was about to embark on the famous and fateful trip to Scotland with the Ruskins, and once arrived, the young man kept up a constant flow of letters to his new friend in London from Glenfinlas, Callander, Perthshire. The correspondence is jocular, familiar and teasing, a great deal about the fishing and a few more serious comments showing how the Pre-Raphaelites admired Leech's work. "We have Punch sent to us, and I cannot resist telling you how good I think your illustrations have been since I left town. I wish I could send any hint worthy of your drawing but I confess myself entirely outwitted."[19]

A fortnight later he was again writing to Leech congratulating him on a Millais-inspired illustration in the periodical: "I was astonished at finding that you had copied my drawing into Punch and at the splendid way it was cut, nothing could be better. If ever I find myself failing with the brush, I shall appeal to you for your influence on

128

behalf of a place in that paper. I send you other drawings of *facts*. Remember, I do you these for yourself, and with no hope that they may appear in Punch, although I shall always be proud to see them there, and glad to think that they may save you the trouble of thinking for yourself when you are weary and bored for want of a subject. I am glad you do not mention my name which would never go with the serious position I occupy in regard to Art. The sketches of the unfortunate officer clinging to his tent post, and beseeching assistance in the recovery of his bedroom, suggested the accompanying drawing of a disaster equally fearful in its consequences."[20] The drawing "Pre-Raphaelite Sketching: inconvenience in windy weather" was not used, but another "Awful protection against midges" showing artists sketching from Nature was in November 1853.

Leech was trying to persuade Millais into the saddle in the autumn of 1853, Millais probably influencing his friend towards fishing and shooting in the Highlands, both of which sports were soon to be utilised for Mr Briggs. "Another year we will journey together", Millais wrote to him at the end of the holiday on 23 October, "as I am sure we should enjoy the same things and get on splendidly."[21] By the March of 1854, Millais was hunting with Leech and Mike Halliday in the Home Counties and that summer they were again together at the Peacock Inn at Baslow in Derbyshire with Mrs Leech and the artist's sister, Esther. It was during that fortnight in July that Millais made his masterly watercolour portrait of Leech, showing him at the height of his powers, relaxed, amused, abstracted for a moment from the illness, nervousness and financial worries that were to ravage his last years (Colour Plate 20, page 131). Miss Leech, who remembered the drawing being done, recalled Millais as "a good tempered unspoilt boy".[22] Leech's regard for Millais outweighed the opprobrium surrounding the desertion of Ruskin by Effie in 1854, the annulment of the marriage the same year and the re-marriage of Effie to Millais in June 1855, not difficult when the art world had made Ruskin the villain of the piece. But Leech's good humour and tact managed to embrace both sides of the faction; he was seeing Millais in London regularly while remaining on the right side of the great critic. "Ruskin can draw well," he is recorded as saying at a *Punch* dinner, but has "more brains than body".[23] He certainly managed this social impasse a great deal more skilfully than the separation of Mr and Mrs Dickens. There he had commended young Dickens for supporting his mother and received a sharp and hurt retort from the novelist!

But what exactly was Leech's attitude to Millais' painting or to that of any of the other young men he would constantly be meeting in the Millais circle? For example he actually visited Holman Hunt at Fairlight when "Our English Coasts" was being painted in 1852. Would Leech have felt any enthusiasm for such a meticulous and brilliantly coloured view of nature? Frith's comments suggest not, although his dissatisfaction with contemporary painting was probably more one of temperament than aesthetics.

20. Typescripts of letters originally in the possession of Sanders of Oxford, 1969.

21. ibid.

22. Leech albums, Bodleian Library, MSS Eng misc e 946/1-7, p. 443.

23. Silver Diary, op. cit., Vol. 2, p. 6.

Excited Gentleman. "THEY'RE OFF!—THEY'RE OFF!"
Quiet Lady. "ARE THEY, DEAR? WON'T YOU HAVE SOME PIE?"

"From the time of my introduction to Leech", Frith writes, "I became gradually very intimate with him, and the more I knew of his nature, the more I became convinced that he totally lacked the disposition for continuous, steady, mechanical industry necessary for success in painting. He constantly ridiculed the care spent on the detail of pictures; finish, in his opinion, was so much waste of time. 'When you can see what a man intends to convey in his picture, you have got all he wants, and all you ought to wish for; all elaboration of an idea after the idea is comprehensible is so much waste of time' — this was his constant cry, a little contradicted by the fact that he constantly tried to paint his ideas, but in a fitful and perfunctory manner."[24] (See illustration left.) On another occasion when he was watching Frith at his easel on a "rather elaborate piece of work", he murmured, "Ah, my Frith, I wasn't created to do that sort of thing! I should never have patience for it."[25]

Leech definitely admired some of Millais' earlier pictures. Millais sent his "Ophelia", "Return of the Dove" and "The Order of Release" to Paris in 1855 and Leech saw them there on a short visit to France in September. "When I was in Paris I saw your pictures," he writes to his friend, "Believe me, out of some thousands of pictures, large, very large, small and very small, they stood out, as your works always do, most conspicuously good."[26]

As far as we can discover from the descriptions of his houses, Leech's walls were not studded with paintings by famous friends; a miniature of his daughter by Millais was a proud possession, otherwise his own works decorated the rooms. It is probable that he grew to admire Millais' work as the sharpness of his Pre-Raphaelitism softened during the 'fifties and the content changed to the more sentimental. In this Leech was typically Victorian. After the 1860 Academy exhibition one finds him most enthusiastically praising Millais' "Black Brunswicker" while finding Egg "stale and conventional".[27] He had obviously questioned Millais closely during the painting of "The Eve of St Agnes" in early 1863 and had attended the Academy private view when it was first shown. During two successive *Punch* dinners he returns to the subject of this new work in April and in May.

"JL tells of Millais painting his St Agnes", Silver confides to his diary, "with a dark lanthern in the moonlight, and discovering that the painted window did not cast a 'bloody light' as Keats and Sir Walter have said it does. No colours at all are cast — only dark and light."[28]

Later he adds: "JL contends that Millais' girl in his St Agnes picture is very pretty. Might have brought in a moonbeam as a high light on her head — marvellous that mermaidish appearance given by the sea-weedy green dress at her feet. Is it true that moonbeams don't carry colour?"[29]

Leech attended most of the major London exhibitions as a compulsive mixer in High Society rather than as a particularly forthright critic. He was present at the International Exhibition of 1862 and specially admired the sets of hunting bronzes shown by the Russian

24. Frith, op. cit., Vol. 2, p. 6.
25. ibid., p. 7.
26. Millais, J.G., *Life and Letters of Sir J.E. Millais,* 1899, Vol. 1, p. 271.
27. Silver Diary, op. cit.: 29 March, 1860.
28. ibid., 15 April, 1863.
29. ibid., 6 May, 1863.

Colour Plate 20. John Leech by Sir John Everett Millais.
Drawing heightened with watercolour, 10½ x 8½ins.
National Portrait Gallery.

30. Silver Diary, op. cit., 8 October, 1862.

31. Frith, op. cit., Vol. 2, p. 247.

artists.[30] A couple of years earlier he had been to see a large painting of Nero contemplating the ruins of Rome by Piloti. Much to his companion Edgar Boehm's astonishment he had suddenly exclaimed, "I would rather have been the painter of that picture than the producer of all the things I have ever perpetrated."[31] Boehm had protested and drawn attention to the glaring errors in this Germanic monstrosity, but Leech seems not to have changed his mind. He was by inclination a middle-class and middle-brow man who happened to be a genius with a pencil, it was typical that he should complain to Henry Silver that the art criticism in the *Times* was "too learned" and couple with this the name of Ruskin. For him his art was purely instinctive, not something over which it was necessary or proper to intellectualise, he seldom refers to it in letters and hardly at all to brother artists. To be earnest or talk cleverly about what he was doing would not only have been out of character, it would have been ungentlemanly, and closed to him some of the best houses in England and Scotland.

* * * * *

Leech's method of work was more or less confined to observation, rudimentary jotting in his notebooks and then two or three hours' concentrated effort at his drawing table. Each of Leech's residences had a work room where he could hide himself away and tackle block by block the weekly *Punch* cuts or the numerous illustrations to the à Beckett *Comic Histories* or the Surtees novels, strangely enough there are few descriptions of these studios where he spent so much time. The one notable exception comes from a contemporary Canadian, Frank Bellew, who visited Leech at 32 Brunswick Square in 1861 or 1862. It is a valuable glimpse for it not only describes his work place but gives a good impression of his comfortable but unpretentious life style.

"The door of John Leech's house in Bedford Square [*sic*] was opened wide by a natty little servant girl, just like one of his own pictures. The hall or entry was as neat as a new paint-box, with numerous door-mats placed here and there where they would do most good. I was shown into a parlour which was a picture in itself, a poesy grateful to four of the five senses; sight, for it was beautiful; smell, for its sweet freshness and fragrant flowers; touch, for its velvet carpet and numerous fleecy mats; and hearing, for its negative virtues of silence and repose. Some water-colours, enlarged copies of his own sketches in *Punch,* stood on the mantelpiece, which was also adorned with statuettes and porcelain vases. Everything in the room betokened good taste and refinement.

"... After I had waited a few minutes the artist himself entered, and conducted me to his workshop, or studio. In this room nothing was visible save a desk, on which lay one block of box-wood, a pencil, and a piece of paper; and covering two sides of the room, rows of large mahogany closets or bookcases, whose dark panelled doors gave no hint of their contents. There was not a print, nor

sketch, nor cast, nor any artist's tool to be seen, save the solitary block, pencil and scrap of paper."[32]

There is a sort of scrupulous neatness about this description that rings true; the freshness of the reception room and the meticulous and almost austere appearance of the work room say much about Leech's attitude to his work. He was intensely dedicated and supremely professional in his approach, but it was the sort of tidy-mindedness that is better on the minutiae of life than in the big decisions. His tremendous care in his dress and his ill-organised finances, are only the other side of this character that could wrestle with a sketch and yet miss the deadline for its delivery. Mark Lemon was quoted as saying Leech was no good at "study"[33] and it was certainly true that he could not concentrate on anything that seemed unimportant to his art, and whether this shows admirable dedication or pure wilfulness, the reader may decide for himself.

With his few jotted notes "carried home in his eye" as he put it to Frank Bellew, he would go to his desk and rough out the main salient facts of his story. These "were generally facts, or founded on fact", he told the same visitor. "Sometimes the germ was very small and sometimes very complex, and he found it a greater mental strain than most people would believe to build up the one or boil down the other so that the point would be immediately apparent in his picture."[34]

This preliminary drawing would be traced in outline and then transferred to the woodblock in the hard pencil he habitually used with its carefully sharpened point. The completed conception would be finished on the wood in the same hard pencil with light and shade carefully indicated and perhaps a little touch of Chinese white heightening to indicate his intention more clearly to the engraver.[35] From the one surviving block left unfinished at his death and from a few extant drawings it is obvious that the blocks left his studio full of a rare delicacy of effect and an amazing power of draughtsmanship. Unhappily this completed realisation was swept away in the engraving and even in the hands of artists that he trusted, like Swain, the extreme precision and refinement of his lines are lost. What has survived best is the preliminary studies in pencil, flowing and loose sketches of his most famous *Punch* cartoons, a face, an arm or a bonnet given in more detail than the rest perhaps, but otherwise essentially Leech's in embryo. As well as these, a great number of traced outlines survived from the transfer process, they are really mechanical and wooden by comparison with the others and they became of interest only after being extravagantly praised by Ruskin. The dispersal of Leech's drawings will be dealt with later, but it would be fair to say that probably the best work disappeared under the graver's tool.

"I have seen Leech make his first sketch (of which I have specimens)," recalled Millais in after years, "and trace them on to the block, scores of times. The first was rapid; but on the wood he was very deliberate, knowing how necessary clearness of execution is to the engraver."[36] Dr John Brown, who never met Leech, commented in his essay on the artist that it was bad production that

32. *Toronto Mail,* 12 September, 1883.
33. Silver Diary, op. cit., 23 February, 1860.
34. *Toronto Mail,* op. cit.
35. Leech albums, op. cit., p. 183.
36. Frith, op. cit., Vol. 2, p. 279.

PRETTY BIRDLING.

spoiled the artist's work. "Had these blocks been carefully and thoughtfully engraved by one hand, and then been printed by the hand instead of the steam press, we might have seen some of the *finesse* and beauty which the drawing showed *before* it was 'cut away'."[37] Hole felt the real enemy was time and the demands of the *Punch* office.

"He was ever on the look-out, listening, musing, realising. 'I am obliged', he said, 'to keep my pencil in exercise, lest it should get above its work.' But the real constraint was in the continuous demand 'nulla dies sine linea'. 'There is always', he sighed, 'a boy from the Punch office, diffusing an odour of damp corduroy through the house, and waiting for fresh supplies.' Sometimes he could work with marvellous rapidity. I have known him finish three drawings on the wood before luncheon. Sometimes he said that his pencil was on strike, that it was a dangerous anarchist, and that he proposed to call out the military."[38] The illustration shown on page 135 appeared in *Punch* in 1846. Leech could laugh at his own shortcomings.

Leech's lack of promptness caused great trouble to his engravers, the chief of whom was Swain. "My work was always against time," he told Frith, "I seldom had more time than two days to engrave one of his drawings in."[39] Swain adopted a Leech style of cutting, the lines were thickened and therefore coarsened to the extent that they more resembled ink drawings, but the personality of the drawing was untouched. In spite of comments by later biographers, Leech complained comparatively seldom in his letters about engravers. Frith reports him saying to a friend admiring a finished drawing, "Ah, wait till you see what it looks like in *Punch* next week," and elsewhere, "I wish you had seen it on the wood; they seem to me to have cut all the prettiness out of the girl's face."[40] But Swain remembered differently. "I always found him kind," he recalled, "and willing to forgive any of my shortcomings in not rendering his touches in all things."[41] The fact that Leech lived just too early to benefit from the process of photographing drawings on the wood is a great sadness. Had he been able to, his own expectations of the completed work might have been met, he would have had the original to check with the engraving, and we should have been the richer by a great store of his drawings. As it was, Leech accepted philosophically the limitations of the engraver with only the slightest cautions: "I have taken some pains with it," he tells Evans of *Punch* about a design, "so pray have it carefully engraved."[42]

Leech's considerable fluency in description and verbal presentation must have helped him continually during his career. Even as the leading caricaturist of the age and probably one of the most sought after in London, he still had to "sell" his work to intractable and touchy publishers like the Ingrams. With *Punch,* a slight sketch or a casual line across the dinner table might be sufficient to convince, but outside that charmed circle Leech had to put forward a plan succinctly and attractively. A letter concerning illustrations for the Christmas Number of *The Illustrated London*

37. Brown, John, *Horae Subsecivae,* 1882, p. 33.

38. Hole, *Memories,* op. cit., p. 27.

39. Frith, op. cit., Vol. 2, p. 51.

40. ibid., pp. 51 and 125.

41. ibid., p. 51.

42. Bodleian Library MS Eng lett d 397, fols 63-142.

OUR ARTIST.

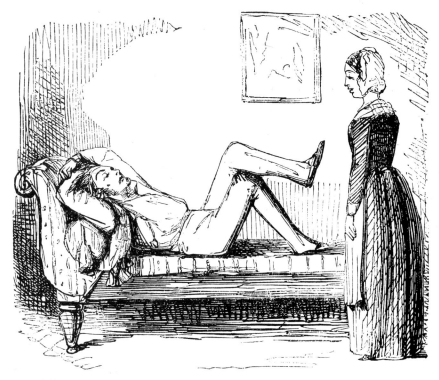

"If you please, Sir, here's the Printer's Boy called again!"
"Oh, bother! Say, I'm busy."

News in 1850, shows Leech as orderly and convincing, even when he is not arguing with crayon and sketch-book handy.[43]

> 31 Notting Hill Terrace
> December 9th 1850

My dear Ingram,

I have seen, and consulted with Mr Tom Taylor upon the subject of the Christmas Illustrations and matters you spoke to me about.

The following subjects have occurred to me. For a tolerably large drawing —

1. Punch (The Show) in the Drawing Room with groups of pretty children, pretty young ladies — and as much comicality as can be got in.
2. Christmas Day. Where one ought *not* to dine. Before the dinner — everything cold — pompous — formal — proud — and uncomfortable — stiff — disagreeable people etc etc.
3. Christmas Day. Where one ought to dine — after dinner — everything kindly, jolly, social and delightful.

43. Evans letters, Harvard University, MS Eng 1028.

A LITTLE BIT OF SENTIMENT.

4. When Christmas Comes but Once a year — The hard working mechanic with roast goose — good humour -kindliness etc etc.

5. Where Christmas Day Never Comes — The wretched hovel — sickness — poverty.

6. The Man who has Nowhere to go on Christmas Day — Walking up and down before the houses of people he does not know intimately enough to visit — The lights and figures seen through the blinds etc etc. All this is of course in the rough, but I think something could be made of the subjects, and I am sure Taylor would do the literary part admirably — The whole would take I should suppose about two pages of your paper — Would that suit you? and what time would you give? —

Yours faithfully
John Leech

The illustrations duly appeared on December 21st in *The Illustrated London News,* where he was an occasional but not frequent contributor from 1845 to 1857.

The captions to the pictures were also a very important part of Leech's genius and ones that he did not neglect. Unlike Charles Keene, Leech generally used his own situational comedies and so the words beneath have all the vitality of the overheard jibe or jest. He seems to have understood much better than his Georgian predecessors or his *Punch* successors, that brevity is the soul of wit. Silver says "he always made his 'legends' as concise and terse as possible, first jotting them down hastily, and condensing while he drew."[44] (See illustration left.) Leech's drawings are humorous from the beginning: "the funny situation is seen clearly at a glance, and wins a laugh without explanatory words."[45] This is much closer to twentieth century work, but even if Leech's legends are subordinate they are never superfluous, they are integral and as we have said give him more the quality of a novelist than most artists. Thackeray was absolutely right to look at the "narratives" of juveniles, butchers' boys and child huntsmen and say "Steele, Fielding, Goldsmith, Dickens, are similarly tender in their pictures of children".[46]

When he was provided with incidents by other people it often showed the speed at which he *could* work. Rather surprisingly Holman Hunt sent him some ideas in this way.

"I seized the pen, and on a page I drew two horizontal lines quite dividing the space. In the top I put: 'Scene — kitchen garden, country cottage. *Dramatis Personae:* Factotum, master entering' and then a line or two of dialogue. The second subject I treated similarly, and the third also, which was not so promising. I enclosed this without a word to Leech, and posted it with my other letters about two in the morning. The following Wednesday the two subjects, admirably treated, were in *Punch* — When next I saw him he was eager with excuses for not having written — He added: 'The letter when it was opened at breakfast was most opportune, for I had to

44. Silver, "Art Life of J.L.," *Magazine of Art,* Vol. 16, 1893, pp. 115-120.

45. ibid.

46. Frith, op. cit., Vol. 2, p. 255.

leave town by five, and I was bound to furnish two designs before going, and I had come down without having the wildest notion what to do. The subjects in your note were ready-made, and I was able to sketch them without a moment's waste of time."[47]

J.C. Horsley, R.A., was another friend who gave Leech ideas but without apparently adding sketches. Horsley had seen a "swell" being offered a string of onions by an itinerant trader and thought the scene perfect for Leech's pencil. When it appeared the "swell" was accompanied by a homely lady, thus eliminating the ludicrous side of the episode; Horsley felt that Leech had totally missed his point!

The images of Leech were so trapped in the Victorian retina that they emerged unconsciously in painters other than Frith. In the summer of 1850, Leech contributed to *Punch* a wood engraving entitled "The Real Street Obstructions" (below). In this he draws attention to the type of minor harassment inflicted by the police, when a public nuisance remains unchallenged. A young and pretty street seller of "sweet Chainey Oranges" is being moved on by a coarse and corpulent police officer, her precious load being spilled, while a barrage of sandwich men and advertisers go unmolested. Leech obviously has felt a sense of outrage about the treatment of this wretched girl, but the idea as well as the indignation were

47. Frith, op. cit., Vol. 2, pp. 223-224.

THE REAL STREET OBSTRUCTIONS

Detail from Ford Madox Brown's Work, *1852.* By permission of Manchester City Art Galleries.

translated into the work of another artist. Ford Madox Brown began his vast canvas "Work" in 1852, two years after the Leech illustration. In the top right background, behind the heads of the thinkers, Carlyle and Maurice, an exactly comparable scene is being enacted. A cockney orange girl is being victimised by a churlish policeman, beyond a line of sandwich men march away up Heath Street, Hampstead (illustration above). This is only one instance of Leech's images finding their way into other artists' works. It would be impossible to say how much credit goes to Leech in the mass of genre subjects of the 1860s by painters such as Redgrave, H.N. O'Neill, A.B. Houghton, John Ritchie, Emily Mary Osborn and George Elgar Hicks, who were prepared to depict contemporary life in a compelling way.

Chapter Seven

SATIRIST OF FASHION

rom the very first Leech was fascinated by the absurdities and excesses of fashion. The early Victorian period was the scene for great beauty in female dress and male costume was neither as drab nor as dreary as is often supposed. Early on in his career, as we have noted, he produced *The Fiddle-Faddle Fashion Book* and the early lithographs pay great attention to both the dandy and the fashionable lady. Leech's acutely observant eye was always watching out for the over-fastidious, the superfinely frivolous, so that he could engage their foibles with his pencil. *Fiddle-Faddle* was done under the influence of Cruikshank, and particularly under that side of Cruikshank that had created the *Monstrosities* plates of the late 'twenties. Leech's approach to fashion was therefore slightly tinged with Regency satire but more liberally diluted with straightforward Victorian incredulity and disapproval! His attitude to caricaturing fashion can be seen very clearly if one looks closely at Leech himself as the fashionable man.

John Leech was something of a dandy in dress, if one takes the Regency view that dandyism is more an attitude than an appearance, relies more on its inconspicuous good taste than on its outward desire to cause a stir. Most accounts of our caricaturist refer to his impeccable appearance and the studied care with which he went about his toilet. When Reynolds Hole asked him to assist at his wedding in 1861, Leech requested long notice of the date " 'because', he said, 'his coat, waistcoat, trousers, and especially his scarf, must be gradually and carefully developed.' He appeared in due course, a combination of good looks, good temper, and good clothes, as my best man."[1] "I should tell you", Millais wrote to Evans, eighteen years after Leech's death, "that he was always careful in *his dress* and always went to the best houses for everything he purchased, possibly from having early in life discovered the wisdom of such a course (see his satire of everything shoddy) but chiefly from inherent good taste — his choice was so *quiet* that one only *felt* he was perfectly attired."[2] This low key elegance seems to be borne out by the surviving photographs, taken in the early 'sixties, and is implied by Millais' stylish portrait of 1854 with its knotted cravat and gold pin and its carefully groomed hair and side-whiskers (Colour Plate 20, page 131).[3] His normal working dress was a black velvet coat "something in shape like a shooting-coat",[4] his only concession

1. Hole, Reynolds, *The Memories of ...,* 1892, p. 43.

2. Evans Letters, Harvard University, MS Eng 1028. Letter from J.E. Millais, 13 February, 1882.

3. National Portrait Gallery.

4. Frith, W.P., *John Leech His Life and Work,* 1891, Vol. 2, p. 91.

TASTE.

to artistic Bohemianism in his own studio.

That Leech was so scrupulous in dress and yet so conservative, does explain why he found the subject so engaging in others. His works are like a register of fashion changes, even when the underlying humour is not specifically about dress. Frith found this as early as 1892 when talking of the artist's *Rising Generation* lithographs. "These works of Leech possess what it is not too much to call an historical interest, as they chronicle truly the dresses of the time. In the object of our young friends admiration, I fancy I see the approach of the crinoline, while her ringlets afford a striking contrast to the fringes of the present day. An old lady would now create a sensation indeed if she appeared in a turban like that which bedecks the sitting figure."[5] Frith was Leech's friend for many years, saw his method of work and appreciated his accuracy. Another contemporary who did not know him, makes the same point; John Brown in his warm essay of *Horae Subsecivae* writes: "Then as to dress; this was one of the things Leech very early mastered and knew the meaning and power of, and it is worth mastering, for in it, the dress, is most of the man both given and received."[6]

Leech was painstaking in his preparations of drawings of historical costume. In 1844 when working on Albert Smith's historical novel, *The Marchioness of Brinvilliers,* he complained both of Smith's late delivery of the manuscript and the sort of accuracy that was expected of him. "Really," he writes, "it is too much to expect that I can throw myself at a moments notice into the seventeenth century, with all its difficulties of costume etc etc."[7] Leech was not specially happy in this sort of illustrating, nor had he a great aptitude for it, but with the modern life subjects he entered into the spirit of the illustration and gave the costume a similar degree of scrutiny.

Among the early lithographs of 1837-38 one, "I say Bob", deals with dandies. "Envy" deals with children's costumes and "Well, I declare, now..." shows the dresses and bonnets of two women in some detail. It is not however until well on in his *Punch* career that Leech starts to satirise costume, possibly the magazine's readership was too radical and not sufficiently *fashionable* itself in the early years, to warrant it. He is also cautious (except in the 1844 *Pocket Book*) about showing feminine peculiarities, the absurdities of male clothes providing him with sufficient fuel from 1845 to 1849. The earliest, "Fashions for 1845", shows an over-zealous salesman trying to sell a cravat pin to a diminutive gentleman. "A pin for your scarf, sir? Here's an article we have sold a great many of!" Needless to say the gold pin is nearly the size of the dandified little gent's head! The pin, such a notable part of Victorian masculine jewellery, appears again in the first half of 1853, where two swells admire a pin with a huge skull to it under the heading "Taste" (margin illustration). As gentlemen's costume became more regularised and more sombre, the young man-about-town seems to have put all his flamboyance into his neckwear, waistcoats and shirting. Leech pounces on all these articles of attire with great glee in the late 1840s and early 1850s, and they erupt like an explosion in many of his jokes. Although the

5. Frith, op. cit., Vol. 1, pp. 58-59.

6. Brown, John, *Horae Subsecivae,* 1882, p. 19.

7. Frith, op. cit., Vol. 1, p. 151.

Colour Plate 21. "Dressing For the Ball in 1857". Frontispiece for Punch's Pocket Book For 1858. *Steel engraving coloured by hand.*

Colour Plate 22. "Some Seaside Fashions for 1863". Frontispiece for Punch's Pocket Book For 1863. *Steel engraving coloured by hand.*

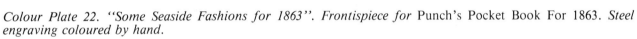

elaborate neckclothes of the Regency had disappeared, there was a return in the 1840s to wide and rather stiff bows, in 1849 Leech sketches them like great wings on his tiny dandies and self-possessed undergraduates. In one cut, the hansom cab can scarcely accommodate the ties of two of his swells, but the zenith of these creations is reached in the summer of 1850 with "A Most Alarming Swelling". A line of four dandies with linked arms parade through the Park with peg-top trousers of incredible weaves, waistcoats of eye-catching patterns and enormous ties. Before one accuses him of wild exaggeration, one does have to remember that Leech's London was *almost* the London of the young "Dizzy" and of Count D'Orsay, whom he knew and entertained. He satirises the elaborate "Joinville" with fringed ends, the all-round collars of the early 'fifties and the shoe-string necktie. Shirts seem to have taken on a new lease of life around 1846 and Leech has them displayed for us in "More Novelty in the Shirt Way" where a bewildering selection of dots, squiggles and zig-zag patterns are shown above a contented little swell gazing at his mirror. In a similar comment on bizarre shirts, a chamber-maid is almost frightened to death by a visitor who appears to be covered in small skulls!

In 1847 the artist has noticed that the tight trousers of the period are being produced in bright colours with bold checks and stripes, typically he introduces "Fashions For Fast Men" in which two clerks discuss in high falutin' language the merits of one over the other. The year before, another of the same breed is being shown a huge and gaudy pattern by a persistent draper: "That's a sweet thing for a waistcoat, sir, and would look uncommon well upon you sir?" The little swell ponders but is obviously clay in the hands of the draper. This mania for broad stripes and checks was the beginning of the craze for "Exhibition" checks which coincided with the Crystal Palace exhibition in 1851.

Some of Leech's earliest contributions to *Punch* include dapper little gents wearing the short overcoat known as the "pea jacket" or "pilot coat" which had been introduced about 1843. The pea jacket was like a donkey jacket but the pilot coat was longer and the artist had enormous fun putting women into them and exaggerating their enormous buttons. A complete contrast to this in 1855 was the excessively long and narrow "Noah's Ark" overcoat for gentlemen, tightly fitted and giving their wearers the appearance of wooden figures; the absurdities of this were brilliantly shown (illustration left).

When he was not directly interesting himself in clothes, Leech was having considerable amusement at the expense of hair styles and fads and fashions in whiskers, notably male ringlets in 1841 and "The Great Moustache Movement" which features from 1853. The fashion until then had been for men of Leech's age to have a curly or waved crop of hair, parted in the middle and falling to a luxuriant growth of side whiskers, but the upper lip was clean-shaven. But after 1853 and accelerated by the military fashions of the Crimean War in 1854, moustaches came back into vogue. Leech tried to grow moustaches himself in 1853, giving rise to a number of *Punch* jokes

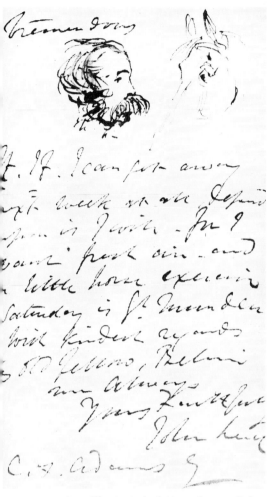

An illustrated letter from John Leech to Charles Adams, 21 January 1854. Dimsdale Collection.

and a self-portrait with moustachios in a letter written to Adams. Discussing a meet where he intends to ride a new horse, he says, "I have been so green myself that I shall want her particularly 'tranquil' — have sacrificed the moustaches for fear of frightening the horses in the field. They were getting too tremendous."[8] (Illustration left.) He was obviously rather half-hearted in his enthusiasm for the new fashion, perhaps he felt it too ostentatious as he implies in a conversation recalled by Edmund Yates. "I quite well recollect in the earliest days of the beard movement his remonstrating with me about my budding moustache 'Its all very well for those fellows', he said, with a glance to a table where Albert Smith and some others were sitting, 'but no gentleman wears one'."[9] "In my opinion," Leech told Frith on another occasion, "only soldiers should be allowed moustachios."[10]

"The Moustache Movement" sketches show Leech at his best, cutting right across the social scale with urchins imitating swells, tradesmen and clerks competing with stubbly growths (below) and juveniles outdoing their fathers. An early one in the summer of 1853 had the moustachioed baker "cutting out" the soldier in the affections of the kitchen-maid, an autumn one shows a whiskery railway official peering like an apparition into a train compartment! There are more excellent ones to follow, the servant who notifies a visitor that Master "ain't allowed to see nobody but his 'airdresser" and "Master Smith" under a garden cloche trying to "Force His Moustachios for the Brown's Party", 1854. "I wear mine because they looks 'ansom, and goes down with the gals," he has a cockney clerk explaining in late 1853. The subject re-appears in 1857 but by

8. Dimsdale Collection, 21 January, 1854.

9. Evans Letters, op. cit. Letter from Edmund Yates, 9 October, 1885.

10. Frith, op. cit., Vol. 2, p. 221.

MOUSTACHE MOVEMENT.

Gent. "I SAY, MOSEY! WHY DON'T YER GO THE 'OLE 'OG, AND LET ALL YER BEARD GROW, LIKE ME?"

Colour Plate 23. "Mr Sponge at Jawleyford Court". Illustration to Mr Sponge's Sporting Tour, *1852.*

TEMPUS EDAX RERUM.

"GOOD GRACIOUS ! IS IT POSSIBLE?—NO ! YES ! NO !—YES ! YES, BY JUPITER, IT'S A GREY HAIR IN MY FAVOURITE WHISKER !"

BLOOMERISM !

Strong-Minded Female. "NOW, DO, PRAY, ALFRED, PUT DOWN THAT FOOLISH NOVEL, AND DO SOMETHING RATIONAL. GO AND PLAY SOMETHING ON THE PIANO; YOU NEVER PRACTISE, NOW YOU'RE MARRIED."

that time the taste for beards is uppermost and has begun to interest Leech too. There is for instance a personable young cleric with a beard in 1861, preaching to a church-full of adoring girls with the caption "What's to become of Captain Heavyswell?"

As the more excessive elements of dandyish dress receded after 1850, Leech concentrated more and more on the ladies; there was certainly plenty to choose from. Among the earliest are a pair of sketches about the chatelaine which came in to favour in early 1849 as an appendage for the lady of the house. Leech has one fashionable female with everything from kettles and hearth brooms to fire tongs and corkscrews dangling from her middle, another "A Blessing to Mothers" has chains attached to dogs, children and toys while she lazily reads a book! This was a very gentle dart at womankind; fiercer satires were to follow.

In 1849, Mrs Amelia Bloomer of New York tried to introduce a "rational" attire for ladies consisting of a short skirt with loose trousers below it, closely gathered round the ankles. It was an extraordinary innovation for the mid-Victorians, and although it was never really popular here, Mrs Bloomer herself visited this country in 1851 in order to promote her invention. Leech had already poked fun at "Rational Dinner Costume" in 1850, so it is hardly surprising that the revolutionary notion of "bloomers" should have appealed to him when the first examples arrived from America. In the second half of 1851 we have "Latest From America, Quite New and Very Chaste", where three scandalised ladies in bonnets look in horror at a shop assistant holding aloft check unmentionables. Later in the year there is "Bloomerism — An American Custom" where a pair of gaunt, bespectacled, cigar-smoking feminists (perhaps intended for Amelia herself) march through the streets in their trousers and skirts, cheered on by urchins.

Bloomerism had become linked in the public mind and perhaps in Leech's with feminism, the adoption of male roles and the world of the blue-stocking. Daumier had peddled some pretty scathing satires on the "new woman" in Les Bas-Bleus, 1844, but with the exception of the "Bloomerism" sketches there are no excursions into literary and learned womanhood in Leech's work. With his pretty and domestic wife, John Leech had no time for women who wanted to oust their husbands, scribble novels or usurp power. The series develops during 1851, reaching a crescendo at the turn of the year with a double page spread of bloomers entitled "Bloomerism — A Dream". Here, prophetically, Leech has his "liberated" females in their ludicrous garb, acting out the roles of police, coachmen, soldiers and dons, complete in the latter case with mortar-boards and parasols! A far more subtle sketch in line and dialogue and for that reason closer to Daumier's prototypes had appeared that autumn. A very masculine wife in the ubiquitous bloomers says to her effeminate husband, "Now, do, pray Alfred, put down that foolish novel, and do something rational. Go and play something on the piano; you never practise, now you're married" (left). But Leech had greatly exaggerated the notion in his drawings.

EASIER SAID THAN DONE.
Master of the House. "Oh, Fred, my Boy—when Dinner is ready, you take Mrs. Furbelow down stairs!"

"Bloomerism" was in its way no more absurd than the rise and growth of the crinoline between 1843 and 1857 when it could be anything from twelve to fifteen feet in circumference. The newly established middle-class that Leech so accurately chronicled, wanted to show off their prosperity and their status, and the crinoline with multiple petticoats and later on a cage, was a good way of doing this. Leech's earliest references to the size, shape, and inconvenience of these accoutrements seems to be in late 1856, and it is the man's point of view he takes up! In "Easier Said Than Done" a young man, almost smothered by a vast crinoline is ordered, "Oh, Fred, My Boy — When dinner is ready, you take Mrs. Furbelow down stairs!" (left). He also pictures crinolines at the ball, 1858, at boating parties, the same year, shop-keepers sheltering under crinolines, 1860, and fishermen using them to signal with, 1863! One of the most celebrated of the 1858 pictures, shows a fashionable lady with a crinoline like a galleon, pausing in front of a gothic porch. "Yes Love," she tells her companion, "a very pretty church, but the door is certainly very narrow!" In another, a harrassed husband, about to go away, is asked to find room for a crinoline in his portmanteau (opposite above) and "Confound the Hoops" of 1858, has the suitor unable to approach the girl of his heart because of her — crinoline! The cage crinoline was made up of a dome of graduated hoops, originally of whale-bone, later of steel and finally of watch-spring, an extremely voluminous bulk which Leech's drawings adequately portray. How closely he followed fashion developments can be judged from the introduction of a new invention. In 1856, a firm patented an inflatable crinoline cage, by which the structure could be blown up through indiarubber tubes to the desired size.[11] Leech's version of this "Dressing for the Ball in 1857" appeared in the *Punch Pocket Book For 1858* which he had prepared at the latter end of 1857 (Colour Plate 21, page 141). A bevy of lovely girls prepare to put on their crinolines while their maids feverishly pump the cages in to shape! According to one authority the system was unsuccessful due to "unexpected punctures".[12] In 1861 "The Modern Governess" is in a crinoline with the globe stretched across it to instruct her pupils; by 1862 the crinolines, or some of them, have been handed on to the servants. We get "The Crinoline For Domestic Use" in which a drudge is reprimanded for wearing such a thing and "Cause and Effect" of 1864 shows a pretty housemaid in a crinoline knocking over everything in the drawing-room!

Was Leech's petite wife behind some of these sallies against the absurdities of fashion? Most men would notice the main movements, but what about details, such as the "off the shoulder" ball dresses of early 1851 or the so called "Zouave" jackets of 1860? One suspects that Mrs Leech may have taken in at least one fashion magazine which her husband studied. One design of 1853, has a clothes-conscious young girl looking at such a Parisian publication and receiving far from encouraging advice from her dowdy grandmother!

Hats certainly did not escape Leech's eye either, they are most pronounced after 1855, when large round hats became popular for the

11. Cunnington, C. Willett and Phillis, *Handbook of English Costume in the Nineteenth Century,* 1966, p. 451.

12. Cunnington et al., op. cit., p. 451.

GOING OUT OF TOWN.

Mary. "IF YOU PLEASE, SIR, MISSUS SAY YOU MUST FIND ROOM FOR THIS IN YOUR PORTMANTEL."

IMITATION IS THE SINCEREST FLATTERY.

Sarah Jane to Betsy Ann. "OH, YES! IF IT COMES TO THAT, YOU KNOW PEOPLE CAN STICK OUT AS MUCH AS OTHER PEOPLE—
I ALWAYS WEARS ONE O' MOTHER'S OLD CLOTHES BASKETS."

PLEASING DELUSION. IN RE THE ROUND HATS.

Female. "WELL! THERE CAN BE NO QUESTION ABOUT ONE THING!—THEY CERTAINLY DO MAKE YOU LOOK YOUNGER!"

seaside or the garden, and one cartoon "Useful If Not Ornamental" has the younger brothers of the house, using a round hat as an archery target. "Scene On The English Coast" (below) has a long line of — round hats! He also fastened on to the shovel-shaped riding hats which were the rage about 1858 for walking costumes; they appear in frequent portrayals of sultry-eyed beauties of the country house and the promenade. Spoon bonnets appear like clockwork in 1861 and the small round pork-pie hats which he first notices in 1859, come to full flower in a charming croquet scene in *Punch's Almanack for 1863*.

At the close of the 'fifties, a fairly novel idea was introduced for walking dresses. The skirts were made short enough to reveal the ankles and could be hitched up becomingly over a scarlet petticoat by a variety of means including a "flounce suspender". Leech's flounces are charmingly raised to reveal ankles in "The Race For a Bathing Machine", 1858, and in the frontispiece to *Punch's Pocket Book* for 1863 (Colour Plate 22, page 141). A similar effort is achieved in his "Common Objects at the Sea-Side — Generally Found Upon the Rocks at Low Water", August 1858. "Dinner Under Difficulties", 1861, has the male guests nearly submerged under the new fangled flounces! "For the unexaggerated truth of this print, I, who write, can vouch," says Frith, "for have I not again and again been obliged to solve the difficulty of using my knife and fork?

SCENE ON THE ENGLISH COAST.

THE RULING PASSION.

"NOW, TELL ME, DEAR, IS THERE ANYTHING NEW IN THE FASHIONS

13. Frith, op. cit., Vol. 2, p. 177.
14. Cunnington, op. cit., and Buck, Anne, *Victorian Costume & Costume Accessories,* 1961.
15. Frith, op. cit., Vol. 2, p. 176.
16. Cooper, Leonard, *R.S. Surtees,* 1952, p. 110.
17. Cuming, E.D., *Robert Smith Surtees (Creator of 'Jorrocks') 1804-1864,* 1924, p. 260.
18. Surtees, R.S., *Mr Sponge's Sporting Tour,* 1852, p. 80.

In spite of the attacks upon it, crinoline had its day — and far too long a day it was."[13]

During Leech's halcyon days, 1843 to 1860, the costumes of the time were perpetually under his gaze, faithfully noticed and relentlessly parodied. Apart from the intended exaggerations, many of the domestic scenes would seem to be very accurate pictures of contemporary fashion. Certain costume historians have actually used Leech designs in their books as a correct barometer of the times.[14] Frith underlines this aspect in 1891, when he says, "from observation I can assure a doubter that Leech has frequently under, rather than over, done the swell of those voluminous skirts."[15]

The descriptions of costume and fashionable attire also play a surprisingly large part in the novels of R.S. Surtees, which Leech was illustrating. The correspondence between artist and writer bristle with such considerations and at least one biographer has suggested that Surtees' interest in dress may have arisen from his meeting with Leech.[16] Did Surtees incorporate such detail in order to make the popularity of *Mr Sponge* certain, with a public accustomed to Leech's social caricatures? Leech was not above introducing his own favourites. "I purpose making the editress of the Swillingford paper (the lady who makes such a hash of the hunt) a Bloomer," he writes to Surtees in May 1852 and sure enough she is introduced as such.[17]

The strong connection is well shown in Surtees' description of the entry of Mr Sponge into the dinner party at Jawleyford Court, so similar to Leech's *Punch* swells.

"Notwithstanding Jawleyford's recommendation to the contrary, Mr Sponge made himself an uncommon swell. He put on a desperately stiff starcher, secured in front with a large gold fox-head pin with carbuncle eyes; a fine, fancy-fronted shirt, with a slight tendency to pink, adorned with mosaic-gold-tethered studs of sparkling diamonds (or French paste, as the case might be); a white waistcoat with fancy buttons; a blue coat with bright plain ones, and a velvet collar, black tights, with broad black-and-white Cranbourne-alley-looking stockings (socks rather), and patent leather pumps with gilt buckles — Sponge was proud of his leg!"[18]

In Colour Plate 23, page 144, Mr Sponge is seen in colour, every item of this precise inventory in place, escorting the stout Mrs Jawleyford in to dinner.

A similar microscopic attention to detail is found in *Ask Mama.* The first glimpse that the Earl of Ladythorne has of the dashing Miss De Glancey is followed by an exact catalogue of what she is wearing, namely the fashionable hunting costume of 1858:

"But though she did not look my lord did, and was much struck with the air and elegance of everything — her mild classic features — her black felt, Queen's-patterned, wide-awake, trimmed with lightish-green velvet, and green cock-feathered plume, tipped with straw colour to match the ribbon that now gently fluttered at her fair neck — her hair, her whip, her gloves, her *tout ensemble.* Her lightish-green habit was the quintessence of a fit, and altogether there was a high-bred finish about her that looked more like Hyde Park than what one usually sees in the country."[19]

Perhaps the last word on Leech as a satirist of fashion should come from Du Maurier who succeeded him. Du Maurier was the most painstaking observer of High Life, his figures exude wealth, style and breeding, and yet it is the mixture of fashion *and* humanity in Leech that appeals to him.

"In his tastes and habits he was by nature aristocratic; he liked the society of those who were well dressed, well bred and refined like himself, and perhaps a trifle conventional; he conformed quite spontaneously and without effort to the upper-class British ideal of his time, and had its likes and dislikes. But his strongest predilections of all are common to the British race; his love of home, his love of sport, his love of the horse and the hound — especially his love of the pretty woman — the pretty woman of the normal, wholesome English type."[20]

And what about Leech's flamboyant swells?

"... How healthy, good-humoured and manly they are, with all their vagaries of dress and jewellery and accent! It is easy to forgive them if they give the whole of their minds to their white neckties, or are dejected because they have lost the little gridiron off their chatelaine, or lose all presence of mind when a smut settles on their noses, and turn faint at the sight of Mrs Gamp's umbrella!"[21]

19. Surtees, R.S., *Ask Mama*, 1858, p. 52.
20. Du Maurier, George, *Social and Pictorial Satire*, 1898, pp. 36-37.
21. ibid., p. 46.

Conversazione of Ladies

Chapter Eight

"PAINTER OF MANKIND"

s the years progressed, John Leech's life was punctuated by more signs of acclaim, more heartfelt affection than any illustrator had heretofore received from his public. The new journalism of which *Punch* was very much a part was one reason for this popularity, so too was the artist's wide range of subject matter, including as it did Surtees' novels, Dickens' stories, R.H. Barham's *Ingoldsby Legends* as well as miscellaneous works by Thomas Hood, Mrs Trollope, W.H. Maxwell and Harriet Becher Stowe. He had been Art Editor of the short-lived *The Month* in 1851[1] and was to occupy a similar place on *Once A Week,* 1859. The appearance of *Pictures of Life and Character* between March 1853 and October 1854, brought him even wider fame. In these oblong quarto books, his best *Punch* work was gathered together for another audience who did not know his engravings in the magazine; a cosmorama of squires, huntsmen, pretty housemaids, urchins, querulous spinsters and swells met inside these covers to divert thousands of Victorian families.

But at the same time Leech himself had grown less satisfied and more unsettled. He had passed his fortieth birthday in 1857 and was certainly not immune from the restlessness and soul-searching brought on by the approach of early middle age. The best years of his life had glided by. Leech was a household name, but there were undercurrents of self-questioning; had he achieved his celebrity in the right way? Was an ephemeral weekly the correct outlet for an artist? Was he able to live in the style he wanted after all this work? It was probably the latter problem that he felt most deeply and which drove him on all the time to fresh endeavours. Twist and turn as he might, he had never been able to free himself from his financial embarrassments or the demands of creditors and relations upon his pocket. His open-hearted frankness which was a virtue for his friends on walking holidays, fishing expeditions or by the seaside, became a vice in matters of business; he describes himself as "a mere child"[2] in such negotiations and frequently behaved with a child's innocence. He was known to be extremely, even unwisely, generous and to have a rather exaggerated sense of duty towards even distant relations. The Brook Green villa, so delightfully satirised in *Punch,* had been a poor investment, and he was still trying to free himself from its debts in 1856, nine years after leaving it![3] At about this time he was forced to borrow two hundred and fifty pounds from Mr Evans of Bradbury

1. *The Month,* July to December 1851, in collaboration with Albert Smith.

2. Hole Letters, Tallents Collection, 9 December, 1862.

3. Bodleian Library MS Eng lett d 397, fols 63-142. Letter 27 June, 1856.

ROOM FOR IMPROVEMENT.

Dealer. "THERE, HE AIN'T A 'ORSE MADE UP FOR SALE.
HE'LL GO ON IMPROVIN' EVERY DAY
YOU KEEP HIM—HE WILL."

and Evans, to help his sister Caroline start a school in Bayswater, the obliging Evans produced the necessary sum but within a twelvemonth he was writing to him again.

"I wish to lend my sister again the sum of two hundred and fifty pounds as you were kind enough to enable me to do some time since, and for the same period namely six months. Will you kindly help me to do so? I don't think there will be any further occasion to necessitate such a loan as I am sure you will be glad to hear that her school answers all, indeed more than her expectations but the disbursements are heavy at first."[4]

It was all the more cruel that he was generally believed to be a very rich man. W.M. Rossetti recorded Holman Hunt saying in 1861, that Leech was earning £2,000 a year at a time when few artists were earning £500.[5] Leech lived well in his Brunswick Square home, he entertained constantly but not extravagantly, managed two family holidays a year, had an occasional visit to Paris. And yet the ordinary annual outgoings of a normal London householder were beyond him. In August 1860, Evans is supplying more loans to pay off the instalments on Leech's insurance policy. "It will be a great weight off my mind if you will kindly consider the matter," he writes pathetically, "for I have really been almost worried to death this last year. I trust however that a few weeks in the North may make me a more useful member of society."[6]

Paradoxically these "weeks in the North", staying with his grand friends actually compounded rather than relieved the situation. Leech was not a typical snob but he was a typical Victorian; he belonged very much to that stratified century where the pressures to conform or sink were so strong. Charming and guileless as he undoubtedly was, he wanted desperately to be accepted by the right people with all the tragic earnestness of the self-made man. He wished above everything to be the country gentleman, to hobnob with lords, to be treated on equal terms by the leisured class, yet gnawing away inside was the feeling that he could never quite attain this, never rid himself of Ludgate Hill, his father's shameful bankruptcy and his pressing money problems. His hunting, shooting and fishing expeditions continued, they furnished him with a lot of material, but he was bound to repay this hospitality in London, bound to buy the costly equipment that went with it, so that his new friends should not suspect he was not a wealthy man. His mares Royal, Rajah and Red Mullet were loaded on to trains as the round of visits went on, to Baron Mayer de Rothschild at Mentmore, to the Duke of Athol in Scotland, the Smythe-Owens at Condover Hall, the Nethercotes at Moulton Grange and the Holes at Caunton Manor. Although these families provided exactly the social milieu in which he liked to move, none of them were for that very reason approachable about his money difficulties. In fact Leech would have been humiliated had they known of his predicament and some of the payments to Old Leech must have been made to keep that particular spectre away from the feast. His extremely close friendship with Reynolds Hole, a friendship which lasted from 1858 until the artist's

4. Bodleian Library, op. cit., 27 February 1857.

5. Rossetti, W.M., *PreRaphaelitism Papers,* 1899, p. 285.

6. Bodleian Library, op. cit., 17 August, 1860.

7. Frith, W.P., *John Leech His Life and Work,* 1891, Vol. 2, p. 280.

8. Hole, Reynolds, *The Memories of ...,* 1892, p. 17.

9. Henry Silver Diary, *Punch* Office, 11 December, 1861.

10. Hole, op. cit., p. 48.

11. *Toronto Mail,* 12 September, 1883.

death, resulted in over a hundred letters but not in a single one is there any overt reference to money. It was only when he was staying at Barkway and hunting with the Puckeridge, "my hunt" as he called it, that he felt free to perch in front of faithful Charley Adams' fireplace, half seated on a table with one leg dangling (a favourite position) and be himself. From Charley, who had known him at the Coffee House, had been behind him during those awful detentions and lent him regular sums over the years, there was nothing to hide.

Leech's natural grace and good manners did not really need any veneer of good breeding and pedigree to go with them, but even if this fantasy was lived half unconsciously, it was lived well. Almost to a man contemporary writers refer to the artist's "gentlemanly" bearing, "the presence of a gentleman, grave and courteous always",[7] or "dressed tastefully and quietly like a gentleman".[8] This striving after another sort of life began to appear more frequently in his conversation as the years went by and was referred to by him at the weekly *Punch* dinners. At one such he had exclaimed that what he most wanted in all the world was £1,000 a year and a country life, to which Thackeray had flatly replied that it could not be done.[9] These thoughts led to long periods of melancholy brooding and pitiable self-doubt about his own work, from which he was only roused by insistent friends. Hole writes of one of these occasions: "Mr Millais, joined us, in our indignant expostulations, and in assuring him that his work gave more pleasure to his fellow-men than all the pictures which were hung up in galleries and in rich men's homes, and therefore were comparatively unseen."[10]

This ruminating melancholy interspersed with moments of gaiety may have all been part of his Irish ancestry, that Celtic inheritance of passions strongly held and moods suddenly changed. He had never been constitutionally very strong in spite of his fine build, he was a constant prey to influenza and coughs and also to boils, evidently brought on by over-work and low resistance, he was also probably a migraine sufferer. He had had several bouts of debility, the worst at the end of 1853 when he was scarcely able to deliver any work for *Punch.* Frank Bellew described him as "somewhat languid, or rather exhausted, in his manner, with a touch of melancholy, and was evidently of a highly nervous organization".[11]

The tension in Leech's life, whether financial, social or artistic, had certainly created the nervousness which in its turn had reacted in physical ailments. His most obvious neurotic complaint was in regard to street noise, he had a strong aversion to the sound of street musicians but particularly to Italian organ-grinders who were pretty numerous in the London suburbs. This phobia first appeared in *Punch* in 1843, when Leech was only twenty-six, with advancing years it became an obsession with him, causing him increasing irritation and distress. His illustrated attacks on these purveyors of cheap music were among the few venomous cuts that he ever executed in *Punch.* Although tired and over-burdened with work, he could shrug the seeming effects of it off with a joke to his colleagues, but he could not so easily escape his public.

Colour Plate 24. "Mornin' My Lord..." Oil sketch for the Egyptian Hall Exhibition, 1862.
21 x 28ins.   Viscount Leverhulme Collection

Colour Plate 25. "While Charles Prefers..." Oil sketch for the Egyptian Hall Exhibition, 1862.
21 x 29ins.   Viscount Leverhulme Collection

JOHN LEECH.

This picture of Leech appeared in the Illustrated Review, *15 November, 1872.*

Even in the days before photographs in the press, Leech's face was sufficiently well known to make him the object of much curiosity. The great caricaturist was watched in the hunting-field, scrutinised by his neighbours and lionised by some hostesses in a way that he often found disagreeable. With so sensitive a temperament, the reserve of so famous a figure was often mistaken for disdain by people meeting him for the first time. His sense of insecurity made him immediately defensive with strangers, more relaxed with acquaintances and children, but only truly at ease with his few intimate friends. "I have heard him described as haughty", Frith wrote, "stand-offish, cold, and so on; and his manner to some of those who may have met him for the first time, occasionally admitted of that construction; but it arose from nervousness, or from an aversion to loud and ill-timed compliment, feeling, as he sincerely did, his 'little sketches' deserved no such eulogium." [12]

Such an unassuming man as Leech, delighted by the simple rather than the sophisticated things of life, engagingly innocent yet painfully brittle, was extremely vulnerable to the criticism, misunderstanding and pressures that his fame brought him. He disliked being recognised by autograph hunters and their like and was quite nettled over boorish remarks about his own work.

"He liked the sympathy of those who could appreciate the intention and execution of his work," wrote Hole, "but his countenance, his mixed expression of indignation and amusement, was a memorable sight to see ... when a vulgar fellow, who travelled with us on the rail, asked him 'how much he got for his funny cuts' and assured him that 'some on 'em was tiptop', though he thought Old Briggs was bosh." [13]

Encounters like this, the desire to protect his social position, the wish to conceal his financial shortcomings, led the artist to become a man with two lives, two separate existences, one which showed a smiling public face, the other an interior look of strained bewilderment. That percipient writer and observer of human nature, Holman Hunt, noticed these two sides when he met Leech with his family at the Crystal Palace, Sydenham, in about 1862. In one of those rare moments when all reticence is thrown away and one man bares his heart to another, Leech poured out his troubles to Hunt, the slavery of his work, the difficulty he had in making ends meet, the lack of appreciation accorded to artists in the country. As suddenly as the curtain had been raised it was lowered again.

"When we neared a large circle of acquaintances in the Palace grounds Leech withdrew his heart far within, out of sight and reach of all present, who looked upon him in no other light than that of the happy bringer of cheerfulness to the large world that loves English humour." [14]

In general the artist's work was not controversial, so that at least he was spared the more vindictive comments of the Victorian art papers. But such adverse criticism as there was, upset him, and could only contribute to his nervous disorders and his physical tiredness. In May 1858, a new illustrated publication called *The Welcome Guest*

12. Frith, op. cit., Vol. 2, p. 240.

13. Hole, op. cit., p. 20.

14. Holman Hunt, W., *Contemporary Review,* 1888, pp. 335-358.

"I BEG YOUR PARDON, MA'AM,
BUT I THINK YOU DROPPED THIS."

made its appearance, it was designed as a cheaper competitor of *Punch* and became a rival of *Once a Week* founded the next year. It was filled with novelettes, gossip and inferior wood engravings. In one of the early numbers there was a wholly unwarranted attack on Leech's work by the scabrous Edmund Yates in which he referred to the artist's work as lacking pity and the artist himself as "a terribly cruel, granite-natured man".

"How mercilessly he satirizes Poverty, and Poverty alone. Poverty of means, Poverty of form and feature, Poverty of wisdom or of training — no matter what, so that it be a phase of human weakness and suffering! A poor holiday serving-wench, consoling herself with a little harmless affectation of gentility; an old woman, whose heart may not yet have withered up in her bosom, striving to conserve some semblance of departed juvenility; a hard-working city wife, who has not had much leisure to pay particular attention to her H's; a scrubby clerk, who can not sit a horse quite as gracefully as a Melton Mowbray squire, or whose legs and whiskers are not quite up to the standard of Horse Guards' perfection; a sorry music master presuming to ride in a cab when he has only sixpence to pay for it. These, and such as these only, are the objects of Mr Leech's unsparing castigation." [15]

Yates concluded his unpleasant article by saying, "If human wickedness were only as detestable in Mr Leech's eyes as human weakness, we might still have a Hogarth among us." As well as ignoring Leech's dislike of idle high life and exploitation, Yates has completely misread the great humanising role that the illustrator was playing in bringing gentle domestic humour to the forefront. Leech's seriousness too is amply displayed in the Crimea and Mutiny engravings. This vitriolic piece may have been penned to show Yates' dislike of *Punch* or to discomfort Leech because he was known to be a close friend of Thackeray. Yates had attacked Thackeray in 1858 and had been dismissed from the Garrick Club; also he was the main instrument in the breach between Thackeray and Dickens. [16] Leech pretended to laugh the whole thing off in a letter to Hole, but it obviously rankled and the latter replied more seriously: "I must confess that my teeth snapped and my toes quivered, and I had not a single thought or feeling which a cool clergyman ought to have, when I re-perused the dirty document in question." [17]

Leech did not forget it either; in a surprising outburst at one of the summer *Punch* dinners at the Star and Garter, Richmond, on 5 July, 1860, he attacked Yates and bravely supported Thackeray. Silver records, "Yates writing about Thackeray in *New York Times* can't be a gentleman says J.L. — Wants kicking. No use using the kid glove style or argument with a Bohemian, must take to the bludgeon to make any impression on such a pack..." [18]

* * * * *

In 1859, an unusual set of circumstances came together which were to give John Leech new hope and which some of his friends believed

15. *The Welcome Guest,* 1859, Vol. 2, p. 20.

16. The attack on Leech actually appears opposite one on Thackeray; strangely enough Yates gives an impression of friendship with Leech in his *Recollections,* 1884.

17. Dewar, George A.B., *The Letters of Samuel Reynolds Hole, Dean of Rochester,* edited with a Memoir, 1907, p. 19.

18. Silver Diary, op. cit., 5 July, 1860.

Old Lady (*loq.*). " BLESS MY HEART ! HOW RIDICULOUSLY SMALL THEY DO MAKE THE EYES OF THE NEEDLES NOW-A-DAYS, TO BE SURE ! "

would change his direction, give him financial security and thereby improved health. In that year the Electro-Block Printing Company of Burleigh Street, Strand, patented a new invention for enlarging woodblock work and then printing it on canvas. Whatever the original point of this invention, it was ideally suited for an artist who had always worked in a smaller scale and still felt unsure of himself painting on a large canvas. It eliminated the more laborious laying in of outline for which Leech had very little patience. Briefly, the impression of a small block was taken on indiarubber and enlarged. This perfect copy was then transferred to the lithographic stone and printed as a ground work, eight times its original size on a large sheet of prepared canvas. All the advantages that Leech could dream of were in this process and it was only a question of his mastering the medium and learning to apply the colour, for him to become what he now most wanted to be, a genre painter in oils!

The indefatigable Mark Lemon is usually credited, probably correctly, with drawing the artist's attention to this invention, but it may have been Reynolds Hole who provided the practical opening. In February 1860, Hole was proposing to give a talk to his parishioners at Caunton and requiring some large diagrams, enquired from Leech in London about the new enlarging process. Leech replied on February 24th:[19]

> My dear Hole,
> I have just heard that the cost for doing the lecture pictures would be from £6 to £7. A very great deal more I should say than you would be inclined to fork out for a village lecture. In a state bordering on frenzy trying to get out of Town.
> Yours sincerely
> J.L.

Three weeks later, the lecture pictures which Hole had apparently ordered, arrived safely and Leech added his own enthusiasm to Hole's, "I am very glad the 'Pictures' arrived in time and were useful. I will speak about another set for you. The additional expense would I should say be trifling. By the way, as regards that 'from a conversation' I had with Evans he I believe has persuaded the patentees of the process that to do these particular sketches was *immensely to their* advantage and the damage will not be altogether more than a pound or so... Really, that same enlarging process is wonderful, is it not?"[20]

Ideas seem to have been crystalising during 1860, no doubt encouraged by Lemon and his other friends. If a good selection of his *Punch* pictures could be satisfactorily enlarged and put on canvas, an exhibition of this work might be staged in London, redounding to Leech's fame and his financial position. It had to be done. The right subjects must be found, they were already known from the *Life and Character,* the best venue for the show must be located and in the meantime Leech must master the techniques of oil. Millais was en-

19. Hole Letters, op. cit., 24 February, 1860.

20. ibid., 5 March, 1860.

IN FOR IT.

"HALLO, SIR! ARE YOU AWARE YOU'RE TRESPASSING THERE?"

listed almost at once and Leech was inculcated into the mysteries of manipulating oils, the use of the brush and the tricky application of flesh tints. Frith, who was not the most objective critic when a brother artist was moving in to oil, remembered these first efforts as crude in the extreme. The coarse outlines of the enlargement were very obvious in these early attempts, Leech filling in the primed white areas with a thin transparent colour and making the pictures look like "indifferent lithographs slightly tinted".[21] This was obviously very unsatisfactory and by degrees during the year, Leech became master of the medium and instead of allowing the thick lines of the printers ink to remain on the canvas, he gradually removed them with turpentine, especially on the faces and figures. He was then free to re-draw them with great care and apply the flesh tints which made the pictures live again as they had first sparkled in the pages of *Punch*.

About sixty social subjects were chosen for enlarging, the majority of them with a sporting flavour to appeal to Leech's huge country based audience. Mr. Briggs was there, so was Tom Noddy and there were fishing, hunting and shooting episodes. The newly printed canvases began to arrive at Brunswick Square in the spring of 1861, which gave the artist exactly a year to complete the mammoth task; the gallery chosen for the show was the Egyptian Hall and the date fixed the month of June 1862. Leech was in London throughout the early part of that summer working on his pictures, struggling with this new dimension in his art, trying to perfect it sufficiently in time. His neat workroom must have gained easels, palettes and tubes of colour as it was changed into a studio in the midst of all this feverish activity. In August he was able to steal away to Lowestoft but probably took some of this work with him as he was obviously getting alarmed. He confided in a letter to Hole on 6th September from Lowestoft, "The picture matters are becoming very serious, and until they are disposed of, my holidays must be very limited."[22] He spoke of shutting himself up in London for the winter.

The autumn was always a bad time for him and doubly so in 1861. It was the moment that the Whitefriars people began to demand ideas for *Punch's Pocket Book* which meant a steel engraving and colour as well as several woodcuts, but it was also the time for *Punch's Almanack* which he always found a great strain. Worse was to come, for in November Surtees began badgering him about a new sporting novel, *Mr Facey Romford's Hounds;* would the illustrations be started by January? Leech's well-meaning attitude was to accept everything and then simply nothing was finished on time and *Facey Romford* was delayed for months because of the oil paintings. It is not difficult to picture the scene at Brunswick Square in early 1862, the gas light burning late into the night, the artist nervous and exhausted, still applying himself to the long series of subjects, Annie Leech worried and saying nothing, fellow artists and friends not admitted. At least he was sufficiently satisfied with his progress in January to ask H.O. Nethercote to visit him in daylight. "I should like to show you some work I have been at",[23] but the following month he revealed the strain to Hole and his desperate hope of

21. Frith, op. cit., Vol. 2, p. 249.

22. Hole Letters, op. cit., 6 September, 1861.

23. Houghton Library, Harvard, letters to H.O. Nethercote, 21 January, 1862.

NO NEWS IS GOOD NEWS (?)

First Old Foozle. "WOULD YOU LIKE TO SEE THE PAPER, SIR? THERE'S NOTHING IN IT."

Second Old Foozle. "THEN WHAT THE DEVIL DID YOU KEEP IT SO LONG FOR?"

financial success. "You have no idea how I am driven with my work — but I am glad to say people like what I have done — Oh! May the British Public generally think well of it — and won't we have a jollification if they do!"[24]

The month of April was even worse, the stacks of waiting canvases, though reduced, were not completed and at this moment both of Leech's children went down with whooping cough and Annie was confined to her room with bronchitis. "My pictures throes are agonising," he told Hole on the 14th, "work never ending,"[25] and to Millais, "I have been so pressed for time I have scarcely known which way to turn."[26] Despite the lack of time and the amount of painting to be done, the artist had to deal too with the mechanics of the exhibition, how the pictures were to be placed, what accommodation the Egyptian Hall would offer and what entrance charge should be made at the gate. Rather surprisingly it was left to him to have small benches made for the galleries so that visitors could rest while viewing the exhibition. There was also the question of the private view and the arrangements for the critics to see the oil sketches, which matters Leech particularly dreaded. He consulted Dickens (who had already seen the pictures) on the last question and received a typical response.[27]

Office of All the Year Round
28 May 1862

My dear Leech

... I wouldn't send vaguely to the Editors of papers and periodicals, *and their friends,* for this reason. That it would involve you in much the same difficulties as a Private View. For example, the Sunday Times takes Dobbs, Hobbs and Snobs, and leaves out Bobbs, and *you* know Bobbs, and Bobbs knows Hobbs, and Bobb's writes to you to know why Hobbs got in, when he (Bobbs) didn't.

Now, I would have No private view whatever — for anybody. I would send cards to all respectable Editors (in the case of Daily Editors at all events, for 2), and I would open on a certain day at a certain hour, and there you have a beginning and end.

I will get Charley Collins to do an article for these pages, and I will go over the Proof, and put in anything that I see wanting.

When the exhibition finally opened to the public in June, it was greeted most enthusiastically by the public. Leech appeared at the gallery on the opening day but after that stayed at home. He had to. The series was still incomplete and some sketches were being added to the walls even while the show was in progress. He managed to get away to Brighton for a few days but still felt the strain of the whole undertaking. "I was so unwell at Brighton (and indeed am now quite unhinged)," he wrote to Hole on June 14th, "that I have not been able to make any social arrangements until now and beside indis-

24. Hole Letters, op. cit., 19 February, 1862.
25. ibid., 10 April, 1862.
26. Author's collection, 14 April, 1862.
27. *Nonsuch Dickens,* Vol. 3, p. 295.

MR. BRIGGS RIDES (!) HOME, AND WONDERS WHAT MRS. BRIGGS WILL SAY.

position I have been so occupied finishing the series that I have been nowhere... You will be glad to know that the Show more than answered our expectations — and altho' at present I have only got a prize headache — the future promises most favourably."[28]

The third week of June was the most memorable because on the 21st Thackeray published his famous article in *The Times* on Leech's sketches in oil. For the first time in Leech's lifetime he set the man's genius in its proper context, he did in this great essay what Charles Baudelaire was to do for Guys, transform an underrated art, the sub-servient craft of illustration into a national resource, a rich chronicle of the times from which other generations would see and understand the Victorians. Thackeray, catalogue in hand, admires, chuckles, but lifts this panorama of national portraits away from the purely humorous into a study of the British character, its compassion as well as its snobbishness, its Hogarthian truthfulness as well as its vulgarity. Leech had been the instructor of the British public, pointing them to a far subtler humour than their grandfathers had known, pointing them to the hidden nuances and signals of a changing society, the tiny inflections of speech, manner and thought that are the greater barometers than brashness and bawdy and part of a real novelist's armoury.

"What he draws he has seen," writes Thackeray. "What he asks you to live in and laugh at and with him, he has laughed at and lived in. It is this wholesomeness, and to use the right word, this goodness that makes Leech more than a drawer of funny pictures, more even than a great artist. It makes him a teacher and an example of virtue in its widest sense, from that of manliness to the sweet devotion of woman, and the loving, open mouth and eyes of *parvula* on your knee."[29]

More unexpectedly Thackeray who had criticised the British caricaturists twenty years before and held up the Frenchmen as the best examples, now turns full circle. Beforehand he had damned the British for visual grossness, now he condemns the French for moral grossness and even for that exaggeration which he had so much dis-liked in Cruikshank.[30]

"How does Gavarni represent the family-father, the sire, the old gentleman in his country? Paterfamilias, in a dyed wig and whiskers, is leering by the side of Mademoiselle Coralie on her sofa in the Rue de Breda; Paterfamilias, with a mask and a nose half-a-yard long, is hobbling after her at the ball. The *enfant terrible* is making Papa and Mamma alike ridiculous by showing us Mamma's lover, who is lurking behind the screen... The fun of the old comedy never seems to end in France; and we have the word of their own satirists, novelists, painters of society, that it is being played from day to day.

"In the works of that barbarian artist Hogarth, the subject which affords such playful sport to the civilised Frenchman is stigmatised as a fearful crime, and is visited by a ghastly retribution. The English savage never thinks of such a crime as funny and a hundred years after Hogarth, our modern 'painter of mankind', still retains his barbarous modesty, is tender with children, decorous before woman,

28. Hole Letters, op. cit., 14 June, 1862.

29. *The Times,* 21 June, 1862.

30. cf. *The Paris Sketch-Book* "Carica-tures and Lithography in Paris".

CRUEL!

Snob. "'AVE A CIGAR, COACHEE?"
Swell 'Busman. "NO, THANKEE—I ONLY SMOKE TOBACCER!"

has never once thought that he had a right or calling to wound the modesty of either."

This may sound as if Leech's art was excessively chauvinistic and unbearably prudish. We know that he was not. His greatest influences had come from the French draughtsmen, his recorded conversations are fairly fresh and indeed uninhibited. No, Leech was one of the almost unconscious architects of a new sophistication, Thackeray and Leech could visualise and verbalise for a society that really believed it was growing up, that really felt it was advancing from giddy adolescence to the sobriety of adulthood. Thackeray emphasises that the exhibition for these very reasons *can* be a family occasion.

"Mothers of families ought to come to this exhibition and bring the children. Then there are the full grown young ladies — the very full-grown young ladies — dancing in the ball-room, or reposing by the sea-shore — the men can peep at whole seraglios of these beauties for the moderate charge of one shilling, and bring away their charming likenesses in the illustrated catalogue (two-and-six)."

But it is as a "natural truth-teller" that Thackeray finds Leech so refreshing and the recognition in every brush stroke that modern life is being mirrored.

"No man has ever depicted the little 'Snob' with such a delightful touch. Leech fondles and dandles this creature as he does the children. To remember one or two of those dear gents is to laugh. To watch them looking at their own portraits in this pleasant gallery will be no small part of the exhibition; and as we can all go and see our neighbours caricatured here, it is just possible that our neighbours may find some smart likenesses of *their* neighbours in these brilliant, life-like, good-natured sketches in oil."

Leech's response to Thackeray's review was heartfelt; Frith says that he "rejoiced like a child" and added "That's like putting a thousand pounds into my pocket".[31]

The exhibition, bolstered by such a piece of writing by such a man as Thackeray was a wild success. John Brown who attended it, described it as "like a theatre" with enthusiastic crowds entertained as one. "The laughter of special, often family groups, broke out opposite each drawing, spread contagiously effervescing throughout, lulling and waxing again and again like waves of the sea."[32] The artist had been typically modest about these efforts; in the preface to the catalogue, in which the main pictures were reproduced in black and white, he wrote, "These sketches have no claim to be regarded or tested as finished pictures. It is impossible for anyone to know the fact better than I do. They have no pretensions to a higher name than that I have given them — SKETCHES IN OIL." To a friend he commented "They are mere sketches, and very crude sketches too, and I have no wish to be made a laughing-stock by calling them what they are not."[33]

What sort of judgement can we make on these pictures more than a hundred years after the exhibition? Fortunately about a score of these oil sketches survive in private collections and one can gain some

31. Frith, op. cit., Vol. 2, p. 258.
32. Brown, John, *Horae Subsecivae*, 1882, p. 22.
33. ibid., p. 20.

impression of the impact that they had on the public of 1862. Assuredly the most colourful and painterly are the hunting subjects where the artist has built up a bit of impasto on the figures and developed subtle tints on the horses' flanks and in the landscape beyond. In "Morning', My Lord! — Glad to see you out again" (page 15 in the catalogue), Leech has greatly enlivened the characters of the Little Gent and His Lordship by the high colouring of the one and the sallow complexion of the other (Colour Plate 24, page 154). The treatment of the blue horizon is excellent and so is the vigorous painting of the breeches and hats, but the fuzzy line of the printer's ink is still visible on the canvas. All of these landscapes are about 20ins. by 25¾ins. (51cm by 65.5cm) and have a 2ins. border of un-painted area on the edge, perhaps to give the sketch-like look that Leech insisted on.

The increased characterisation of the faces is marked also in "Indignant Master of Hounds", a considerable advance from the wood engraving. As Leech had said in his preface, the pictures were to be "susceptible of such modifications and painstaking as I might deem to be improvements". With "Frederick — A Very Big Boy" Leech has handled the landscape with its winter woods with great delicacy, the sky a rich purple to light blue most carefully observed,

"A Nice Bracing Day at the Seaside." Oil sketch for the Egyptian Hall Exhibition in 1862. 16½ x 24½ins.
Private Collection

A Brilliant Idea —

Matilda "Oh, look ye here Tommy! S'pose we play at your being the big footman, and me and Lizerbuth'll be the fine ladies in the Carridge!"

Colour Plate 26. "A Brilliant Idea". Oil sketch for the Egyptian Hall Exhibition in 1862. 15 x 12¾ins.
                                        Victoria and Albert Museum

A WATERING-PLACE YARN.

Oh! I beg your panding Captin but could you oblige me with my little account

AN EYE TO BUSINESS.

34. Victoria and Albert Museum Collection.

the movement and portrayal of the dog splendidly done. There is also an immense amount of movement and life in the purely social scenes. Leech brings a great deal of motion and texture into the crinolines and in ''A Shocking Young Lady Indeed'' there is a really convincing bit of painting in the over-dresses of the ladies. In the charming ''The Fair Toxopholite'' there are superb contrasts in the fresh colouring, the purples of the dresses and the deep blacks of the shawls. The seaside subjects have a wonderful sense of wind and ozone; in ''While Charles prefers a quiet corner out of the wind'' the girl's dress has a vivid green colour and there is a particularly nice application of tints in the distant coastline (Colour Plate 25, page 154). But in this same picture the brush strokes to railings and stone-work seem thin. Leech is happiest in the larger landscape subjects where there is air and space; the small upright pictures appear closer to the ordinary hand-coloured print.

There seems little doubt that Leech not only enjoyed the seaside holiday but popularised it through his *Punch* work and his oil sketches. No less than twenty-five of the subjects exhibited at the Egyptian Hall were of beach scenes, ladies entering the bathing machines, groups on the sea-front, families taking trips round the bay or strolling along the esplanades.

There is a pleasant contrast between a windy day on the pier represented by ''A Nice Bracing Day at The Seaside'' (see illustration page 162) with dresses billowing out, hats flying off and ''Atlantic'' rollers in the background and the similar scene on a calmer day — ''A Problem For Young Ladies'' (page 167). In both cases the characterisations of the holiday spirit are superb, the ecstatic looks of the children, the beaming old men, the grim determination of the spinsters to enjoy themselves or look as if they were! Quintessentially British too are the distantly breaking waves in the one and the harbour seen against chalk cliffs in the other. Leech chronicled it all, even the unutterable boredom of wet days with disconsolate individuals staring out of rain festooned windows!

These activities with buckets and spades, sandcastles, toy yachts, hoops and balls, became a traditional part of the British summer during Leech's lifetime. The Georgians established the resorts, the Victorians moved them down to the sands with John Leech at their head. Even the souvenirs had his mark upon them, for the earliest picture-postcards were in fact decorated writing papers in which seaside scenes by Leech were often imitated or cheaply engraved for headings. Frith's ''Ramsgate Sands'' apart, these sketches remain the most vivid and intimate studies of the Victorians in holiday mood to have survived; it is for once our great-grandparents off their guard! If Dickens created the Old World Christmas, Leech equally well can be credited with establishing the seaside holiday.

It is difficult to know exactly what prices were being paid for the pictures, but one small upright one entitled ''A Brilliant Idea'' still has its original Egyptian Hall label fixed to it. This records that Mr Dudley Denton paid 40 guineas for it on 24 July, 1862, a far from inconsiderable price for a sketch measuring 14ins. by 9½ins.[34] (Colour

COMMON OBJECTS AT THE SEA-SIDE.

Boy. "OH! LOOK HERE, MA! I'VE CAUGHT A FISH JUST LIKE THOSE THINGAMIES IN MY BED AT OUR LODGINGS!"

THE SEA-SIDE SEASON.

DELICATE STATE OF THE HIPPOPOTAMUS. IT IS ORDERED CHANGE OF AIR, AND A LITTLE SEA-BATHING.

Colour Plate 27. *"Biggin Farm, Anstey, Hertfordshire". A rare oil painting by John Leech, showing his brother-in-law Captain Eaton, riding in a favourite part of the Puckeridge Hunt near Charles Adams' home. 10 x 14½ins.*   Dimsdale Collection

Colour Plate 28. *"The Raking Chestnut". Another rare oil painting by John Leech of a Hertfordshire scene. The intrepid rider is the artist's friend, Mike Halliday. 10 x 14½ins.*   Dimsdale Collection

"A Problem For Young Ladies." Oil sketch for the Egyptian Hall Exhibition, 1862. 16½ x 24½ins.

Private Collection

Plate 26, page 163.)

During the summer months, "Sketches In Oil" drew vast numbers of people and made for the artist a sum of nearly £5,000. Of the sixty canvases exhibited only a handful remained to be finally sold at the artist's sale and a further stream of commissions came in for other favourite *Punch* subjects. On 24th June, Leech told Evans that Lord Powerscourt had ordered a complete set of Briggs as well as reserving one canvas in the exhibition.[35] The extraordinary energy that he had mustered for the exhibition was completely dissipated by the middle of the summer and his strength taxed beyond endurance.

Hole invited the artist to Caunton Manor at the end of June, but Leech was emotionally and physically drained and his health did not appear to improve. The street noises and in particular the organ grinders in Brunswick Square, had persuaded him to move and he had discovered a handsome Georgian house in The Terrace, Kensington, where he felt he might escape his tormentors in a quieter neighbourhood. The success at the Egyptian Hall gave him enough courage to embark on this venture and an added attraction must have been the close proximity of his old friends, Thackeray and Millais.

Lemon, who had been one of the instigators of the oil sketches,

35. Bodleian Library, op. cit., 25 June, 1862.

NOT YET.

"MUSIC HATH CHARMS," &c.

must have wondered if he had done the right thing when he regarded his haggard and nervous friend still plagued and worried by work. More serious even for him was the fact that though Leech appeared to be more financially secure, he was less able to do *Punch* work and the contributions were seriously dropping off in June, July and August. He had confessed in a letter to Hole that his long confinement over the oils had made him "not the thing at all".[36] Lemon again took the initiative, decided that Leech must get away for a holiday and that he, Lemon, would be his companion.

On 7th August Leech was at Folkestone with his family, Lemon joined him there and shortly afterwards they crossed to Dieppe and took a train to Paris. On arrival there was good news awaiting Leech and he immediately dashed off a letter to Evans at Whitefriars.[37]

> Monday
> Paris, Galignani's
>
> My dear Evans,
>   Many thanks for your note & inclosure [*sic*]. We are off in twenty minutes for Biarritz — I see, & am very glad to see a paragraph in Galignani's taken from the Morning Post of Wednesday 3rd stating that H.R.H. The Prince of Wales has been to see the Sketches — As you are in London probably you do not know this — but it is a pity it was not in The Times — I wish the paragraph had been sent to P.H. Square — If inserted it would have been worth ten million francs, Mark is quite jolly & sends his best love & mine
>   Believe me Yours ever
>   J L.

The journey was very enjoyable, Lemon squeezed his immense girth into a French railway carriage, Leech began drawing once more and the two friends visited Bordeaux as well as Biarritz and watched a bull-fight at Bayonne. He was absolutely horrified by this spectacle: "When I tell you that, besides *six* bulls, *seven* horses were sacrificed for the afternoon's entertainment, you will imagine what an exhibition it was — to say nothing of such a trifle as one man being nearly gored to death..."[38] This carnage was drawn and engraved for an autumn issue of *Punch*. More to his taste were bathes in the Bay of Biscay, and the White Burgundy of the area which Leech loved to sample and which as a connoisseur he pronounced "first rate". Lemon and he played japes on one another, Leech teased Lemon about his snoring and Lemon got his own back by telling the chambermaid that his companion was a famous "somnambulist"! They returned in time for the *Punch* dinner on September 18th, and everybody breathed a sigh of relief that Leech appeared to be more like his old self; it was a reprieve for Leech and for *Punch*.

Thackeray's review of the "Sketches" had drawn the crowds, but it was the criticism in *All The Year Round,* promised by Dickens,

36. Hole Letters, op. cit., 14 June, 1862.
37. Bodleian Library, op. cit.
38. Hole, op. cit., pp. 48-49.

that gave the most considered opinion of the new show. The reviewer was Charles Alston Collins, a friend of Dickens, the brother of Wilkie Collins, and a good critic and essayist. Most important of all he was a painter and a Pre-Raphaelite, so that one gets from him what has been missing before, the Pre-Raphaelite view of John Leech.

Perhaps at Dickens' suggestion (and to counter Edmund Yates' attack of two years earlier), Collins began his notice with a description of Leech's more serious works not on exhibition at the Egyptian Hall. Collins obviously felt along with the other Pre-Raphaelites, that scenes of modern life were very important and that Leech's were distinctive for their morality, humanity and penetration. "To teach in this way", he writes, "is one of Mr Leech's prerogatives, and one which we are disposed strongly to contend for, in claiming for him a position far above that of a simple caricaturist or a skilful draughtsman." Collins lists a number of the artist's most trenchant pieces of social criticism, the Jewish clothier, the miser, the elderly rake and the Sunday question, where a pluralist parson replete with comforts, cannot understand why the working man needs the Crystal Palace open on the Sabbath. "These are grim subjects for a humorist to handle," comments Collins, "but they are dealt with in a manner that leaves no doubt as to the strength of him who, when he lays aside the cap and bells, can speak very gravely and

"Crinolines on the Water." Waterman: "There is no call to be afeard while we're licensed to carry six." Oil sketch for the Egyptian Hall Exhibition, 1862. 21 x 31½ins.

Collection of Lady Flett

MR. BRIGGS, AS HE APPEARED COMING TO THE BROOK. IN THE DISTANCE MAY BE OBSERVED HIS OPPONENT, WHO HAS A NASTY FALL, BUT FORTUNATELY TUMBLES ON HIS HEAD.

to the purpose." Collins like many contemporaries refers to Leech's cut on prostitution as "that terrible Haymarket drama" and considers it both unforgettable and proof of the artist's strength.

Collins is also the only writer to mention the pressure of work on the wretched artist, the strain of the public demand and his restless searching after fresh material. It was an odd interpolation in a review and one must suspect Dickens' hand in it. "Consider how such a labourer as this has no rest," Collins writes. "His hours of relaxation are not his own even; for then, too, he must be always on the watch, lest a good thing should escape. If Mr Leech goes out hunting, or makes an excursion to the Derby, or is off to the moors, he can still be hardly said to be making a holiday. He carries his task-master, the Public, with him, and though, doubtless, the complete fitness of his nature must sweeten such labour to him, though he must always have the satisfaction of feeling how entirely he has discovered the exact part he has to play in the world, and that he is playing it with all his might, still, labour is labour, and the wear and tear of a month of such work must be more than is spread over the whole lifetime of a large portion of those persons who turn over the pages of Mr Leech's books, and think how easy it must have been to get them up."[39]

As a good Pre-Raphaelite, Collins dwells on Leech's essential truth to nature. "The shades in the landscapes show to advantage even half across the exhibition room," he tells his readers and elsewhere mentions "the slate-coloured sky merged in the horizon at one side is admirably broad in its effect." As a painter, Collins seems to be most appreciative that Leech who has toiled for years over box-wood blocks, a few square inches in extent, can yet produce "this quality of broad and general effect" which "always tell well, and seem expressly designed to do so". There is also a new point brought out by Collins, that the Victorian public were seeing the actual brush-work of *their* artist for the first time. At the Egyptian Hall his admirers were "being brought face to face with the actual work of Mr Leech's hand ... this gives the exhibition an especial interest."

Looking back over the whole of Leech's work, Frith felt that the Sketches in Oil had been a popular rather than an artistic triumph. The whole exhibition was success enough to be moved from the Egyptian Hall in the autumn and put on display for a few further weeks at the Auction Mart Gallery near the Royal Exchange, but still Frith felt that the pictures "did not increase Leech's reputation".[40] But he does mention some other oil paintings executed with the brush on canvas and not done with the aid of the enlargement process. These must have been painted at Barkway in the late 1850s when Leech was feeling his way in oils and presented to his old friend Charley Adams. "Instead of a garish stain of washy colour merely passed over an engraving," Frith writes, "these small sporting subjects are painted in a good solid style, well drawn and carefully finished; carrying with them the conviction, to my mind, that Leech might possibly have been as great with the brush as he was with the lead pencil."[41] Fortunately this splendid pair of paintings survive in the collection of Charles Adams' descendants. The subjects are

39. *All The Year Round*, 2 July, 1862, pp. 390-394.

40. A catalogue in the Dimsdale Collection bears the name "Egyptian Hall, Piccadilly" but one in Cambridge University Library that of "Auction Mart Gallery". A large revised catalogue in July, contained opinions of the press and the note that the show was "Open daily from 10 to 5, on dark days brilliantly lighted by gas".

41. Frith, op. cit., Vol. 2, p. 258.

"Biggin Farm, Anstey, Hertfordshire" and "the Raking Chestnut" (Colour Plates 27 and 28, page 166), both showing well known scenes in the landscape of the Puckeridge country which Leech knew and loved so well. The painting of the farm is particularly lush in its handling, the colours have an almost Pre-Raphaelite quality in their brightness and the form and texture of the fields is minutely observed. The second picture has a superbly painted grey sky as backdrop and quite strong impasto treatment, not at all typical of either the sporting paintings of this date or the rather dry Oil Sketches. These are sparkling and lovely scenes which belong clearly to the English sporting tradition of the Alken Brothers, Marshall and Wolstenholme, their fluid paint work looking forward in an uncanny way to early sketches by Munnings. The masterly touches on the roof of Anstey Farm, the winter trees, the distant fields, make one wonder if the laborious enlarging process was necessary at all. Perhaps it *was* because of the volume of work involved and the fact that oil paint is not ideal for portraying the immediacy of Leech's humour, by reason of its slow application and large scale.

Leech made £5,000 out his exhibitions, a fact that was known to his friends; perhaps Mark Lemon alone knew that £3,000 of it went at once to pay his family debts.[42]

42. Silver, op. cit., 1 November, 1864.

MR. BRIGGS, AS HE APPEARED IN THE BROOK.

Chapter Nine

BLOOMSBURY TO KENSINGTON

mong the memories of Leech that were stored up by his friends, many were centred on the artist in his family circle, seated by his own fireside, entertaining at his own table, surrounded by his two children and their friends, whom he adored. The picture of Leech the family man is an attractive one, but in the earliest part of that married life, John and Annie suffered a tragedy which left them for many years without a child at all. Leech's increasing number of childhood illustrations in the 1840s and his work on a further children's book *Master Jacky* in the 1850s, symbolised his own childlessness. Like Doyle's preoccupation with story books, Leech's droll juveniles, cockney girls and pretty misses became a substitute for the hankerings after that longed-for child. "Mrs Lemon," wrote Hole, "the wife of the editor of *Punch* and designated sometimes by irreverent minds as Judy, told me that Leech was sadly disappointed in the first part of his married life that he had no children."[1]

The Leeches were married for five years before they had their first child. Mrs Leech became pregnant in 1847 and the child was expected in September. With this in mind they had considered it quite possible to accompany Dickens on his northern tour, where the company of amateur actors were playing *Every Man In His Humour* and *Turning The Tables* at Manchester. Leech, as a part of the troupe, moved on to Liverpool in early August where they opened for a benefit night on behalf of the writer Leigh Hunt. It was following this, that Annie Leech began to feel ill and Leech cut short the stay so that he might take her back to London. Travelling by the Great Central Railway, the Leeches reached Euston on 9th August and Leech was so alarmed by the imminence of his wife's labour, that they put up at the Victoria Hotel, Euston Square. There, on the same day, Annie gave birth to a daughter Rose Annie, much to the amazement of Dickens. "What a tremendous chance that Leech's little girl was not born on the Railway!" he wrote, "I trust in God, having gone so far, all will go on well and happily."[2] Leech himself at once wrote to Charley Adams at Barkway, "You will be glad to hear that I have got a little daughter and that both mother and child are both doing well — Mrs Leech was taken ill at the end of our trip to Liverpool (where as perhaps you are aware Dickens, and some of us had been playing for Leigh Hunt's benefit) and she was confined at the Victoria Hotel, Euston Square, where she now is — I thought you would like to hear

1. Hole, Reynolds, *The Memories of ...*, 1892, p. 40.

2. *Nonsuch Dickens,* Vol. 2, p. 46.

MR. PUNCH AT HOME.

3. Dimsdale Collection, 9 August, 1847.

4. ibid., 26 August, 1847.

5. ibid., 16 September, 1847.

6. Forster Collection, Victoria and Albert Museum Library 48 B 28 and 48 E 4.

7. Dimsdale Collection, 30 May, 1848.

8. ibid., n.d.

9. *Punch,* Vol. 26, p. 116.

the news so I send off these few lines."[3] Three weeks later he told Charley that mother and daughter "are both 'going on' famously"[4] but by September it was simply "my wife and little one are both going on as well as possible."[5] Perhaps the premature Rose Annie was a rather sickly child, for she seems to have been continually ill although her father was inordinately proud of her. "I should be truly most delighted to see you," he told Forster, "I would show you too that wonderful baby you have heard so much of — and which (as Jerrold says) is now visible to the naked eye."[6]

By the Spring of 1848 Rose Annie was badly ailing and though Leech was still writing to Adams in jocular vein, it was Mark Lemon who passed on the bad news at the end of May. "You will be grieved I know to hear that poor Jack has been in a world of trouble about his little girl — In fact I do not think she will live over this day — He is sorely distressed about it."[7] Lemon followed this with another letter on the same day, "You will be glad to hear that Jack's little girl is better today & there's now some faint hope of the recovery." Although little Rose Annie survived, it was not to be for long and she died of one of the many infant diseases to which Victorian children were prone in March 1849. The charming juvenile sketches of 1848, so delightfully autobiographical, come to a sudden halt, as Leech and his wife come to terms with this loss.

Charley Adams seems to have been specially sensitive to the Leeches' childlessness, and even more so after 1850 when he lost his own son. That year he "lent" his eldest daughter Charlotte Elizabeth, "Chatty", to the Leeches and they took her on holiday to Broadstairs. "Mrs Leech and Chatty with me will return for good to Notting Hill on Saturday," he told Adams in a letter, "when we shall be glad to have her with us as long as you can spare her. Apropos of dear Chatty I am sure her mamma will be glad to hear that she was uninterruptedly cheerful and well and has certainly proved herself one of the best tempered, best hearted little creatures possible."[8] The closeness between the two families is probably best shown by the rare and very lovely pencil and watercolour portrait of Adams' little girl Annie (Colour Plate 29, page 183). Made in the middle 1850s, it demonstrates what mastery Leech had in the field of child portraiture; the subject was Leech's godchild.

But it was after they had left Brook Green for 31 Notting Hill Terrace and then moved on to the handsome brick house, 32 Brunswick Square, that their second daughter was born after a lapse of nearly five years. Ada Rose Leech was born at her parents' house in February 1854 and Leech, so overjoyed, began chronicling her existence in the pages of *Punch.* A group of wide-eyed and tight-bonneted ladies are shown cooing over a tiny baby with typical Leech expressions — a disgruntled boy comments under his breath "I think it's a nasty, ugly little beast, for all the world like a cat or a monkey!"[9] If Leech could enjoy the humour of parenthood in this way, he obviously enjoyed too the role of fond father; his illustrations of children are often the most memorable in these years and friends so often recollected him surrounded by children. The

longed-for son came in August 1855 when John Charles Warrington Leech was born at the same address. The artist must have written ecstatically to Millais who wrote back in the same spirit: "I must write and congratulate you upon your good fortune in having a son and heir to inherit his Papa's great name and fortune, I quaff a beaker to his health. May he live long, ride good horses and go across country like a man."[10] It was about this time that Millais did a miniature of little Ada with her father's hand coming in to the picture, long a treasured family possession.[11]

Leech's family was thus completed by the two "chicks" as he called them (Dickens called them "the Darlings") and the devoted and indulgent father was not only using their antics as model and inspiration but continually reporting their latest doings to fellow artists and the *Punch* table. According to Frith, the little boy became "the darling of his father's heart" and at Brunswick Square liked to copy his father in every possible way. At the age of five he asked to have a velvet coat made for him like his father's, "and he might have been seen on most mornings, palette in hand, standing before a little easel, working away at copies of the engravings in the *Illustrated London News,* which he coloured literally with all the colours of the rainbow, whilst the father sat by with block and pencil."[12] The family called the little boy "Bouge" or "Bougie", perhaps a corruption of "Baby", and many of the anecdotes use that affectionate term.

One story quoted by Frith shows how much his own children were the personification of his illustrations. A lady lunching with him at Brunswick Square noted that the children (unusually) ate at the same time as the parents. "Now, children, say your grace," Leech had gently ordered. Both children began to say it together as fast as they could. Leech said when they had finished: "Well run — Ada first, Bougie a good second!"[13]

Leech had this astonishing empathy with children, perhaps because he was at heart a very simple man, perhaps because his humour and delight were so spontaneous and fresh like the delight of a child. Charley Adams' daughter "Chatty", so popular a little guest on Leech's holidays, remembered that Leech could sympathise and comfort rather than scold, after she had got a thorough wetting by the sea. "I have a happy recollection of being snugly tucked up on his knee for some hours after the event, while he continued his drawing."[14] He also used his pencil on his own children when he felt it appropriate. "Leech had an original and effective method of reprimanding his children," Hole recalled. "If their faces were distorted by anger, by a rebellious temper, or a sullen mood, he took out his sketch-book, transferred their lineaments, with a slight exaggeration — to paper, and showed them, to their shameful confusion, how ugly naughtiness was!"[15]

The *Punch* men were frequently regaled by the witticisms of the Leech children and even the *bons mots* of Annie, as on the occasion when Leech, reading the newspaper over the breakfast-table was disturbed by infant chatter and his wife said "Hush Ada, don't you

10. Typescripts of letters originally in the possession of Sanders of Oxford, 1969.

11. Hole, op. cit., p. 42.

12. Frith, W.P., *John Leech His Life and Work,* 1891, Vol. 2, p. 91.

13. ibid., p. 92.

14. ibid., pp. 92-93.

15. Hole, op. cit., p. 41.

Ruggles. "HOLD HARD, MASTER GEORGE. IT'S TOO WIDE, AND UNCOMMON DEEP!"
Master George. "ALL RIGHT, RUGGLES! WE CAN BOTH *SWIM*!"

DOING IT THOROUGHLY.

Old Gent. "I SAY, MY LITTLE MAN, YOU SHOULD ALWAYS HOLD YOUR PONY TOGETHER GOING UP HILL, AND OVER PLOUGHED LAND!"
Young Nimrod. "ALL RIGHT, OLD COCK! DON'T YOU TEACH YOUR GRANDMOTHER TO SUCK EGGS! THERE'S MY MAN BY THE HAYSTACK WITH MY SECOND HORSE!"

AN EXCELLENT WINE.

"THE BEST OF CLARET IS, THAT YOU MAY DRINK ANY (hic) QUANTITY YOU LIKE, WITHOUT FEELING ILL."

16. Henry Silver Diary, *Punch* Office, 5 February, 1862.

17. ibid., 9 December, 1863.

18. ibid., 2 October, 1858.

19. Hole Letters, Tallents Collection, op cit., Walter Wren to Hole, 25 April, 1894.

20. The terrace was re-numbered in 1895 and demolished in 1963. Kensington Public Library.

21. Frith, op. cit., Vol. 2, p. 128.

hear Papa is reading!"[16]

The life in most of his later establishments was comfortable rather than luxurious, as we have seen Frank Bellew had found 32 Brunswick Square plain and neat, rather than rich and expensive; he was nevertheless keeping an extra maid-servant in Bloomsbury and employing a governess for the children. Annie ran a well-ordered household, a far cry from their life in Powis Place in the early 'forties where bachelorish Leech invited a hoard of old sparks to breakfast without telling her, and the leg of lamb had to be cut up and boiled![17]

On the contrary, Leech's hospitality was thought to be very good, his dinners excellent and his cellar exceptional. Tom Taylor considered that John Leech had the best beer and claret in London[18] and one would hardly expect the son of a former hotelier and wine merchant to serve anything else, though Frith questions it. He was fastidious about the choice of wines with various viands and desserts and the way that they were served. Thirty years after his death, one of Charley Adams' cousins remembered best Leech's advice on food and drink "I learned from him, not to give my friends 'dinner' wines & 'dessert' ditto — & to make salad."[19]

The dinner parties he gave at 31 Notting Hill Terrace (now Holland Park Avenue)[20] were pleasant affairs. The house, a Regency stucco one forming part of a row, looked directly into the park of Holland House, which used to touch the road at this point. For his friends it was a balm to come into this semi-rural atmosphere, eat well and talk convivially. The first time Frith went there was for a supper given by the Leeches to coincide with the Highland Games taking place in Holland Park opposite and on this occasion he met Dickens' friend the Rev. White, who as a great connoisseur of port made their host a little nervous. Frith writes, "Leech's dinners, without being too lavish or extravagant, were always unexceptionable as to food, and notably so as to wine." On another evening, the Leeches, who never had a man servant in the house, had asked ten or a dozen people to dinner and had enlisted the help of a local man to serve. They had chosen the local parish clerk, "a solemn person who was not too proud to add to his stipend by going out to wait".[21] The guests, who knew Leech's love of punctuality were amazed to be kept waiting, the conversation languished and flagged altogether, consternation showing in Leech's face. Finally Dickens or Jerrold had jumped up and exclaimed:

"Well, it's getting late: I'm afraid I must go. Thank you, dear boy, for a delightful evening: the dinner was capital, the turtle first rate — never tasted finer salmon: and as to the champagne —"

This piece of bravado lessened the tension and there was a roar of laughter from the guests standing around. At that very moment the grave and black clad parish clerk appeared to announce "Dinner is served" to which Leech's friends had replied with a chorus of "Amen". As Frith implies, it was a scene worthy of our friend Briggs.

The artist was quite downright over questions of cuisine and at a Thackeray dinner he was heard to remark that "Turtle is one of the

WONDERFUL INTELLIGENT CHILD.

— "ROSE, WILL YOU HAVE SOME DINNER?"
Rose. "HAVE HAD MY DINNER."
— "WHAT HAVE YOU HAD FOR DINNER?"
Rose. "SOMETHING THAT BEGINS WITH AN S!"
— "AND WHAT BEGINS WITH AN S!"
Rose. "COLD BEEF!"

22. Silver, op cit., 22 July, 1863.

23. Silver, Henry, "The Home Life of J.L.", *Art Journal,* Vol. 16, 1893, p. 167.

24. Frith, op. cit., Vol. 2, p. 35.

25. Hodder, George, *Memories of My Time,* 1870, p. 87.

26. Silver Diary, op. cit., 23 May, 1863.

27. ibid., 21 March, 1860.

few things there's no mistake about'', [22] and he was always watching the diet in the nursery. Henry Silver, who knew Leech well in his later years and became a close friend of Mrs Leech records one such incident.

"Once at Brighton, I remember, 'Bouge' and Ada were invited to a children's party, and were specially enjoined to be careful what they ate there, as the house had repute for rather gorgeous cookery. On their return they were quite hungry, finding nothing they dare eat, except some microscopic sandwiches. 'They offered us champagne papa, but, of course, we didn't take it, for we don't get it at home, you know,' said Miss Ada, like a martyr. 'And they handed us some tiny little birds, all wrapped up in vine leaves; but we didn't touch them either, though Bouge said he would like to.' And here Miss Ada turned her big eyes on the other little martyr. 'Ortolans no doubt,' said Leech, 'funny giving children ortolans! Well, Ada, you were quite right not to let Bouge eat them. They are merely lumps of fat, and might have disagreed with him. Still, it seems a pity you were not allowed to pocket some. They might have come in handy, for we've rather a poor dinner'.'' [23]

Leech was not by nature a great party-goer and would probably have remained by his own fireside if he had followed his basic inclinations. Du Maurier, a generation later, was to find all his material at dinner parties, Leech found much of his at home. But mixing with the right people and being seen in the best houses was a need, which, by the late 'fifties had become an addiction. If, as was very often the case, an invitation came from Little Holland House or Mrs Milner Gibson in Wilton Crescent, Leech felt compelled to be there. He was a good listener rather than a good talker, he would think a long time before capping a discussion with a sensible remark at the *Punch* Wednesday dinners. At Augustus Egg's dinner parties he could even be prevailed upon to sing his favourite song, a melancholy ballad called "King Death" and on one occasion Dickens called out to him "There, that will do, if you go on any longer, you will make me cry." [24]

After a rendering of "King Death" at Bouverie Street, George Hodder recalls an amusing incident: "On one occasion, when he had sung this song with even more than his usual vigour, Douglas Jerrold exclaimed 'I say, Leech, if you had the same opportunity of exercising your voice as you have of using your pencil, how it would *draw!*'.'' [25] As a matter of fact Leech strongly disliked Jerrold and would not have courted his friendship; for him Jerrold was a dangerous radical who had brought him into fierce arguments in the early days of *Punch,* [26] over questions of patriotism and people's rights. Although Leech was ostensibly apolitical and was criticised by Taylor for not using his vote in 1860, [27] that gentle face held behind it all sorts of stern convictions. He openly disliked the petty British shopkeeper, was antagonistic to the Jews and privately criticised the Prince Consort as a foreigner. But it was radicalism among his contemporaries that made him seethe and he had sufficient of that to put up with until Thackeray invaded *Punch.*

Moloch and his Victims.

An illustration from The Haunted Man.

His political nose was only occasionally put out of joint where his work was concerned but in 1847/48 while undertaking the tricky work on Dickens' book *The Haunted Man,* he became very perturbed. Despite the superb interpretive work on his drawings by the engraver Linton, Leech would not countenance Linton's socialism, voiced so loudly during this time of revolution; in a letter to Forster he gives Linton very short shrift.[28]

> My dear Forster,
>   I have quite done with the book and return it herewith — With regard to the second drawing I am now upon it, and I hope to have it finished by this afternoon sometime, when I will bring it or send it to you — I think I shall place the block in the hands of Swain, who is not likely to be making fine republican speeches, and consequently more likely to engrave it properly — Patriotism is a very noble feeling and speechifying very well in its way, and in proper places, but I hate, abhor and detest, some meddlers and mischief makers, so down with L-nt-n
>   Yours Faithfully
>   John Leech

Linton later wrote radical pamphlets. Albert Smith, novelist and *Punch* contributor, on the other hand was far less dangerous, an amiable and rather vulgar Londoner who was a master of journalistic prose. Smith irritated Leech by being over familiar and referring to him across the table as "Jack", a name reserved for his oldest friends. Jerrold was provoked by this to say to Leech "How long is it necessary for a man to know you before he can call you 'Jack'?" After this Smith was less free with that name.[29] Frith is probably right in thinking that Leech distanced himself from some of the *Punch* characters, preferring the impeccable Millais and the gentlemanly Tenniel.

Even on holiday and in the various rented lodgings that he took at Broadstairs, Dover, Brighton, Lowestoft, Scarborough and Whitby, he liked to be surrounded by friends, although he was never the centre of a coterie as Dickens was. Hole talks of the "clever guests whom he delighted to gather round him" and mentions in particular "Thackeray, Millais, Adams, his oldest ... Lemon, Shirley Brooks, and Tom Taylor — three successive editors of *Punch;* Douglas Jerrold and Percival Leigh; Tenniel, Holman Hunt, Lucas, Knox (on the staff) and others whose names I forget."[30]

At Notting Hill Terrace or Brunswick Square, he was at the centre of his family circle, restricting his "bachelor" activities to Saturday nights at the Garrick Club where Thackeray addressed him as "the great cawickachawist of the Age". The old Garrick Club was in King Street and one of Leech's close friends, Alex A. Hare, called it "an institution apart... There was a degree of intimacy or 'abandon' amongst them (the members) the like of which would be vainly sought for in any existing Club of which I have knowledge." Somewhat surprisingly he adds "This was just the place for Leech."[31]

28. Forster Collection, op. cit., (Forster 239).

29. Frith, op. cit., Vol. 2, p. 129.

30. Hole, *Memories,* op. cit., p. 30.

31. Evans Letters, Harvard University, MS Eng. 1028, letter from A.A. Hare, 14 March, 1886.

On Sunday afternoons he might ramble around the Zoological Gardens with Thackeray, staring at the animals and enjoying the company of his old friend.[32] Both the Leeches were regular theatregoers, John was an avowed Shakespearian — "Shakespeare was an universal genius and could feel and write about anything" he told Henry Silver[33] and of a new production he wrote to Forster, "I saw 'King Lear' last night. I think it finer than 'Macbeth' and I thought Macbeth the finest thing I had ever seen."[34] He was a frequenter of philharmonic concerts at the Crystal Palace, the Italian opera and sometimes more raucous entertainments. Yates reports seeing him at Evan's late Joys (a music hall) at the western corner of the Covent Garden piazza, where performers sang, imitated birds and did comic vocals. "The public thronged to the concert-room — there was a private supper room in the gallery, looking down on the hall through a grille, where ladies could hear the songs and could see without being seen ... Thackeray was constantly there ... very occasionally Leech."[35]

The fact that Leech's influence on the arts extended to the theatre is nicely brought out in a passing mention in Herman Merivale and Frank T. Marzial's *Life of W.M. Thackeray*. Knowing how much Leech admired Sothern, the actor's portrayal of "Lord Dundreary", Thackeray got them together across the dinner table. Leech was both astonished and delighted to hear that Sothern had modelled the character on "a close and constant study of the artist's 'swells' in *Punch*".

He was on terms with many of London's leading actors. One was Ben Webster of the Haymarket Theatre, for whom he made a lively little ink drawing in 1849, possibly incorporating a portrait of the comedian (illustration page 181). With typical punning intent, Leech has drawn on the reverse a spider's web, a fly caught in it, a greedy looking spider and entitled it "A Web Stir".

His taste in books was that of the conventional, novel-reading Victorian, the classics of the previous century — he once told Forster that he could not have Boswell's *Life of Johnson* back because Annie was reading it — and the recently published works of his friends. "*The Newcomes* is a wonderful book," he writes to Millais, "particularly the latter part of it — the old colonel's 'Adsum'! What genuine pathos! I dined with Thackeray the day before he started for America. I don't think he liked leaving England. Would that he were back working away at another book."[36] Elsewhere in his pages of *Punch* there are references to popular books. On 28 April, 1860, he refers to George Eliot's best-seller, *The Mill on the Floss,* published earlier that year. The scene is of two sisters in a drawing-room.

Constance (literary)	"Have you read this account of 'The Mill on the Floss' dear?"
Edith (literal)	"No, indeed, I have not; and I wonder that you can find anything to interest you in the description of a disgusting prize-fight!"

A similar amusing incident is depicted a year later on 6 April, 1861, coinciding with the fever of interest in Wilkie Collins' popular

32. Brown, John, *Horae Subsecivae,* 1882, p. 37.

33. Silver Diary, op. cit., 28 June, 1860.

34. Forster Collection, op. cit. (Forster 240).

35. Yates, Edmund, *Recollections,* 1884, Vol. I, p. 171.

36. Millais, J.G., *Life and Letters of Sir J.E. Millais,* 1899, Vol. 1, p. 272.

HAVING HOOKED A "FISH," HE IS LANDED TO PLAY IT.—THE FISH RUNS AWAY WITH HIM—AND MR. B. IS DRAGGED ABOUT A MILE AND A HALF OVER WHAT HE CONSIDERS A RATHER DIFFICULT COUNTRY.—

MR. BRIGGS HAS A DAY'S SALMON-FISHING.

THE FISH HAVING REFRESHED HIMSELF, AND RECOVERED HIS SPIRITS, BOLTS AGAIN WITH MR. B.

A pen and brush drawing made for the actor Ben Webster. 5¼ x 5½ins.   Author's Collection

thriller. "Awful Apparition" shows Mrs Tomkins suddenly appearing in her husband's study with night-dress and candle and commanding "How much longer are you to sit up with that 'Woman in White'?" Tomkins is of course frightened into a fit! A similar example of Leech's off-the-cuff humour across the dinner table is provided by another punning reference to this book. The *cause célèbre* of 1862 was the daring exhibition of "The White Girl" by the young James McNeil Whistler at a gallery in Berners Street. Leech, who apparently went to see it and referred to it as "girl in night-clothes shown in Berners St", did not join in the controversy over whether it was meant to represent "The Woman in White". But at the *Punch* dinner he wittily suggested that if there was any doubt about it, it could be called "No Name" (another of Collins' books).[37]

If Leech's social attitudes were those of an old fashioned Tory, what Silver could describe as "the clubbish view of things",[38] his deeper convictions, if they surfaced at all, were less typical of his age. There is no evidence that he was an ardent church-goer in an age of conventional church-going, no suggestion that he felt strongly about drink in an age of teetotalism, scant evidence that he involved himself in any particular philanthropy among London's burgeoning charities. His belief was that conscience alone was a sufficient guide: "If I do wrong I feel ashamed and sorry," he told Silver, "and my conscience tells me that for my own happiness I had best do right."[39] This might have shocked some of his readers, and they would have been more shocked if they had suspected that their favourite carica-

37. Silver Diary, op. cit., 16 July, 1862.
38. ibid., 19 January, 1859.
39. ibid., 27 November, 1861.

HOWEVER, IN MUCH LESS TIME THAN IT HAS TAKEN TO MAKE THIS IMPER-FECT SKETCH—ACCOUTRED, AS HE IS—HE PLUNGES IN—AND AFTER A DESPERATE ENCOUNTER, HE SECURES A MAGNIFICENT SALMON, FOR WHICH HE DECLARES HE WOULD NOT TAKE A GUINEA A POUND !—AND IT IS NOW STUFFED IN THE GLASS-CASE OVER THE ONE WHICH CONTAINS HIS LATE FAVOURITE SPOTTED HUNTER.

turist saw nothing wrong in Mormonism "in pt of the plurality of wives".[40] Leech's simple approach was not to interfere with anyone if they did not interfere with him, but he would not tolerate cant or hypocrisy. He attended a seance at Knox's in August 1860 and tried to expose the fraudulence of the medium, Mrs Marshall, and was duly as he put it "wrapped out of the room".[41] But when the Darwinian debate was at its height, Leech could clearly not see why people felt so strongly and he gently pokes fun in *Punch* of 25 May, 1860. For Leech, the family man, his horizons could be the whole of Victorian London (Colour Plates 30 opposite and 31, page 186), but they could equally be the dimensions of his own parlour with the velvet curtains tightly drawn (Colour Plate 32, page 186).

* * * * *

Essential to the artist too, were the excursions out of London to revitalise his pencil. Millais introduced Leech to salmon fishing at Stoball, Perthshire, in 1855. It was not only a sport which he was anxious to take up, but one at which he felt sure Briggs would be an excellent novice! First of all he had tried his hand at casting, but either the flies were insufficiently good or their movements too mechanical, for he caught nothing. He then resorted to harling and sat for days in a boat in the vain hope that a fish might come and hook itself.

"Just below the dyke at Stanley the line suddenly straightened; Leech snatched up the rod, and away went a clean-run 25 pounder with the hook in his gills! Then the struggle began, and great excitement for the fishermen, as this bit of Stanley water is a rough place, full of rushing streams and deep holes, in which are sharp shelving rocks, from which the quarry must be got away at once or he would certainly cut the line.

"After allowing him one good run, Leech scrambled out amongst the rocks and stones of the Stoball shore, and the fish making straight down stream, dragged him helter-skelter over boulders and through bushes, till he was nearly at his last gasp. Then, luckily for him, the salmon retreated into 'The Devils Hole', and sulked there for half an hour. The angler then recovered breath, and ultimately, at the bottom of Stanley Water, my father gaffed the fish, to the great delight of 'Mr Briggs', as subsequently portrayed in *Punch*."[42] (See illustrations above left and page 180.)

These Scottish visits were the breath of life to a naturally active man. During the 1855 trip, the magnificent landscape and splendid sport had lured Leech into a dreamy reverie in the woods near Blair Athol. Quite unknowingly, he wandered into the private acres of the Duke of Athol and into the middle of one of his grace's deer drives. The duke, who came face to face with Leech, was absolutely furious, shouted at him at the top of his voice and swore at him in Scottish. Leech, such a nervous and timid fellow, fled before this onslaught. The duke did not know the name of the intruder, not until, some months later the whole scene appeared immortalised by Leech in

40. Silver Diary, op. cit., 5 March, 1862.
41. ibid., 1 August, 1860.
42. Millais, op. cit., Vol. 1, p. 267.

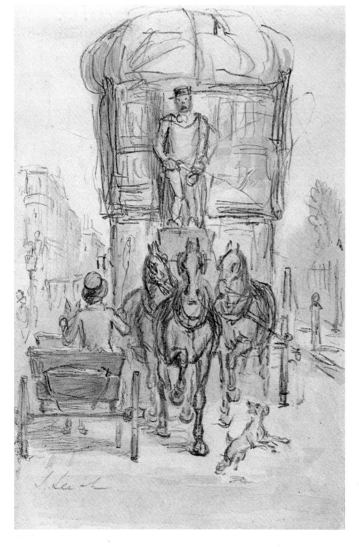

Colour Plate 29. A miniature in pencil and watercolour of Charles Adams' daughter Annie. The artist was her godfather. 4¼ x 2⅜ins. Dimsdale Collection

Colour Plate 30. Preliminary drawing for 'Might is Right' which appeared in Punch *in 1853. Pencil and watercolour. 7 x 5¼ins.* Victoria and Albert Museum

"BUY A LITTLE DORG, MAR'M?"

Punch as "A Scotch Dog in a Manger"!

The following year, 1856, Millais and Leech were again in Perthshire and this time they were invited by the duke to one of the deer drives. Leech was horrified, he stubbornly refused to go until Millais practically dragged him over to Blair. The duke was well aware what Leech had drawn, but had sufficient sense of humour to say nothing at first. But when the sport was under way, and the duke was alone with Leech in a "butt" he suddenly put a pistol to Leech's head and said that *now* he had him at his mercy. Leech was so terrified that he missed his shot! [43]

He enjoyed immensely the grandeur and luxury of staying at Blair, but could not according to Hole overcome his dislike of late meals and his aversion to pet dogs. "He was delighted with the scenery and the gracious hospitality, but his spirit was perturbed by the lateness of the dinner hour, which depended upon the ducal siesta, and was sometimes delayed until 9 p.m., and also by the presence at the dinner-table of a small but obese dog, who, as the footmen took up large hot-water dishes and handed them to the company, watched his opportunity, and crawled from one vacant space to another, that he might enjoy the warmer locality." [44] On his journey south from this visit he penned the following lines to Mark Lemon. [45]

Station Hotel
York
Sunday

My dear Mark,

I am here en route for London, where I hope to be tomorrow evening. My house is not ready for me so I must put up for the moment at the Kings Cross Hotel — a great bore but I was anxious to come south as the weather was getting cold — We have had on the whole however beautiful days and am all, I think, better for the change — Last week I was so hurried about from place that I could not possibly manage to send you anything, but I have collected a lot of material which will I think be novel and useful for P.P. I went on Monday again to Blair and saw everything that could be seen about there — Driving etc. The Dook so gracious nothing could be like it — in fact I should have thoroughly enjoyed myself had it not been for several shocks which we have all alike received and which make me look at things from the reverse of a comic point of view —

Let me see you as soon as you conveniently can when I come to Town — I propose stopping at the Gt Northern Hotel because it is near my house and I shall be either there or in Brunswick Sq. — Tuesday and Wednesday —

With our kind regards to you and yours
Believe me
Yours always
JL

43. Frith (op. cit.) tells a slightly different version of this story, Vol. 2, p. 116.

44. Hole, *Memories,* op. cit., p. 36.

45. Author's collection.

HOW DO *YOU* LIKE IT

Although Leech apparently disliked letter writing, many of his surviving epistles are vividly told in the most lovely English as F.G. Kitton has pointed out. One written to Millais shows how close was that friendship and how much he wanted to share his latest fishing adventures with him.[46]

32 Brunswick Square,
June 14th 1855.

My Dear Millais, — I return the insurance paper filled up, to the best of my belief, properly — though perhaps with regard to the question, 'Is there any peculiarity in his configuration?' I ought to have been more explicit. However, when you go before the 'Board' they will be able to judge of your tendency to corpulence and what may be called your general 'stumpy' (if I may use a vulgar but expressive word) appearance — I might, too, have attended to your strikingly socratic profile; but the answer I have returned will, I daresay, answer the purpose.

I came to town the very day you left for the North, and called at your chambers, missing you by a few hours only — How much I should have liked to give you a shake of the hand, and to wish *viva voce* health and happiness to you! I do most cordially wish you may have both for many years... Last week I went out pike-fishing at a most beautiful place called Fillgate, with one Joliffe, of whom you have, I think, heard me speak. He was in the 4th Light Dragoons and was in the ever-memorable Balaclava Charge. He gave me a vivid description of the dreadful business. Altogether I have rarely had a more pleasant day. We behaved, I am afraid, in a most unsportsmanlike manner, for he was anxious to thin the pond of fish, and determined to set trimmers. About four and twenty of these devices were put in all over the water, and it was exciting enough to paddle after them as the bait on each of them was carried off by Mr Jack. You would have enjoyed it immensely, only you would have jumped out of the boat. And we caught a 'bold biting Perch' sir! — such a one as I have only seen stuffed in the fishing-tackle shops, and which I always believed to be manufactured by the carpenter or umbrella maker. He weighed three pounds, and *not* fisherman's weight. Let me hear from you sometimes. This I know, is asking a good deal under the circumstances, for cannot your time be much more agreeably employed than in writing to

Yours always, my dear fellow
John Leech

Just as Millais had appeared in Leech's earliest middle age and become his friend, so too Reynolds Hole arrived on the scene in 1858 and greatly cheered his last years. Hole, two years Leech's junior,

46. Millais, op. cit., Vol. 1, p. 270.

Colour Plate 31. Sketch of a lady and coachman for one of Leech's Punch *subjects. Pencil and watercolour. 3½ x 2¼ins.*
Victoria and Albert Museum

Colour Plate 32. Sketch of three figures taking refreshment for an unidentified illustration. Pencil and watercolour. 3½ x 3½ins.
Victoria and Albert Museum

was one of that peculiarly Victorian species, the landed parson. The wealthy incumbent of his own living in Nottinghamshire, Hole could afford to live in a mansion rather than a vicarage and was able to spend much of his time in civilised pursuits rather than in the grind of parish duties. He was a good sportsman, an excellent performer in the hunting-field, a man of letters and a very considerable expert in matters of horticulture. The first two were to bind him irresistably to the heart of John Leech, the third was to produce a pleasant partnership, the last probably not interesting the artist greatly.[47] Hole could easily be considered a rather worldly cleric, with his estates, hunters in the stable, servants in the house and the time to write beautiful letters to friends and witty articles for *Punch*. But he was an active churchman, wrote hymns, published sermons and was an accomplished platform preacher; it was this side of him that eventually gained him the Deanery of Rochester.

For a long time Hole had admired the *Punch* artist's work, especially the hunting cuts one suspects, and when Leech accompanied Adams on a day out with the Belvoir, Hole had an opportunity to meet him. "I had always longed to grasp the hand which diffused so much pure enjoyment," he wrote afterwards, "and taught men how to be both merry and wise, and it was an epoch

47. Leech did in fact produce a steel engraving of a rose bush for one of Hole's Rose Annuals in November 1862. Hole Letters, Tallents Collection.

Preliminary study of a horseman for a Punch *illustration. Pencil. 5 x 7ins.*   Author's Collection

in my life, a green spot on the path of time, to look on his kindly, intellectual handsome face.''[48] Leech was well known for not liking sudden introductions to admiring strangers, particularly if they had been watching him previously in the hunting-field. But he must have recognised a kindred spirit in the jolly enthusiastic parson who was almost his contemporary in age. He accepted an invitation to Caunton Manor almost at once and Hole, who afterwards became President of the Rose Society, laid on an unofficial rose show in the grounds, so that his neighbours might meet Leech.

"I invited all my neighbours to meet Leech at a garden party, my annual Fête des Roses, of which I had then three or four thousand trees; and, in memory of the fair ladies, who admired him, and the flowers, and the cooling cups, he afterwards made a charming picture of Mr Punch, crowned with a wealth of roses and surrounded by smiling Hebes, offering sherry-cobblers, fanning him, and shading from the sun.''[49]

It must have been very shortly after this visit, that the idea of a holiday with this new-found friend entered Leech's mind; anyway it was he that made the suggestion. "Leech proposed that we should take a fortnight's holiday in Ireland, and I accepted his invitation with an eager gladness, which was somewhat subdued when he suggested, 'You should write, and I will illustrate, an account of our little tour.' ''[50] This was to become *A Little Tour in Ireland,* one of the most enchanting of Leech's works and his only one in the fashionable form of a travelogue. He may have been spurred on by Thackeray's fictitious travelogues, Doyle had also tried this genre and later illustrators (notably Caldecott) followed on. *A Little Tour* was to be a faithful record of comings and goings, doings and happenings in that *other* island which the English found so puzzling and with which Leech claimed kinship. It was one of those sudden holidays that work. Leech was at Scarborough in early August 1858, just settling plans and thinking about the journey. "I am already beginning to funk the sea passage," he told Hole, "or rather voyage, four hours, oh dear! Suppose we make up our minds *not* to go until the channel is perfectly tranquil. We are out pleasuring you know. I know of nothing that combines the ridiculous with the truly miserable so much as a man, with no power in his legs, staring fixedly at a horrid steamboat basin. Ugh!"[51]

The two friends set out from Caunton Manor, travelling first to Chester — "The Rows of Chester are very picturesque and quaint, but do not make a favourable impression upon a giant with a new hat" — and then to Bangor and Holyhead. The crossing to Kingstown was not as terrible as Leech feared and the following morning they were booking in to Morrisson's Hotel, Dublin. Hole went about with a copy of Swift under his arm, Leech with his sketch-book under his, and saw together Trinity College, Phoenix Park, Killiney and Porto-Bello. *A Little Tour* when it appeared, was slightly disguised as the rambles of two undergraduates, but the characters of Leech and Hole are visible throughout. From Dublin they travelled by the Midland Great Western to Galway, where they admired the fishing

48. Hole, *Memories,* op. cit., p. 16.
49. ibid., pp. 19-20.
50. ibid., p. 33.
51. Hole Letters, Tallents Collection, 5 August, 1858.

Illustrations from A Little Tour, *"my friend Frank C—" and "there was in Ireland an old breed of swine . . ."*

girls on the Claddagh and travelled on by jaunting car to Oughterarde and Clifden in Connemara. Leech's fishing expeditions at Kylemore were superbly illustrated in the book, before they left for Limerick. "Limerick — Justly celebrated for its Hooks, it is far more to be admired for its Eyes, for, although the former are the best in all the world, the latter are much more killing!" is a good example of Hole's facetious style. Alongside is a beguiling Irish beauty from the pencil of Leech! There was still time in this hectic fortnight to see Killarney and the Gap of Dunloe, Glengarriff and Cork, before returning by rail to Dublin. There they were able to enjoy Donnybrook Fair before taking the steamer for England. Leech returned the following April with Mark Lemon and Evans to get more information for his designs or as he put it "rub up my Galway experience".[52]

From Kylemore, Leech sent Hole some jolly letters describing this return.[53]

My dear Hole,

Evans, who is commander in chief of the writing paper, is busy in his room cleaning himself after a walk across the bog. If I ask for writing materials I should probably get whisky and hot water, so you will excuse me for sending you a few hurried lines in pencil. We are at Kylemore. Having been favoured with beautiful weather, that is beautiful for these parts, we have of course been wet through but altogether have got on famously. I should have tried for a salmon today, but — you will hardly believe it — somehow or other the boat was out of repair. It is to be put to rights in the course of the day, and I go on board tomorrow, armed to the teeth. Lord Bacon thinks we may be tolerably safe on the lake provided we do not cough or sneeze! Certainly the vessel does not look at present very water tight.

Up at half past six in a great state of excitement. New rod. Best gut and *the* fly — And spite of wind and weather I go with Lord Bacon and Johnny Joyce into the boat to which much has been done, but alas! Three boats length from the shore and Johnny's rollock gives way. So we have to 'give it up this while'. We try again after breakfast, and as that same is on the table I will give this to the postman, a nice little girl who will take it (I hope) to Letterpost.

On his return to Brunswick Square, Leech wrote frequently to Hole to keep him posted on the progress of *A Little Tour.* "I am hard at work on the frontispiece. I found it impossible to get the number of Claddagh figures I wished in one page, so there will be a plate about two pages and a half, to pull out Pocket Book fashion. This will enable me to get many more subjects into it, and Evans agrees with me that it is desirable to do so. You will think so too, I hope. I cannot help saying how much I like your work upon going

52. Hole Letters, op. cit., 10 February, 1859.

53. ibid., 8 April, 1859.

An illustration from A Little Tour, *"But the Irish waiter is, notwithstanding, a capital fellow ..."*

over it again, and I only trust I may be able to do my part worthily — Of this, you may be assured, no pains shall be spared as far as I am concerned. Evans and Lemon both saw my watercolour sketch of the Claddagh and gave me the greatest encouragement."[54]

The venture was such a success that it really cemented the friendship between them, the book was published in the late summer and generally acclaimed, even in Ireland. Looking at the neat little cloth-bound volume with its folding coloured frontispiece and numerous wood engravings, one can only regret that they did not do more in this genre. Many of the larger plates are vintage Leech, but there are some initial letters and headings, such as that for Chapter XIII and the full page "The Tunnel, Killarney to Glengarriff" which are pure romantic landscape and look forward to the illustrators of the 1860s. Hole was extremely hopeful that their book would be followed by *"A Little Tour in Holland"*,[55] but Leech's increasing ill health and the 1862 exhibition intervened to prevent it.

Leech sometimes took with him on his longer trips, a mahogany box containing fresh wood-blocks, pencils and other aids to work. The presence of this celebrated "mahogany box" in their houses was a good omen to his friends; it was the highest compliment he could pay in wishing to work in the peace and quiet of their homes. Hole suggested that he bring his tools to Caunton on a visit in October 1859.[56]

> My dear Leech, I have so much to say that I shall not attempt anything of the kind. The chief thing on my mind is to ask you (and if you knew how really anxious I am on the point, you would not refuse, tho' you are such a granite-hearted old ruffian) to *come here in November and do the Almanac.* I can easily prove that it is your duty to do so. I. You cannot get the little oxygen, which there is to be got in Novr, except in the country. II. You want all the oxygen there is in the firmament to do justice to the Almanac. III. We have horses and dogs and every adjunct of country life. IV. You will be removed from the cares of housekeeping. V. It is proved that Caunton is singularly adapted for the realisations of Art, all critics at home and abroad uniting in the assertion that the three drawings finished by you in one morning here were the best (with the trifling exception of 3 little sketches of my own) ever done in the same period of time. No but *really* will you bring the mahogany box and come?

Caunton became a home to the exhausted Leech, second only to Barkway, Hole introduced him to archery, a sport which appears from time to time in the pictures and perhaps to croquet which he played on the spacious lawns with the rector and his young wife.

But most people remembered Leech neither on his travels in Ireland nor at his friends' homes, but as Brown put it "at his own fireside and in the nursery when baby was washed".[57] Naturally the

54. Hole Letters, op. cit., 21 April, 1859.

55. Dewar, George A.B., *The Letters of Samuel Reynolds Hole, Dean of Rochester,* edited with a Memoir, 1907, p. 20.

56. Hole Letters, Tallents Collection, 12 October, 1859.

57. Brown, op. cit., p. 25.

A ROMANCE OF ROAST DUCKS.

"MY DARLING, WILL YOU TAKE A LITTLE OF THE—A—THE STUFFING?"
"I WILL, DEAR, IF YOU DO; BUT IF YOU DON'T, I WON'T."

most clear recollections of that life come from 7, The Terrace, Kensington, Leech's last home. The new house was sufficiently large for the Leech family to entertain more than ever before and faithful Henry Silver was often invited.

"Like most men of good sense, and what then was deemed good breeding, Leech had a great dislike to being hurried at his dinner. A lark pudding was a common dish with him on Sundays: for, though detesting a cold dinner, he had a great dislike to give his cook much work on Sunday. But he would linger lovingly over this one dish, probing to its juicy depths, and picking choice tit-bits for his wife, or for the guest (for there was rarely more than one) who had the good luck to be present."[58]

The fact that Leech, the country lover, had never had much of a garden was amply compensated for in this new house. "The rule prohibiting cold dinners was not observed in summer time, especially when he had moved from Brunswick Square to Kensington," Henry Silver records. "Here he often gave a garden party, which was far more pleasant than is usual for such merry-makings. A plateful of good soup and a slice of cold roast beef were served instead of ices and slices of sponge cake; and half a score of guests were asked instead of half a hundred. Thackeray avowed a special fondness for these parties, and, living close at hand, was often able to be present. The garden was a well nigh country garden then, flycatchers and blackbirds used frequently to build there... Indeed, under the weeping ash-tree, where the festive board was spread, all was so cosy and so quiet that you might have heard an 'h' drop if a cockney had been present."[59]

58. Silver, "The Home Life of J.L.", op. cit., p. 166.

59. ibid., p. 166.

DOMESTIC BLISS.

Head of the Family. "FOR WHAT WE ARE GOING TO RECEIVE, MAKE US TRULY THANKFUL.—HEM! COLD MUTTON AGAIN!"

Wife of his Bussum. "AND A VERY GOOD DINNER TOO, ALEXANDER. *SOMEBODY* MUST BE ECONOMICAL. *PEOPLE* CAN'T EXPECT TO HAVE *RICHMOND* AND *GREENWICH* DINNERS OUT OF THE LITTLE HOUSEKEEPING MONEY I HAVE."

Chapter Ten

DECLINE

The years 1863 to 1864 were the Indian Summer of Leech's activity. For the most part the quality of his work remained undiminished although he himself was slowly failing in health. The greatest consolation for him after the super-abundance of work on the oil sketches in early 1862, was the move to his new home in Kensington, already referred to. The family had left Brunswick Square for the last time in early October and he packed Annie and the children off to Folkestone, joining them with John Tenniel on about the 8th. They moved on to 136 Marina, St Leonards-on-Sea, for the whole month of November, and though Leech was confidently predicting they would be in 6 The Terrace soon, they were still at St Leonards on December 4th.[1]

He himself returned to London to camp out in the house and inspect progress. "I think by degrees I shall be able to make it pretty comfortable," he remarked to Adams in a letter.[2]

No 6 was a large early Georgian house which Holman Hunt called "Dutch", a reference to its picturesque mellow brick, tile roof and white sash windows, just beginning to come into vogue as part of the Queen Anne revival (see opposite). It was the one house occupied by the artist which was sufficiently large to allow him a plan of his own devising; it was spacious enough for children's rooms and reception rooms to be separate and he had a superb studio for himself on the top floor.

Hunt visited him there and as well as noticing Leech's immense pride and pleasure in the place, described its atmosphere.

"I dined with him soon after he settled there; he gloried in the quaintness and spaciousness of the house, and said that in his large bedroom he felt like the Prince of Orange going to rest. He had decked it with appropriate furniture, an old Hollander's picture of birds, chosen by Millais, with other things to fit it for an artist's home, were in their proper places."[3]

Most enjoyable of all was the mature old London garden behind the house, where his children could play and he could wander round his bedded plants and fruit trees. "Our garden is now in its full beauty," he told Hole in June 1863, "if that is any temptation to you", or again teasing Hole the great rose-grower "if we can't grow Roses, we can as I know show Ribstone Pippins against anyone."[4]

One of the extraordinary charms of the Kensington House was its

1. Dimsdale Collection.

2. ibid., 27 November, 1862.

3. Holman Hunt, W., *Contemporary Review,* 1888, pp. 335-353.

4. Hole Letters, Tallents Collection, 22 October, 1862.

No 6 The Terrace, Kensington, the house which Leech purchased in 1862 and where he died two years later.
Royal Borough of Kensington and Chelsea Libraries

The garden at No 6 The Terrace, Kensington. Leech gave summer parties here attended by his friend W.M. Thackeray.
Royal Borough of Kensington and Chelsea Libraries

great informality. His children were always hopping about and yet at the same time the great literati of the land might be standing in the hall, stepping over a top or avoiding a toy horse; children were both seen and heard at The Terrace.

"...thither we were bidden on Wednesday the 25th of February (1863) to his little fair-haired daughter's birthday party," Silver remembered. "Ada would be nine years old, and she was her father's special favourite; although her coming to the world had lost him a day's hunting. For just before her birth he and Millais, who rode often with him, had just pulled on their hunting boots and were waiting for their horses, when suddenly the nurse summoned him to go off for the doctor!

"I came a little late on the evening of the party, and found Shirley (Brooks) standing at the door of the front drawing-room.

" 'Look,' said he, 'the Guildhall's come to Kensington. There stands Gog and Magog!'

"The older guests, the 'grown-ups' as they're called now, were gathered in the front room; and in the other, which was larger, were the children dancing. At the corners facing us, and towering above the little dancers, stood Thackeray and 'Big' Higgins of the *Times,* the famous 'Jacob Omnium'. They were both of them four inches more than six feet high, and were alike benignly smiling on the merry-makers. It was a pretty scene, and when I told the happy hostess of Shirley's happy thought, she promised 'John' should make a sketch of it. But I fear he never did so."[5]

Hunt also witnessed a gentle argument between Leech and his friend Millais one day when he called at the new studio. Leech was still finishing off many of the oil sketches commissioned during the exhibition and Millais had come to offer advice. The resulting dialogue recalled by Hunt shows Leech at his most fanciful and whimsical, betraying that almost child-like love of what he was doing, so evident in his works.

"The palette being produced, it had upon it some dry patches of pigment systematically arranged, and now dry from the last days of painting, 'Why, what's the good of preserving morsels of old paint like these? All of them together when new would not cost fourpence!' said the impulsive painter. Leech pleaded: 'I know, my dear fellow, but, 'pon my honour, it's not out of stinginess, it is only because I haven't the heart to scrape up into a mess the beautiful little buds and blossoms of sweet colour; often, it is true, they get dry, as now, and they have to be thrown away, but then they have lost their preciousness independently of my choice, and I have no self-reproach. I could not help feeling real pain if I wasted them while yet they were alive, as they seem to be when fresh, It seems foolish, I know,' he added, 'but I can't help the childishness, I really can't.' "[6]

Although romantic in this sense, he was also intensely interested in technique so that the enlargement process and the translation of *Punch* illustrations into genre paintings was more than an achievement, it was a continuing experiment. One letter to an unnamed correspondent at about this time suggests that he was beginning to

5. Layard, G.S., *Shirley Brooks — A Great Punch Editor,* pp. 204-205.

6 Holman, Hunt, op. cit., pp. 335-353.

Mr. Scrawley takes a quiet room in which to write his prize ode on Burns, but finds he has made a mistake.

Colour Plate 33. A small sketch showing the consequences of noisy neighbours, a recurring theme in Leech's work. Pencil and watercolour. 6⅜ x 5½ins. Victoria and Albert Museum

Colour Plate 34. "The Mermaid's Haunt", from John Leech's Social Subjects, *lithograph by Thos. Agnew & Sons, published 2 January, 1865.*

The Mermaid's Haunt.

THE VALENTINE.

Little Foot Page. "I SAY, MARIA, WHAT'S A RHYME TO CUPID?"
Maria. "WHY, STUPID RHYMES TO CUPID—DON'T IT, STUPID?"

7. Victoria and Albert Museum Library, October 1862.

8. Henry Silver Diary, *Punch* Office, 6 May, 1863.

9. ibid., 3 June, 1863.

10. Hole, Reynolds, *The Memories of ...*, 1892, p. 49.

think of using watercolour paint as an alternative for some enlargements, it also shows the interest he had in the technical side of the work.

"I have requested Messrs Bradbury & Evans to forward to you a couple of subjects — one, a wood engraving from Punch, the other an Etching from an illustrated book — which I shall be obliged by your enlarging as agreed. I have also directed Messrs Winsor & Newton to send you two canvases stained, but unfortunately I left Town without preparing them with size — now, may I trespass upon you so far as to beg that you will prepare them before making your enlargement — a little isinglass, melted, not too thick & washed with a small sponge dipped in a little pea flower over the canvas. —

"I have found to produce a very nice surface that will take watercolour well — but I dare say you know all this better than I do, I shall be very glad to hear that you have got these matters safely & are at work satisfactorily."[7]

The early months of 1863 produced a fine crop of *Punch* work, horse-dealing and hunting subjects in January, the servants' hall and a family christening providing fresh stimulation in the Spring. He had been to see in late 1861 the astonishing stage success of "Lord Dundreary" in Tom Taylor's play *Our American Cousin* at the Haymarket. "Dundreary" whiskers were copied and "Dundreary" jokes made and he contributed one to *Punch* on 31 January. Also featured were political cuts about Sunday closing, an old bête noire of the artist, and some harsh observations on his old adversary, Napoleon III, in February. There was really no intimation as yet that the recovery following the holiday in Biarritz was not complete; on March 11th he was hunting at Barkway, while Mrs Leech watched the Prince of Wales' wedding from the *Punch* office, and a month later he was hunting at Caunton with the Holes.

As the spring progressed Leech's friends began to be aware of a gradual fragility in the artist and a more acute reaction to and obsession with his neuroses. Its most noticeable symptoms were a growing shortness of temper and rather bitter remarks at the *Punch* dinners, neither of which were typical of the benign and genial Jack Leech that they had all known. On 6 May, just after the opening of the Academy exhibition, Leech said "it was sickening to see Eastlake & Co stretching their hands out to shake the Prince of Wales's on Saturday" and to listen to "Melted Butter speeches in profusion".[8] About a month later he was confessing with desperation that street noises were killing him and they were "driving him to suicide".[9]

In the second week of June Leech left with Millais for a salmon fishing tour in Scotland, it was to be a respite from the arduous weekly work and the stuffiness and grime of London in summer. It may even have been Thackeray's suggestion for he had drawn Hole's attention to Leech's appearance with the plea "get John Leech out of London".[10] This trip, the last that the two friends were to make together, was not an unqualified success. On arrival at their lodgings in the Highlands, Leech found plasterers at work on the building and was nearly driven mad by the din in the one place he had expected

"DON'T MOVE THERE, WE SHALL CLEAR YOU!

TO BE SOLD—THE PROPERTY OF AN OFFICER GOING ABROAD.

197

PATERFAMILIAS, WHOSE PET AVERSION IS STREET MUSIC, GOES TO THE SEA-SIDE, HOPING TO ESCAPE FROM THE NUISANCE. HE IS AT BREAK-FAST,—BEAUTIFUL VIEW, NEW-LAID EGG, &C. &C.—WHEN—

OH, HORROR!

11. Holman Hunt, op. cit., pp. 335-352.

12. Silver Diary, op. cit., 8 July, 1863.

13. ibid., 12 August, 1863.

quiet. He was back on 22 July to dine with Thackeray at Palace Green, but even the new house at nearby Kensington High Street was proving a problem to the wretched man.

Although the house was set in a terrace, it was surrounded at a distance by a maze of small streets, mews cottages, alleys and lanes, which were the perfect haven for organ-grinders and their juvenile admirers. The fact that Leech's work room was at the very top of the house, meant that he was often within earshot of three or four of these menaces at the same moment, all playing different tunes. When Leech sent out one of his servants to protest, more often than not the organ-grinder could not be found, hidden away as he was in some stable-yard or distant court. Leech, like so many people with an obsession began to be tiresome to the neighbours, Kensington residents who had little sympathy with the nervous temperament of the great man and did not intend to be dictated to by a newcomer. Hunt remember that one lady in a house opposite said "she had no patience with Mr Leech's nervousness, and that he must learn to get over it, for she should have any musicians who liked to come into her front garden, where they could not be interfered with."[11] Hunt protested but she would not change her views and the Italians played in the street from dawn to sunset, churning out their melodies, and giving no intermission, except on Sundays as required by law. If this was not enough, he had actually been conscious of day-time banging, somewhere at the back of his premises, soon after the family moved in. To his dismay he had discovered that a wheelwright had a knocking shop in a building abutting the property at No 6. At great expense to himself, he had been obliged to buy the man out and seek new premises for him in order to gain a little peace of mind.[12]

In August there was a sharp attack in *Punch* by him on street music, "Faust and the Organ Grinders". A group of sallow fellows invade a quiet neighbourhood which is obviously Kensington, the caption reads "From a Study Window" and the considerable text compares these street folk to Faust in the Gounod opera (then playing) where the doctor sells his soul while hearing street music! Certainly Leech's problems were growing. Later in the month he took his family for a holiday to Worthing, where he became terribly bothered by itinerant open air preachers on the sands, so he moved to Lansdown Place, Brighton, where costermongers nearly drove him away. Both incidents feature in *Punch,* the preachers on 22 August and the costermongers in November, as Silver put it "Leech finds a nuisance everywhere poor devil!" (Colour Plate 33, page 195).[13]

From this month onwards, the artist was quite ill and remained away from London for the next five months. There were two spells at Brighton, the second in Marine Parade in November, and in between these seaside convalescences, visits to Caunton Manor and Glenn Hall, Leicester. Despite the strain, both physical and mental, he managed to do the weekly *Punch* work and struggle up to town for at least five of the *Punch* dinners, and the occasional supper party at the Garrick. One such supreme effort was to attend Founder's Day at Charterhouse on 12 December, 1863. Thackeray was there and the

HOW No. 4 ENJOYED HIMSELF,

AND

HOW No. 8 SUFFERED IN CONSEQUENCE.

14. Merivale, H. and Marzials, F.T., *Life of William Makepeace Thackeray,* p. 215.

15. Leech Albums.

16. Silver Diary, op. cit., 13 January, 1864.

17. ibid., 20 April, 1864.

18. ibid., 16 March, 1864.

two old friends sat together during the ceremonies and the novelist delivered an oration.

Two weeks later, Thackeray was dead, and the shocked Leech was being shown into the writer's bedroom, the morning after he had passed away. "His arms and face were very rigid," he afterwards told Anthony Trollope.[14] Scarcely recovered from his summer's illness, Leech was again plunged into gloom and despondency. He did however rouse himself sufficiently to be a help to the Thackeray family; naturally his work suffered because of this.[15]

> 6 The Terrace,
> Kensington,
> Dec 24 1863.
>
> My dear Mark,
> You will be shocked as I have just been to hear of poor Thackeray's sudden illness and *death* — I have been round to see his Mother and she wishes me to see their legal adviser directly. Under these most distressing circumstances — I must really leave off what I am about —
> Always Yours
> John Leech

When he returned to No 6 in January 1864, there was a noticeable change in him and at forty-six he had the appearance of an old man, the similarity being more marked by his depression and grief. There was now no Thackeray at Palace Green and he told Silver that he could not sleep without dreaming of his dead friend and his nights were so disturbed that he had to leave Annie and sleep in another bedroom on his own.[16] Worse was to follow. Surtees, who had been corresponding with him regularly, moved to Brighton in early March and died there very suddenly on the 16th. It was a tragedy that *Facey Romford's Hounds* was to be finished without the author, but much more so for Leech for there would be no more celebrations "under the scarlet cover". There were further irritations that sprung from the artist's strained nerves, squabbles with the Kensington shopkeepers who he imagined were uncivil to him, arguments about pet dogs that barked and more unpleasant encounters with the organ-grinders. Silver recounts one such:

"JL still nervous about himself, defied by 2 organ men yesterday who called him 'You bly sht' 'You bly bg' etc in the choicest Billingsgate. Said if he hadn't feared the excitement he would have knocked them down."[17] (See illustration on page 200.)

These aggravations and exhaustions made him extremely ill-tempered and he began to indulge in personalities at the *Punch* dinners, referring to the Royal Academician, Herbert, as an "Affected Roman Catholic" who "went to Paris for a week and now speaks broken English".[18] On 27 April there was a serious outburst in which Leech attacked Evans (his publisher *and* benefactor) for daring to alter the wrapper for *Facey Romford's Hounds* and making

FOREIGN ENLISTMENT.

If we must have it—for Goodness Sake begin with the Organ Men.

One of Leech's attacks on street musicians, a symptom of his growing ill health and susceptibility to noise. Punch, *December 1854.*

it fit only for a public house. After Leech's stormy departure, the others discussed the situation.

"We all agree that Leech is out of health," records Silver, "and should take rest — but Mark thinks he wouldn't give up his dinner engagements. To get into society has been the aim of his life, and now he seems to have lost all taste for enjoyment. He has always been a spoilt child says Mark, lets petty worries master him, and it is sad to think his great gifts have not made him a more happy man."[19]

Although Lemon's comments seem rather harsh, they were probably voiced in the heat of the moment and do not convey his real concern. Lemon must have been well aware that Leech had had a mild heart attack at the end of the winter, as communicated by the artist in a letter to Nethercote. "The other day I went for a day in Hertfordshire, and going only half way across a field — I was seized with a spasm in my chest & throat which I thought would have choked me — and this I have found lately comes on upon the slightest excitement or exertion."[20]

19. Silver Diary, op. cit., 27 April, 1864.
20. Houghton Library, Harvard University, Aut File, Leech to Nethercote, 23 March, 1864.

The quarrel at the *Punch* table on 27 April, almost certainly prompted Lemon to write an appeal to M.T. Bass, MP, the influential campaigner against street noise, on 22 May. Bass's bill to contain the nuisance was only just going through the Houses of Parliament (to be celebrated by Leech in his memorable cartoon "Three Cheers for Bass and His Barrel of Beer & Out with the Foreign Ruffian and His Barrel Organ", 28 May, 1864) but alas the damage had already been done. Having run through a number of medical men, Leech had settled on the services of Dr, afterwards Sir Richard, Quain, a physician to the Brompton Hospital. "The Doctor I have seen last," Leech wrote confidently to Hole, "and who seems to be the only one who understands my case, gives me great hope, but he insists upon my going to Homburg, and to abide by the discipline exercised there, for three or four weeks — and I am to do no work while I am there. . . .but when I return to England, as I hope to do, a cheerier and stronger 'cove', then if you will have me — why there is nothing I should like better than to come to you. . ."[21]

Dickens had already supported Bass's Bill with a letter signed jointly by Leech and others[22] and clearly felt that the prospect of the holiday and the successful legislation were having a tonic effect on his friend. "You looked, and evidently were, at least 1000 per cent better today, than when I saw you last."[23]

Meanwhile Lemon did all that he could do under the circumstances by writing to Bass, explaining the case and trusting that it would add ammunition to the case of the bill.[24]

Punch Office
85 Fleet Street
23d May 1864

Sir, — I venture upon what might possibly be considered an impertinence, were not the object of my note of public interest.

I am so greatly interested in the success of your measure for the regulation of street music that I am desirous of strengthening your hands by putting you in possession of some facts within my knowledge. I formerly lived in Gordon Street, Gordon Square, but was compelled to quit London to escape the distressing consequences of street music, although Gordon Street was comparatively a quiet locality. A dear friend of mine, and one to whom the public has been indebted for more than 20 years for weekly supplies of innocent amusement, and whose name will find a place in the history of Art, has not been so fortunate. He lived in Brunswick Square, and remained there until the nervous system was so seriously affected by the continual disturbance to which he was subjected while at work that he was compelled to abandon a most desirable home, and seek a retreat in Kensington. After expending considerable sums to make his present residence convenient for his art work — placing double windows to the front of this house

21. Hole Letters, Tallents Collection, 17 May, 1864.

22. *Nonsuch Dickens,* op. cit., Vol. 3, p. 387.

23. ibid., p. 389.

24. Quoted in full in *The Times,* 31 October, 1864.

&c; he is again driven from his home by the continual visitation of street bands and organ-grinders. The effect upon his health produced — on my honour, by the causes I have named — is so serious that he is forbidden to take horse exercise or indulge in fast walking, as a palpitation of the heart has been produced — a form of *angina pectoris,* I believe, and his friends are most anxiously concerned for his safety. He is ordered to Homburg, and I know that the expatriation will entail a loss of nearly £50 a week upon him just at present. I am sure I need not withhold from you the name of this poor gentleman — it is Mr John Leech.

If those gentlemen who laugh at complaints such as this letter contains were to know what are the natural penalties of constant brainwork, they would not encourage or defend such unnecessary inflictions as street music entails upon some of the benefactors of their age. Such men are the last to interfere with the enjoyments of their poorer fellow-labourers .... All they ask is to have the same immunity from the annoyances of street music as the rest of the community have from dustmen's bells, post horns, and other unnecessary disturbances. The objection to street noises is not a matter of taste. It involves the progress of honest labour and the avoidance of great mental affliction.
Apologizing for the liberty I have taken,
Mark Lemon.

It was obviously important for the wretched Leech to have a travelling companion on this arduous journey through Europe; fortunately a long standing friend and fellow artist, Alfred Elmore RA, volunteered. It was still up to Leech to make the arrangements and he consulted another invalid, Thackeray's friend, M.I. Higgins, who frequently visited Germany. He then sent the following letter in a surprisingly legible hand.[25]

6 The Terrace
Kensington
London
June 11 1864

Madame,
My friend Mr M.I. Higgins permits me to introduce myself to you, and to request that you will be kind enough to provide me & a friend with two, good, quiet bedrooms, & a sitting room if you have them disengaged. We start from England on Thursday next and come as quick as possible by way of Brussels to Homburg — Mr Higgins lives in Eaton Square and tells me that he has been at your house frequently — and has been most comfortable — Will you kindly let me have a letter by return of Post —
and Believe me
Yours Truly
John Leech.

25. Author's Collection.

The two artists left England on about 16 June, having had a send-off from *Punch* the previous night with all members of the Table shaking him by the hand.[26] His friends had already noticed a more confident air and better spirits when he had finally made the decision to go and so they were hoping for great things.[27] The two men arrived in Homburg by the 18th of the month and Leech, though comfortably housed, wrote to say that he was disgusted by the gambling women there; he added that he had played the tables himself and generally won, but only for very small stakes. After nearly a month at Homburg, he was advised to go on to Schwalbach and try the mud bath cure, supposed to be very restorative because of the iron in the water. "You sit in mud for 24 hours and come out an Ironclad" Leech jokingly told his *Punch* friends in a letter.[28] By the second week of August he was home again with, despite warnings, overflowing sketch-books and in particular a scheme for a double page of *Punch* showing the Weinbrunnen at Schwalbach — it was to be his last major work (see below).

There were *Punch* dinners on September 21st and 28th but Leech attended neither, having decided to go on a family holiday with

26. Silver Diary, op. cit., 15 June, 1864.

27. ibid., 11 May, 1864.

28. ibid., 20 July, 1864.

"Schwalbach", a large wood engraving done for Punch *in the autumn of 1864. Leech took the cure in this German resort in a vain attempt to recover his health.*

Annie, Ada and Bouge to Whitby, his favourite northern resort. There he was delighted to be joined by Shirley Brooks and his wife and the youngest member of the *Punch* team, George Du Maurier, who was in some ways a natural successor. Du Maurier remembered that in walks and talks he was "the most delightful companion, and the most 'lovable' of men".[29] But he also noticed that "he seemed very languid and weak, and I had the sorrowful presentiment that much more work would not be forthcoming from him — but little expected that the end was so near."[30]

Schemes were talked of by which the burden could be taken off him; he should leave *Punch,* he should work in the country, he should only do what he was able to tackle. Millais in particular had realised that to continue a normal life in town was impossible, because his friend clung to him in the street and had to be guided about. "He became so nervous latterly," said Millais, "that he used to take my arm when walking together, jerking it perceptibly when any sudden noise or any vehicle passing rapidly near us and lingering an unnecessary time at the street crossings."[31] One idea which was probably under way by the middle of 1864 was to reproduce a dozen of the most famous Leech sporting subjects in colour lithography for a much wider audience than the oil sketches could reach. The firm of Agnew's handled this profitable venture and *John Leech's Social Subjects, Sports and Pastimes* and *John Leech — His Celebrated Hunting Subjects* were published on 2 January, 1865. The prints when issued were of a very high technical excellence, some hand tinted, but others printed from as many as twelve to fifteen separate lithographic stones. The subjects were often the same as the famous oil sketches with slight variations, but it is difficult to estimate how much say the ailing man had in their preparation. An example of these prints is shown as Colour Plate 34, page 195.

Leech returned from Whitby on 3 October and attended the *Punch* dinners on 12 October and the following week. At the latter he seemed unwell and almost dazed. Shirley Brooks found that "He complained of illness and pain, and I saw it was difficult to make him grasp the meaning of things that were said to him without two or three repetitions. He left early with Tom Taylor."[32]

Events moved speedily in the last week of October, Leech felt increasingly unwell and on Friday, 28 October, had a consultation with Dr Quain who once more prescribed rest and in particular that he should "Cease to work and dismiss anxiety".[33] It was really an empty appeal to a man who was worried about himself, worried about his family and most of all worried by the large sums of money demanded from him on all sides. He simply returned home to The Terrace, sent a message to *Punch* for them to collect his next drawing and began to sketch out on the block a woman and a dog with his usual dexterity (illustrations opposite). After a short time however his strength ebbed away completely and he retired to bed; for the first time in twenty-three years the *Punch* messenger was sent away empty handed.

On Saturday, 29 October, Mrs Leech had organised a small children's party for her son and daughter. Perhaps in the hopes that

29. Frith, W.P., *John Leech His Life and Work,* 1891, Vol. 2, p. 271.

30. Evans letters, Harvard University, Harvard MS Eng 1028, letter from Du Maurier, 4 October, 1886.

31. ibid., letter from Sir J.E. Millais, 31 October, 1882.

32. Layard, G.S., op. cit., p. 218.

33. Frith, op. cit., Vol. 2, p. 298.

A preparatory sketch for a Punch *drawing, October 1864. 5⅜ x 7⅜ins.*   Charterhouse School

An original drawing on the wood block by Leech based on the foregoing sketch. It is the only surviving wood block of the artist's and he was working on it at the time of his death.   Charterhouse School

Statuette of John Leech by Sir Edgar Boehm RA, 1862. Height 20¾ins.   Dimsdale Collection

such a normal domestic scene would quieten John down and help to allay the fears of the children, the party was still held though Leech was far from well. He begged to be allowed to continue the drawing on the block and got so far out of bed as propping himself up on a nearby couch. The children arrived in the afternoon for the party and Mrs Leech superintended this and the arrival of Shirley Brooks and Evans from the *Punch* office, who were alarmed about the news. They found Annie Leech in tears but as she had recently persuaded John back to bed and had given him an opiate, they felt after waiting for three-quarters of an hour, that it was best not to disturb him.

About an hour later at 7 o'clock, he woke up and seeming discomposed called out for his father, sister and Millais. John Millais had returned from the Continent that very day and was expecting to dine at The Terrace, but on calling earlier had been told that he was not able to do so. So he was very alarmed to be summoned shortly afterwards by a housemaid to his friend's bedside. "The next moment Millais was off, and running through the streets of Kensington he mounted the stairs of his old friend's room, and found him lying across the bed, quite still and warm, but to all appearance dead, the belief in the house being that he expired at the moment of his friend's arrival."[34] It was high Victorian drama, the tinkling sound of the children's party below, a scene that the artist had depicted so often, the great Pre-Raphaelite painter bending over the bed, family and domestics hushed on the stairs. But it was also high Victorian tragedy, for the great jester of their generation was dead, the victim of the life and the society that he loved.

* * * * *

On the Sunday morning, 30 October, Millais, Percival Leigh, Shirley Brooks and Charles Eaton were all at The Terrace and visited the death bed. "We went in and saw him," Brooks wrote, "He looked noble in his calm; the hair and whiskers put back gave up his fine forehead and handsome features, and the eternal stillness gave his face an elevated expression. I looked a very long time on my old friend's face."[35] Millais at once took an active part in helping Annie Leech, he sealed the artist's studio door at her request and within a day he had superintended Edgar Boehm in taking a death mask in the bedroom in his presence.[36] Boehm had already made a statuette of the artist, which had been modelled from the life at Leech's own house in 1862 (left). The death mask was later turned into a bust which Boehm executed for the Royal Academy of 1865; it is now in the National Portrait Gallery.

Meanwhile the news had spread fast, Mark Lemon wrote at once to Charley Adams from the Bedford Hotel, Covent Garden, Hole was informed at Caunton Manor and Dickens heard about it in Kent. "I was at Gad's Hill staying with Charles Dickens when Leech died," Frank Stone recalled, "We were at dinner, a telegram arrived which Dickens opened with a face suddenly saddened 'Leech dead' he said, and could say no more."[37] Journalists such as E.S. Dallas for *The*

34. Millais, J.G., *Life and Letters of Sir J.E. Millais,* 1899, Vol. 1, p. 274.

35. Layard, G.S., op. cit., p. 220.

36. Evans letters, op. cit., letter from Sir J.E. Millais, 31 October, 1882.

37. ibid., letter from Frank Stone, n.d.

THE WEDDING DAY—FIRST ANNIVERSARY.

Cornhill, Shirley Brooks for *Punch,* John Brown for *The North British Review,* waited with pens poised to write lengthy and heartfelt appreciations, some London papers including *The Times,* the *Evening Star* and the *Saturday Review* were quick to publish obituaries.

On 1 November all the *Punch* men met together to arrange a funeral for the great man which would accord with his place in the country's memory and with the wishes of the Leech family. Perhaps unintentionally they made it the moment for their own tributes, their own frustrated feelings. "Then we revert to poor Leech," records Silver, "his voluntas was stronger than his arbitrium says P[ercival] L[eigh] — he could deny none, not excepting himself, and laments those dear old days when Leech first married and what a pleasant little unaffected wife he had and how delightful were the little homely banquets of mutton and gin and water to which she welcomed his friends. P.L. tells of the old father calling on him this morning and bow wowing about the article in the Times which implied that family money matters had injured Leech's health. 'You must write and contradict this Mr Leigh.' 'I shall be most happy to do so sir, if you will supply me with some facts on which I may refute the statement.' . . . Old Leech was Keeper of the London Coffee House, And M.L. says he knows that Leech accepted bills for the old man and his daughters for £3000 or so, which swept away the sum he received for his first 100 paintings. While J.L. was at Homburg the father called to borrow £50 of old Joyce and then of M.L. and hearing this made J.L. very indignant and angry, and M.L. seeing how agitated he was said 'Your duty is to work for your wife and children, and not let your mind be harrassed, and if buttoning up your pockets leads to a quarrel with your father, I still should advise you to button them up.' "[38]

The funeral took place at Kensal Green on 4 November, 1864, a large crowd of public mourners joining the family and the great figures in filing through the neo-classical gates of the cemetery behind the cortège. It was a bitterly cold afternoon (Lemon caught a chill there which lasted for weeks) but it did not deter all his closest friends and Reynolds Hole read the service in the chapel and the prayers at the graveside. The pall-bearers were Mark Lemon, Shirley Brooks, Tom Taylor, J.E. Millais RA, Horace Mayhew, M. Evans, John Tenniel, F.C. Burnand, Henry Silver and Samuel Lucas, all distinguished by their black arm-bands with 'JL' picked out in silver. The coffin was followed by old John Leech, Dr Quain, Charles Keene, George Du Maurier, Charles Dickens, W.H. Russell of *The Times,* Percival Leigh, Edmund Yates, Charley Adams, H.K. Browne, Thomas Landseer ARA, George Cruikshank, Marcus Stone, J. Philip RA and W.P. Frith RA. Leech was laid to rest in the London cemetery only one stone away from his old friend Thackeray.

Leech had, as we know, some slight premonition of death, but he had the invalid's abundant hope as well. Almost the last recorded words to his wife were — "But I can do some work yet. And at any rate, thank Heaven! they needn't send the hat round."[39]

38. Silver Diary, op. cit., 1 November, 1864.

39. Silver, Henry, "The Home Life of John Leech", *Magazine of Art,* Vol. 16, p. 168.

Chapter Eleven

PASSING THE HAT ROUND

nce the funeral had taken place and the first tributes had been printed in the press, there was time for the men of *Punch* to assess the future without Leech and for his family to begin to rebuild their lives. The first question was more easily answered; the magazine had already schooled up two fine successors, Du Maurier whom Leech had befriended and Charles Keene whom he had actively encouraged. Moreover *Punch* seemed to have struck exactly the right note in its short, even stark, obituary notice printed on November 12th. Within black borders and beneath the artist's name and dates, Brooks had composed the following:

"The simplest words are best where all words are vain. Ten days ago a great artist, in the noon of life, and with his glorious mental faculties in full power, but with the shade of physical infirmity darkening upon him, took his accustomed place among friends who have this day held his pall. Some of them had been fellow-workers with him for a quarter of a century, others for fewer years; but to know him well was to love him dearly, and all in whose name these lines are written mourn as for a brother. His monument is in the volumes of which this is one sad leaf, and in a hundred works which, at this hour, few will not remember more easily than those who have just left his grave. While society, whose every phase he has illustrated with a truth, a grace, and a tenderness heretofore unknown to satiric art, gladly and proudly takes charge of his fame, they whose pride in the genius of a great associate was equalled by their affection for an attached friend would leave on record that they have known no kindlier, more refined, or more generous nature than that of him who has been thus early called to his rest. November 4th."

It was also Shirley Brooks who was asked to contribute the first full scale memoir of Leech for *The Illustrated London News*. Thomas Parry wrote to him on 31 October, "Poor Leech's portrait will be engraved in 'The News' after the manner of that of Thackeray. Will you do for Leech what you did for Thackeray?"[1] The engraved portrait was to be taken from the best photograph available and Mason Jackson was to engrave it for the paper. Whether Parry had intended such a detailed biography is not certain, but he was very pleased with it when it arrived in early November. "Shirley Brooks has written a beautiful memoir, boldly individualising himself and his friends," he told Lemon. Mason Jackson's attempts with the portrait were not so successful. "The

1. Shirley Brooks letters, Harvard. Letter from Thomas Parry, 31 October, 1864.

John Leech. A photograph by Maclean, Melhuish & Haes. About 1862. Leech's favourite working dress was a velvet jacket.
National Portrait Gallery

first drawing on the wood was a failure," he confided to Lemon, "so the whole thing had to be postponed a week; it will appear in the next number."[2]

The engraving as published, was very striking, and was based on a photograph of Leech taken by Messrs Maclean, Melhuish and Haes of the Haymarket. It shows Leech, no longer youthful, but with the grave and kindly expression of a man used to watching humanity for a long time and therefore tolerant and patient of its foibles. Another photograph of him, taken by Henna and Kent in the last two years of his life was published at about the same time by W.H. Mason's Repository of the Arts, Brighton, presumably as the result of popular demand. Brooks actually touches on the artist's attitude to photographic portraiture, which perhaps accounts for a dearth of such studies.[3]

"It was part of Leech's retiring nature to hate personal publicity, and he had a strong objection to seeing portraits of himself exposed in shop-windows. It would be vain in these days for a 'celebrity' to attempt altogether to avoid such popularity, or I think John Leech would have done so; but I know that he rejected in most instances, the applications of photographic artists. But several admirable likenesses of him were executed, ..."[4] (Illustration left and page 210.)

It was on record that old Mr Leech when he saw it, pronounced the *News* engraving to be the best speaking likeness of his son ever produced. He sent it to Reynolds Hole with the pencilled note "an exact likeness: the best extant".[5]

"He was the truest of gentlemen," wrote Brooks of Leech in his essay, "but who that was not a gentleman could have produced that exquisite series of feminine portraiture in which English beauty and grace have received a justice never extended before? The English woman has lost her best friend — And why speak of the English children whom he drew so lovingly? I have them here only to add that I think he loved a child with an affection which, did I try to characterise it in a word, I might be thought to exaggerate. Need I add that all the children loved *him*?"[6]

Brooks, as the result of this article and the benevolent engraving of Leech above it, like a presence, was the recipient of a good deal of fan mail. It is all the more intriguing that this Victorian post-bag survived, because the letters are not just from the great and the influential, but from ordinary citizens who loved and mourned Leech. There were autograph hunters of course, but much more impressive, letters from men who had been touched by his drawings such as this one.[7]

Sir,

Although I am but a very obscure individual, yet I feel constrained to write this to tell you how much obliged I am personally, for the simple and unaffected narrative you furnished me, as one of the readers of this day's Illustrated London News, touching your departed but ever to be remembered friend John Leech.

2. Brooks letters, op. cit., 13 November, 1864.

3. Photographic portraits were also taken by J. and C. Watkins (Maas Collection) and Silvy (N.P.G.).

4. *Illustrated London News,* 19 November, 1864.

5. Hole, Reynolds, *The Memories of ...,* 1892, p. 17.

6. *I.L.N.,* op. cit.

7. Brooks letters, op. cit., 19 November, 1864.

*John Leech. A photograph by J. &
C. Watkins. About 1862.*
National Portrait Gallery

Many, many times, whilst admiring those delightful sketches of his — so wonderfully natural and true — have I wished to be able to see and to know more about him — or even to look at his portrait — so deeply impressed have I been and often wondered how a man with such great genius and fame could preserve such a shyness and modesty of publicity.

I was persuaded he was a true gentleman and although your confirmation of this and his other virtues are now gratefully received yet I would wish to have learned it under less melancholy circumstances.

We shall sadly miss at Christmas those pure and sparkling pictures, but what a vacancy will there be at the great artist's own hearth! What a loss for his dear ones!

I am quite an outsider sir, but I feel that I could mingle my tears with theirs.

I seek no acknowledgement of this, but only desire to be considered as a brother mourner, but still,
Your grateful and humble servant
James Warley.

A friend of Brooks, Madame Sainton-Dolby the opera singer, put it slightly differently. "To you, his friend, the loss must indeed be great. Mr Mark Lemon also will feel what a gap there is in the administration of his office. I fancy when we met at Whitby you had some foreshadowing of this calamity and I was not surprised when I took up the paper and saw all was over."[8]

E.S. Dallas also approached Brooks to help him with his article for *The Cornhill Magazine* and Reynolds Hole wrote admiringly from Caunton on 7 December, suggesting, amid his fulsome congratulations, a few ideas for the future. "... all seem to like your words the better, because written, as you say, 'currente calamo', fresh, unstudied, without a syllable of 'mere verbiage', the tinsel cloak of compliment — There have been many pleasant memories (who wrote, and wrote so well that one in 'the Cornhill'?) and I hope for many more. I shall probably add my tiny mite of praise hereafter, having so many records of him — 150 letters, several containing illustrations — ample entries in my Diaries of our meetings here and elsewhere — and such vivid memories of his dear presence, kindly words and deeds!"[9]

Hole was, therefore, the first man in Leech's circle to consider writing something more extensive than an obituary, within six weeks of the artist's death. He was an extremely well fitted man to do so. He knew Leech intimately, had rubbed shoulders with most of the principal characters in the story and had a pleasant, easy-going style of writing. He began in December contacting the closest of Leech's friends, attempting to call in both recollections and letters for a projected work. Brooks was aiding him in mid-December, forwarding a memoir that had been advertised by Hotten of Piccadilly[10] and at about the same time Hole corresponded with Dickens.

8. Brooks letters, op. cit., 20 November, 1864.

9. ibid.

10. Dewar, G.A.B., *The Letters of Samuel Reynolds Hole, Dean of Rochester*, 1907, p. 35.

ROOTI-TOOIT—I'VE GOT CHER!

The novelist replied to this preliminary enquiry straightway :[11]

> Gad's Hill,
> Higham-By-Rochester,
> Kent.
> Tuesday, December 20 1864.
>
> My dear Sir — I am very much interested in your letter, for the love of our departed friend, for the promise it holds out of a good record of his life and work, and for the remembrance of a very pathetic voice, which I heard at his grave.
>
> There is not in my possession one single note of his writing. A year or two ago, shocked by the misuse of the private letters of public men, which I constantly observed, I destroyed a very large and very rare mass of correspondence. It was not done without pain, you may believe, but, the first reluctance conquered, I have steadily abided by my determination to keep no letters by me, and to consign all such papers to the fire. I therefore fear that I can render you no help at all. All that I could tell you of Leech you know...
>
> Your reference to my books is truly gratifying to me, and I hope this sad occasion may be the means of bringing us into personal relations, which may not lessen your pleasure in them — Believe me, dear sir, very faithfully yours
>
> Charles Dickens.

This rather unco-operative letter can hardly have encouraged Hole to continue; he would have been even less encouraged had he known what Dickens was thinking and saying behind his back. Obsessed by the celebrity's right to privacy, even after his death, the novelist took an attitude that no modern biographer would countenance for a moment. On Christmas Eve, he wrote to Shirley Brooks to put him fully in the picture.

"Of course I wrote immediately to the gentleman who read the service so pathetically at poor Leech's grave, And of course (much respecting his affectionate earnestness) I did *not* tell him what I nevertheless think, that it is a pity to write that kind of Biography at all. It seems to me that such a man's life is always best told in his works. The notice in *Punch* was in the best taste, and told all that our friend has left untold of himself which it concerned to the public to know."[12]

Neither Brooks nor anybody else seems to have hinted at this mild disapproval from Dickens, and Hole proceeded undeterred during the first few weeks of 1865; he met Charley Adams in London in January and persuaded him to lend him the extensive correspondence of their dead friend. He combined this meeting with visits to the British Museum for research, as he told his wife.

"I was quite bewildered at first, but settled down to my work

11. Hole, *Memories,* op. cit., p. 90.
12. *Nonsuch Dickens,* Vol. 3, p. 407.

shortly, and looked thro' some folios of caricatures, to give me some idea of the style of those humorous artists who preceded dear John Leech.

"... I had no time to fill my engagement with Millais, but I dined with Adams, Leech's oldest friend, and he can give more information than any other man concerning his early life. He is going to send me all his correspondence, sketches etc, and seems to sympathise in my project with all his heart."[13]

Hole was also visiting and writing down memories of the Leech family. Old Mr Leech and the Misses Leech, who had caused the artist so many headaches during his short lifetime, were now emerging as Leech's greatest champions, nurturers and encouragers. No attention from the artistic world was too much for them, they hobnobbed with all the great critics, discovered an excessive closeness with Leech and were presumably gratified with Hole's continuing interest. He wrote to his wife after such a call in the early months of 1865.

"I had such a happy evening, yesterday, dining with the father, mother, and five sisters of my dear friend, and seeing the most interesting and precious memorials of him, sketches made by him when he was hardly more than a year older than our pet, letters to his parents when he first went to school, the first drawings of his boyhood, the first that were ever published, and many more art treasures. A coach and four drawn and painted when he was seven years old is wonderfully full of spirit and power and at 16 you would call him a finished artist. Miss Leech gave me a coloured sketch done by him at that age, which shows the highest talent, and which I shall have engraved for my book."[14]

Reynolds Hole obviously pursued the determination to finish his book during the next year or two, borrowing rare volumes from Adams, constantly on the look out for fresh anecdotes from *Punch* friends and actually receiving a very full assessment of the illustrator's work from Richard Westmacott RA.[15] But the problems of Leech's loyal friends were to become much more complex than mere biography writing. Each in turn, Millais, Adams, Brooks, Silver and Hole, becoming embroiled in the family difficulties. Hole put the matter straight with Adams a year later.

"The fact is that, altho' I have collected a large quantity of material, and made many notes, though I have thought much of the subject and though my love for dear John Leech is as warm and true as ever, I do not feel that I can write anything worthy of him, and I have regretfully and reluctantly given up my wish. At the very time of this resolution, Dr Brown of Edinburgh, the author of 'Horae Subsecivae', 'Rab and his friends' & of the best article written upon Leech (in the North British Review) writes to me, expressing his wish to undertake a Memoir; and he will do it a hundred times more cleverly than I could hope to do. He is coming here, next month for a discussion. *May I show him your Scrap books & letters or shall I return them at once?* ... I feel sure that Dr Brown will write such a book as ever they who loved Leech the most will welcome."[16]

13. Dewar, G.A.B., op. cit., p. 30.
14. ibid., p. 37.
15. Richard Westmacott RA, 1799-1872, Sculptor.
16. Dimsdale Collection. 16 May, 1866.

Colour Plate 35. 'Mr Briggs Goes Out With The Brighton Harriers' I. Oil sketch sold at the 1865 sale of the artist's studio. 23½ x 15¼ins. Private Collection

Colour Plate 36. 'Mr Briggs Goes Out With The Brighton Harriers' II. The pair to Colour Plate 35 sold on the same occasion. 23½ x 15¼ins. Private Collection

In fact Brown, like Hole, was to be hesitant at the prospect of a biography. He merely extended his memoir to include Hole's charming but very brief essay "De Amicitia". They both had set the seal on a reluctance to write a life of Leech that was to dog his admirers for the next thirty years. Brown's *John Leech and Other Papers* did not appear until 1882, eighteen years after the artist's death, and F.G. Kitton's biography in 1883, nineteen years afterwards; by that time many recollections were dim and many intimate friends were dead.

* * * * *

When Reynolds Hole wrote to Brooks on 7 December, 1864, he asked "Do you know how his widow and children are provided for? Their comfort is a matter of material interest, and if not secured, should be forthwith."[17] It was obvious that Hole did not know the true situation, perhaps nobody could have done, but it gradually came out that far from being comfortably provided for, Annie Leech would have little enough to live on. When the will was proved by the widow on 29 November, 1864, as sole executrix, the testator had left effects somewhat under £6,000. Everybody had hoped that she would have been able to stay on at The Terrace, Kensington, the ideal solution being for Charles Eaton, Leech's bachelor brother-in-law to set up house there with his sister. But fresh facts were brought out into the daylight as they usually are on such occasions; Brooks mentions them in his reply.

"As regards his property," Brooks wrote, "I am as yet but ill-informed, but I have reason to believe that Mrs Leech will not be so well situated as *one* hoped and believed. Friends are applying to Lord Palmerston for a pension for her, and I think would not do what *he*, as you know, would have so much detested, were it not needful. Another matter, strictly of course entre nous, has been revealed. It was believed that Charles Eaton would do a great deal for her, and I think she hoped that he would live with her, and thus that the house might be retained. He *may* do something, but it seems that he has been privately married for about two years — I suppose 'ineligibly', as he has kept it secret. I cannot hear whether there are children, but in any case this fact is against Mrs Leech. Millais anticipates the obtaining a great sum for the drawings. I hope he does not exaggerate their market value — but even if he does not, I conclude that the Agnews have a heavy claim, which I make no doubt those shrewd Swedenborgians will duly set up. On the whole, my impression is that the family will have little more than a competence, but I speak without book, as yet. When I hear more I will let you know."[18]

Millais who was proving an outstanding friend to Annie Leech, saw two avenues open to the family; first to seek recourse from the government in acknowledging the nation's debt to Leech with financial help to the widow, secondly to organise a sale of Leech's remaining assets, his oil sketches and drawings, perhaps with a well-

17. Brooks letters, op. cit.
18. Hole Letters, Tallents Collection, 9 December, 1864.

publicised exhibition preceding it. He began in December 1864 by writing to prominent men as well as to personal friends to press for a state pension for Mrs Leech. Doyle joined enthusiastically in these efforts and an attempt was made to enlist Dickens' support in the hopes that he would personally write to the Prime Minister. Dickens proved as cautious as ever:[19]

> Gad's Hill Place
> Higham-By-Rochester
> Sunday, December 18th 1864
> My dear Millais, — There are certain personal private circumstances which would render my writing to Lord Palmerston, *separately and from myself alone,* in the matter of the pension, a proceeding in more than questionable taste. Besides which I feel perfectly certain that a reminder from me would not help the powerful case. I should have been glad to sign the memorial, but I have not the least doubt that the letter from myself singly is best avoided. If I had any, I would disregard the other considerations and send it; but I have none, and I am quite convinced that I am right,
> You are a generous and true friend to Mrs Leech,
> Faithfully Yours ever,
> Charles Dickens.

The chief obstacle to any help seemed to be not unwillingness, but the fact that procedures only existed for giving state pensions to the families of literary men. But Millais had powerful connections and with the aid of the Prince and Princess of Wales, Lord Palmerston and Lord Shaftesbury, he eventually was able to ensure that Leech's wretched descendants had a piece of the Victorian pie; the two children *were* awarded a pension of £50 a year for life. By these various measures, Millais told Hole that he hoped the widow might have about £500 a year.[20] Hole described Annie that month as "so sweetly sorrowful in her widow's dress that it is heartbreaking to see her and her fatherless children".[21] It was in fact in June 1866 when John Warrington Leech entered Charterhouse School, that Palmerston's successor, Lord John Russell, added a presentation to the pension enabling the son to pay for his schooling.[22]

But all Annie's friends could throw their greatest endeavours into the exhibition and sale of the pictures. The residue of preparatory drawings, watercolours and rough drafts, covering the whole period of Leech's working life, still remained locked away in the attic studio in Kensington. There were in addition forty-six sketches in oil, some of which had been exhibited at the Egyptian Hall, but at least three of them, produced by the enlarging process, had never been seen before. Millais and Mrs Leech also found eight pictures in oil, part of a new series, and presumably part of the experiments in straight oil on canvas technique that the artist was making at the time of his

19. Millais, J.G., *Life and Letters of Sir J.E. Millais,* 1899, Vol. 1, p. 274.

20. Dewar, G.A.B., op. cit., p. 32.

21. ibid.

22. Brown, John, *Horae Subsecivae,* 1882, p. 22.

Colour Plate 37. Unfinished oil sketch of 'Tom Noddy'. 19 x 15½ins.   Private Collection

Queen Elizabeth and Sir Walter Raleigh.

Colour Plate 38. One of the hand coloured illustrations for The Comic History of England *which appeared in twenty monthly numbers in 1847-48.*

death. There was more than enough to make a very substantial sale, even when portfolios, single sketches and sheets of studies were taken into account. Bradbury and Evans, the proprietors of *Punch,* still owned the copyright of most of the material and their close association with Messrs Agnew from 1865 probably resulted in that firm's involvement with the sale. Although Christie's were to handle the spring sale, William Agnew seems to have dealt with the private view and exhibition of the work for five days previous to the auction on April 25th, 26th and 27th. It was he that asked Shirley Brooks to write a preface to the catalogue and it was he that was the prime mover behind efforts to ensure that the artistic establishment of London was present. "Mr Evans tells me you have asked for the addresses of Garrick Club members to be sent to me," Agnew wrote to Brooks on 11 April. "Cards will be sent to each, the sale will require all the support and influence that can be called to bear upon it."[23] Christie's, like the rest of the art world, treated the sale exceptionally generously, very few of the 656 items were heavily lotted together, surely a rare occurrence in the Victorian sale-room, and the three days of the sale gave everybody a chance. *Punch* published its own announcement on the 22nd in which it drew readers' attention to the purpose of the sale, "for the sake of those whom he best loved, those for whom his splendid faculties were ever employed, those whose proudest inheritance is his name". The appeal ended with the statement that the pleasure in owning one of Leech's original works would be doubled by knowing that its purchase helped his family. Annie Leech was living with Charles Eaton at Watford during these months and he wrote to Brooks to thank him "for the very kindly way in which all you have written has been done".[24]

When the private view opened at Christie's Great Rooms, 8 King Street, St James's, on the morning of Wednesday, 19 April, 1865, the fashionable visitors mixing in the foyer, top-hatted gentlemen and shawl-clad ladies, would have seen one of the greatest assemblies of an illustrator's work ever brought together. These were not just the finished sketches that they had enjoyed at the Egyptian Hall, the canvases toiled over, sweated over and repeatedly taken up, but the bare bones, the laboratory notes so to speak, of the artist who had immortalised their times. On the walls were the first prescient lines of the great popular classics of their generation, the exquisite pencillings of *The Ingoldsby Legends,* early tentative compositions for the *Comic Histories* (an example is shown in Colour Plate 38 opposite), the original schemes for *Jorrocks,* for *Ask Mama,* for *Facey Romford's Hounds* and other sporting novels. There was the embryo figure of Mr Briggs, lightly laid on the paper before he had become a Victorian legend, "Mr Briggs as He appeared from Six in the Morning till Three in the Afternoon" and "Mr B having hooked a Fish". Many famous political drawings were hanging together there, the memorable "Mother Church Putting Her House In Order", "This is The Boy Who Called Up No Popery And Then Ran Away" and most famous of all the cartoon based on a Cruikshank original, "The Fagin of France After Condemnation". There were thirteen

23. Brooks letters, op. cit.
24. ibid.

CATALOGUE

OF

THE WHOLE

OF THE

ORIGINAL SKETCHES

Made by that highly-talented Artist,

JOHN LEECH;

COMPRISING

The ORIGINAL DESIGNS for the POLITICAL CARTOONS and PICTURES of
LIFE and CHARACTER which have appeared in 'PUNCH' during the last
Twenty Years ;

ALSO,

The Designs for the Comic Histories, Ingoldsby Legends, Jorrock's
Hunt, Ask Mamma, Mr. Facey Romford's Hounds,
and other Sporting Novels ;

SOME DRAWINGS IN WATER-COLOURS,

AND PICTURES IN OIL:

Which (by order of the Executrix)

Will be Sold by Auction, by

MESSRS. CHRISTIE, MANSON & WOODS,

AT THEIR GREAT ROOMS,

8, KING STREET, ST. JAMES'S SQUARE,

On TUESDAY, APRIL 25, 1865,

And Two following Days,

AT ONE O'CLOCK PRECISELY.

May be viewed Friday, Saturday, and Monday preceding; and Catalogues
had of Messrs. T. AGNEW & SONS, Manchester and Liverpool ; Mr. J.
C. GRUNDY, Manchester ; Mr. HOLMES, Birmingham ; and of Messrs. CHRISTIE,
MANSON and WOODS' Offices, 8, King Street, St. James's Square, S.W.

*Leech sale catalogue, Christie's,
Tuesday, April 25, 1865.*

albums displayed, one of them containing the original sketches for *Mr Sponge's Sporting Tour,* another with one hundred and twenty sketches in it for *Bentley's Miscellany* and others with designs for *Christopher Tadpole* and "Mrs Caudle's" *Punch* series. The real prizes of the day were thought to be the oil sketches however; they included "Miss Matilda", "Putting His Foot In It", "Fast Young Lady" and "The Fair Toxopholites" (the *Punch* version is shown opposite), most of the equestrian subjects having long since been sold by the artist. Included rather sombrely at the extreme end of the sale were Leech's simple studio furnishings, a capital easel by Winsor & Newton, two mahogany easels and a mahogany table.

Brooks' eloquent preface emphasised to the viewers the uniqueness of their opportunity in that it could never be repeated. The sketches he claimed "are intensely interesting, not merely as the originals of the pictures that have delighted millions and have become the property of the world, but as showing the mode in which John Leech worked and thought out his exquisitely truthful conceptions, and as proof that he was as mindful of the pictorial as of the satiric requisitions of the art of which he was so great a master."[25]

The sale commencing on the 25th April could hardly have exceeded the hopes of Brooks, Annie Leech or William Agnew; it was an important social event, Christie's rooms were thronged, and most of the famous names of the period were either present or represented. Hole was there and met Leech's friend Speaker Denison in the mêlée. "It is a most interesting exhibition," he reported to his wife, "and includes specimens of the great artist's genius of every description, from the merest pencil sketch to the finished picture in oils. I met the Speaker, who wished me to buy two or three small things for him."[26]

The first day, mostly drawings, was a dealers' day. Flatou, the illiterate dealer in drawings, was in the front row; alongside were Gladwell of Gracechurch Street, McLean the printseller (Leech's earliest patron), Old White of Maddox Street, a Pre-Raphaelite specialist, and Joseph Poole of Pall Mall. Other contenders were Colnaghi, William Vokins of Oxford Street and Lloyd the print-sellers, who had bought the copyright of "Ramsgate Sands". The first lot went for a mere five guineas, but the average bidding was higher, Flatou paying fifteen guineas for "A Steeple Chase" and "A Look at the country" and Colnaghi paying eleven guineas for one drawing, "A sketch from the Scarborough Strand". Many of the sketches were under ten guineas but practically none were knocked down for three guineas or less. A recurring feature of this and the two succeeding days was the number of figure studies bought by the genre painters of the time. Not surprisingly Leech had a good following among them. George Elgar Hicks bought a total of fourteen lots during the sale, some indication perhaps of his debt to Leech in modern life subjects. Henry O'Neill bought six lots on the first day and nine subsequently. Other artists participating were Henry Morton and the sporting artist, Benjamin Robert Herring, who bought "When it is foggy in London it is delightful in Brighton" for £115 10s!

25. Christie's catalogue, 25 April, 1865.
26. Dewar, G.A.B., op. cit., p. 34.

218

Dickens had written to W.H. Wills on 22 April, "You want to bid for something at poor Leech's sale. I ditto. Forster (as he writes me from Bath this morning) ditto. Let us three go into one boat, and charter Schloss accordingly." Schloss' name does not appear in the list of purchasers, so Dickens may have used another dealer as he undoubtedly bought some drawings.[27]

The second days and third days sales were the days for the lions, Gambart, the prince of the London art world, was there, so were Millais, Bicknell the patron of David Roberts, Disraeli, Reynolds Hole, Charley Adams, Frederick Leighton, Mayhew, Martin Tupper, Lord Stanley of Alderley, Gladstone, Samuel Lucas, all making at least one purchase. The Queen may have been represented by Colonel Oliphant, although none of his recorded purchases appears to be in the Royal Collection. However, one made by Halliday "Every Inch A Sailor", Lot 603, is now in the Collection.[28] Millais, loyal to the last, acquired two pencil drawings, an oil painting "Romance and Reality" which cost him sixty-three guineas,

27. *Nonsuch Dickens,* Vol. 3, p. 420. Sketches of Volunteer subjects by Leech were sold at Dickens' sale, Christie's, 9th July, 1870.

28. Royal Library Album, Windsor.

THE FAIR TOXOPHILITES.

Constance. "OH, MAMMA! I'M SO DELIGHTED. I HAVE JUST MADE THE BEST GOLD, AND WON THE BEAUTIFUL BRACELET GIVEN BY CAPTAIN RIFLES."

Lucy (disappointed). "WELL, CONSTANCE, I THINK YOU HAD BETTER NOT SAY MUCH ABOUT IT. YOU KNOW IT WAS A FLUKE! FOR YOU TOLD ME YOU ALWAYS SHOT WITH YOUR EYES SHUT, AS YOU FEEL SO VERY NERVOUS!"

a portfolio of sketches at £17 6s 6d and an obviously favourite subject "Mr Briggs Shooting — Seven Sketches in One Frame", fifteen guineas. Agnew's bought "Punch's Ball" perhaps in recognition of all the celebrated characters represented for forty-two guineas, and a considerable surprise was the £60 18s and £20 paid by W.E. Gladstone for the oil sketches "A Young Gentleman Who Fancies He is Alone" and "Married for Money" respectively. The highest price of the entire session was the £112 7s paid by Herring and Sam Lucas for "Briggs in the Highlands", followed by the £110 15s paid by Mr Shoolbred for "Mr Briggs Goes Out with the Brighton Harriers", a pair of oil sketches (Colour Plates 35 and 36, page 213);[29] Colonel Oliphant paid £99 15s for a single oil sketch at the end of the sale. A very fine oil sketch of a "Tom Noddy" subject did not however appear in the sale, perhaps because it was unfinished; it is now in a private collection (Colour Plate 37, page 216).

The whole event must have been considered highly successful, the amount raised being something approaching £7,000 for the Leech estate. But if this is viewed in comparison with the prices commanded by some Victorian painters, it is less remarkable. Two years previously, the same Mr Bicknell who attended the Leech sale had paid £3,097 10s for Landseer's "Harvest in the Highlands" and Millais' "The black Brunswicker" admired by Leech, had been sold to C. Plint in 1862 for £819. Most of his old friends were optimistic, Reynolds Hole commented to his wife, "The sale has gone off most successfully. The pencil sketch of Jo Johnson and my Carrie sold for Twelve guineas."[30] Lord Ronald Gower who attended the sale acknowledged himself astonished that the prices were so high, so did George Hodder.[31] Another paper mentioned even more gratifying results — "at the sale of the late John Leech's drawings the Prince of Wales was one of the largest buyers. The specimens selected have recently been framed, and now hang upon the walls of the prince's favourite apartment in Marlborough House."[32] Another newspaper had it on authority that the Queen considered Mr Leech an "extraordinary artist".[33]

Annie Leech probably remained in Kensington until the end of 1865 and then may have lived with her sisters-in-law at 31 Gloucester Square. After the success of the Christie sale, the Misses Leech began to have ideas that further sales of drawings might greatly benefit *them*. A second and far less spectacular sale was organised by Christie's for 21 June, 1866, and an exhibition of the works to be disposed of was held, this time in the Misses Leeches own house. Miss Caroline Leech emerges as the guardian of Leech's reputation, organising this sale, untiring in her efforts to raise money and a continual harasser of the artist's long-suffering friends. She issued tickets for the exhibition and enlisted the support of William Holman Hunt in seeing that the right artists and the right critics came to see it. Hunt did his best for them by writing to F.G. Collins to whom he had already commented on Leech as that "good fellow" whose work "will be sustained and possibly improved in the extent of its favour by time".[34]

29. Now in the collection of Martin Horrocks Esq.

30. Dewar, G.A.B., op. cit., p. 37.

31. Hodder, George, *Memories of My Time,* 1870, p. 83.

32. *Morning Post,* 31 March, 1866.

33. Leech albums, Bodleian Library, MSS Eng misc e 946/1-7, unnamed newspaper cutting.

34. Holman Hunt letters, Bodleian Library, MS Don e. 66 fol 107. Hunt to Collins, 21 November, 1864.

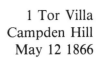

1 Tor Villa
Campden Hill
May 12 1866

My dear Fred,

The sisters of Leech have some very interesting drawings and tracings made by their brother. They date from his 5th and 6th year to his last days. The Misses keep a school and evidently are far from overstocked with the means to meet all their liabilities, and the drawings are therefore to be converted into money — coming so long after the large and celebrated collection sold at Christie's last year there may be some especial need of assistance for them — They are to be seen now by the friends to whom tickets have been sent on Wednesday and Saturday afternoons after 2 until the 30th May. It occurs to me that you ought to see them, more of course for the sake of the sisters than your own. Most of the subjects you will know already in some shape or other. I enclose you my card for your use should you by chance want to see the drawings next Wednesday on that day I doubt not my name as that of a friend to whom the ladies have spoken for advice in the matter would serve — after that I will if you will allow me write to ask that a proper invitation be sent to you. The works are to be sold in King Street, St James's sometime later in the season.

If you still have your money this is the time to invest. Even the steady sound things are depreciated to the lowest point known for years so you could not be in much fear that they could go lower.[35]

A steady flow of respectful critics were ushered through the Miss Leeches' sitting-rooms in the closing days of May, no doubt as adulatory and reverential as the ladies required. The sale at Christie's on 21 June made a very unremarkable showing compared with its predecessor. Of the 189 lots, most were small drawings, there were eleven coloured sketches only and five albums. Herring was once more a successful bidder, but apart from him, Lord S. Kerr was the only distinguished bidder, the rest of the works going to the trade. The total was somewhat over £400, not taking into account the various outlays to the auctioneers, printers of cards and other incidentals.

Leech's son was happily settled at Charterhouse that summer and for the next two years there was a lull in the family's life if not in their fortunes. Annie Leech had never been strong and the worst happened, when, debilitated and drained by shock and anxiety, she died in June 1868. The two children were left orphans at the ages of fourteen and twelve, and though not penniless were thrown back on the resources of Old Leech and their aunts. That stubborn old gentleman was all ready to create more difficulties, but fortunately Millais and Hole stepped into the breach.

35. Holman Hunt letters, op. cit., fol. 139.

Lucy. " WELL, REGINALD, AND WHEN DO YOU GO BACK TO SCHOOL ?"
Reginald. " OH ! THE DAY AFTER TO-MORROW !—AND AIN'T IT A BORE, JUST
AS ONE'S HUNTERS ARE IN SUCH SPLENDID CONDITION ? "

7 Cromwell Place,
South Kensington,
13 June 1868.

Dear Hole,

There seems to be some difficulty about the appointment of a guardian to Leech's Children, as the old gentleman opposes all the persons suggested by the children. It will be desirable to mention more than one and as you were about their father's greatest friend Chas Eaton is anxious to name you also for the Vice-Chancellor (Matins) to choose from — you being a Clergyman & the children wishing that you should be their guardian equally with myself. It will greatly facilitate matters if you will undertake the duty. Please write an answer to *Chas Eaton* 5 Allan Terrace, Kensington — the Vice-Chancellor has given a fortnight to decide.

Yours faithfully
J. Everett Millais. [36]

Ada and Bouge, placed under the watchful eye of the Royal Academician, the parson and their uncle Charles Eaton, seem to have completed schooling smoothly during the next two years, holidays in London being interspersed with holidays at Caunton. Ada became part of the family at Caunton for ten years, sharing the life of the pretty Nottinghamshire village and becoming well-loved by its inhabitants. According to tradition, Reynolds Hole actually built the "gardener's cottage" opposite the entrance to the Manor for the Misses Leech, so that they could live near their niece for a time. [37] But with the Misses Leech, the guardians had no authority and they were most industriously putting their heads together to see how more money could be raised from the *disjecta membra* of poor brother John.

It was only a question of time before John Ruskin, kind-hearted and an easy prey to importunate females, became sucked into the Leech family's very public passing of the hat. An admirer of Leech who had come on the scene very late, Ruskin was by 1872, offering the ladies his fullest support. They had decided to hold another exhibition, this time of John Leech's outlines, at the Architectural Gallery, 9 Conduit Street, in the hopes of raising funds. A committee was formed with this purpose, as the *Times* put it, "that the collection may, by subscription or otherwise, be acquired as a whole for the nation". [38] Ruskin wrote a letter in support of the project, paying compliment to Caroline Leech in passing and praising highly the outlines on display. This letter was prefixed to the catalogue. But what were John Leech's outlines? We have already seen that Leech made pencil sketches of his subjects, then traced them on to the block and then sent the completed drawing on the block through to the engravers. The drawings were mostly dispersed in the 1865 and 1866 sales, but the outline tracings were kept back at that time, presumably as they were considered too trifling. The fact that they had survived at all was remarkable, but Miss Leech's friend, the Rev.

36. Hole Letters, Tallents Collection.
37. Information kindly given to me by Mrs Mary Hole.
38. *The Times,* 8 May, 1872.

Traced outline sketch for Mr Briggs subject. Ruskin championed these outline sketches and eventually purchased them for his Sheffield Museum.

Reading University

39. Charterhouse School Archives, Letter to Stokes, 26 December, 1906.

40. *Catalogue of the Exhibition of Outlines by the late John Leech, at the Gallery, 9 Conduit Street, Regent Street.* 1872. Reprinted in *Arrows of the Chase,* 1880, pp. 161-162.

Gerald S. Davies, left on record why this had happened and why Miss Leech's holograph appears on them. "The handwriting", he says in a letter, "has this historical interest that these 'transfers' done on tracing paper were when they had served their purpose thrown into the waste paper basket. The sister got the reversion of these baskets (the wife kept most of the other pencillings) treasured them and arranged them. Else they would have perished being held of no account by J.L."[39] So that a comprehensive collection of Leech's outlines "preserved by John Leech's sisters with loving care, carefully mounted, and inscribed with their proper titles and references" were now being offered to the nation as the artist's crowning achievement!

Ruskin's praise of these second rate tracings, which the artist had considered as merely mechanical, was quite extraordinary. "It is merely and simply a matter of public concern that the value of these drawings should be known and measures taken for their acquisition," protests the great critic, "or, at least, for obtaining a characteristic selection from them, as a national property. It cannot be necessary for me, or for anyone now to praise John Leech. Admittedly it contains the finest definition and natural history of the classes of our society, the kindest and subtlest analysis of its foibles, the tenderest flattery of its pretty and well-bred ways with which the modesty of subservient genius ever amused or immortalised careless matters. But it is not generally known how much more valuable, as art, the first sketches for the woodcuts were than the finished drawings, even before those drawings sustained loss in engraving."[40]

However, the drawings under the public scutiny in the

Architectural Gallery were neither the first sketches of Leech's brain nor the finished work. They were a link in the process and a vital one in understanding the technique, but they could not possibly be classed alongside "the best outlines of Italian masters with the silver-point" in the way Ruskin proceeded to do. Oblivious to the superb work which had come under the hammer in the earlier sales, Ruskin confidently expected that each provincial town would rally support for these overrated outline sketches. "I want to see the collection divided, dated carefully, and selected portions placed in good light, in a quite permanent arrangement in each of our great towns, in con-nexion with their drawing schools."[41]

G.A. Sala was outspoken about the Ruskin statements saying that the "illustrious art critic was found to be so good natured as to say that these drawings (which might have been executed by a sharp parlourmaid) reminded him of the silver-point outlines made by some great masters of the Renaissance."[42] *The Spectator* also criticised the fact that there was no shading in the outlines giving "a partial and incomplete view of John Leech's art..."[43]

Admirable though Ruskin's attempts were, they failed for exactly the same reason that they failed ten years later; the drawings were simply not worthy to represent the artist. That second attempt was made in 1882 after the Misses Leech had moved to Brighton and become the even more jealous preservers of the Leech memory. They still had the outlines, but had quarelled bitterly with Shirley Brooks and other artist friends of their brother. "My experience is that there is much less enthusiasm amongst artists (painters especially) than in any other class with regard to my brother's works," Caroline Leech wrote to George Evans in about 1882. "It is perhaps natural that they who bestow so much time and labour upon one picture should rather envy John Leech's power of producing such wonderful things *without the least effort*" (author's italics).[44] Such lack of under-standing of the artist was typical of Leech's family. George Evans was the one man among Leech's following whom Miss Leech had approved as a biographer of her brother, and who was at that date assiduously collecting material; coincidentally F.G. Kitton was also collecting information for his memoir.[45]

It is true that Caroline Leech, now well into her sixties was having to weather some dreadful calamities. Leech's son, having left Charterhouse in April 1873 (where he won the Leech drawing prize), went to Lincolnshire to study agriculture for a year or two near Caunton. Developing ill health, he was advised to go to Australia and work in a more temperate climate, but while sailing off Port Adelaide on 29th March 1876, the boat was wrecked and he and a companion were drowned. He was not quite twenty years of age. The following January Charles Eaton died, the only surviving uncle, leaving Millais as Ada Leech's sole guardian. "You have, indeed, been unfortunate," Millais wrote to her on 10 January, 1877, "but at your age you may look for a happy career yet."[46] Ada was extremely lucky; growing up in the civilised surroundings of Caunton Manor, the Holes' gardens and woods were hers in all but name and in the

41. Catalogue, 1872, op. cit.

42. Leech albums, op. cit., possibly from *The Illustrated London News.*

43. *The Spectator,* 13 March, 1875.

44. Leech albums, op. cit.

45. F.G. Kitton, *John Leech, Artist and Humourist: a biographical Sketch ... London ... 1883.* New Edition revised, 1884.

46. Millais *Life,* op. cit. p. 276.

Another of the traced outline sketches purchased by Ruskin.
Reading University

winter of 1879-80 she had travelled with her friends to the south of France and visited Mentone.[47] With Ada's future in mind, Miss Leech made renewed attempts through Ruskin to dispose of the rough outlines in 1882. It was now even more imperative that some money should be forthcoming because in October 1881 Ada had married Mr W.T. Gillett and was hoping to have a permanent residence.

Ruskin, aware of the impecunious state of Miss Leech, mentioned the artist in two of his Oxford lectures on 7 and 11 December, 1883, hoping perhaps that fresh notice would draw attention to the outlines. On the selfsame day as the first of these lectures, Ruskin instructed his trustee, George Baker, to pay £50 for "drawings by John Leech bought for Sheffield Museum".[48] Although this purchase was for his museum at Sheffield, Ruskin probably studied the drawings at Brantwood before passing them on. A letter to his valet, about December 1883, mentions "the two volumes of drawings by Mr Leech...are to...be sent to Sheffield Museum."[49]

Two months later there were more attempts to sell the remaining drawings owned by Miss Leech, to the nation. On 4 and 6 February, 1884, Sidney Colvin of the British Museum politely but firmly declined the outlines due to "the character of the drawings themselves".[50] There were more hopeful signs from the provinces. George Evans, the Manchester based biographer, attempted to start a

47. Mrs Mary Hole Collection. Letter from L. Lear, 11 January, 1880.

48. Spence, Margaret "Ruskin's Guild of St George", *John Ryland's Library Bulletin,* Sept. 1957, pp. 177-178.

49. Letter in possession of Francis Edwards Ltd, 1980.

50. Leech albums, op. cit.

subscription in his native city in April 1884. This met with some criticism once again over the nature of the material in representing the great illustrator and caricaturist. Frederick Shields voiced the same theme — "To the public the woodcuts from the drawings are far more interesting than the skilful & wondrous hints of the SK sketches which waste their swift sure line on any but the artistic eye."[51]

However, in Nottingham a group of thirty-two admirers subscribed together and bought a selection of fifty drawings for the Castle Museum for just over £100. This may have been at the instigation of Reynolds Hole who had considerable influence as a Nottinghamshire landowner.

Miss Leech and her sisters were granted civil pensions of £35 a year each in 1885 and shortly afterwards they made a last attempt at appealing to Brighton friends. A committee was formed under Lord Aberdare, including the faithful George Evans, Graily Hewitt, F. Meadows White Q.C. and others to start a fund for the Misses Leech "who have striven bravely and under many disadvantages" and are now "in such straitened circumstances".[52] By the time that this appeal had been circulated, the old ladies may have felt their long search after money had hardly been worth it. On 30 January, 1885, Ada Rose Gillett, their only niece and Leech's only surviving child, died in childbirth at their Brighton home. The surviving infant, Dorothy Gillett became Leech's only living descendant.

51. Evans Letters, Harvard MS Eng 1028, letter from F.J. Shields, c.1884.

52. Copy of this prospectus at *Punch* office.

"Mr. Briggs comtemplates a day's fishing". Drawing, 8¾ x 10¾ins.
Barber Institute, Birmingham University

Chapter Twelve

LEECH'S LEGACY

hat lasting influence did John Leech have on the arts of illustration and humorous drawing in this country? If we take into account that he was as famous in his day as Heath Robinson in the 1920s, Low in the 1930s and Giles in the 1980s — all rolled into one — he must have had a prodigious impact! But *our* view of Leech's place in nineteenth century art is quite different from that of his contemporaries; where he has survived most readily in the public mind, in *Sponge,* in *Handley Cross,* in a scattering of *Punch* 'cuts, we tend to see him as closer to his barbed and grotesque predecessors and a world apart from the polished ink work of Du Maurier. This is of course a complete travesty of his role. His weekly devotees in the magazines and monthly admirers in the serial novels, saw him principally as the great humaniser of comic invention, the man that had taught them to laugh without gratuitous unkindness or grotesque exaggeration of form. For the Victorians, Leech was not only modern and new-fashioned in his outlook, he was totally one of themselves.

Although he grew up when the political and social burlesques of the Regency were at their height, he never belonged in any direct sense to that tradition, he had rejected the humour of Seymour and remained on distant terms with the vanguard caricaturist of that school, Cruikshank. Frith, discussing Leech's famous forbears, wonders with some justification whether he can be considered a caricaturist at all. Hogarth was a name that sprang to the mind of the Victorian writer by way of comparison, perhaps because he too had painted London streets, perhaps because most of his work was also known through engravings. "The name of caricaturist is as inappropriate to Leech as it is to Hogarth," Frith states, "though instances may be found, as in Hogarth, of occasional indulgence in exaggeration."[1] Hogarth is a recurring name when nineteenth century critics talk of our illustrator, Thackeray had mentioned it in his famous essay of 21 June, 1862, Samuel Lucas felt in 1864 that Leech lacked the serious moral purpose of Hogarth, whereas the French critic, Filon, was sure that he was haunted by Hogarth's spirit.[2] Both were near the mark, because Lucas could sense but not see Leech's uniquely different way of moralising, Filon, the objective foreigner, could value that satire which was unlike ordinary caricature. As Frith pointed out, Leech was in essence dealing with the

1. Frith, W.P., *John Leech His Life and Work,* 1891, Vol. 2, p. 97.

2. Filon, A., *Caricature en Angleterre,* 1902, p. 265.

THE TOO FAITHFUL TALBOTYPE.

Georgina (in riding habit). "WELL DEAR! I DECLARE IT'S THE VERY IMAGE OF YOU! I NEVER!"
Sarah Jane (who insists upon seeing the plate). "LIKE ME! FOR GOODNESS SAKE DON'T BE RIDICULOUS, GEORGINA. I THINK IT'S PERFECTLY ABSURD! WHY, IT HAS GIVEN ME A STUPID LITTLE TURN-UP NOSE, AND A MOUTH THAT'S ABSOLUTELY ENORMOUS!"

follies of his time, Hogarth with the vices of his. Hogarth was a fighter for a cause, Leech was a commentator on life. This analogy holds when we come to the caricature proper in the hands of Gillray, Rowlandson and Cruikshank, the fierce partisanship and bitter sarcasm were unacceptable to Leech's generation, just as the invective of Byron softened to the sedentary *Princess* of Tennyson and the rantings of *Shandy* turned into Thackeray's well-behaved short stories. Samuel Lucas as an older man, could see more clearly than most the totally new path that Leech was treading.

"Those only who remember what our caricaturists were fifty or sixty years since will appreciate the refinement which he has substituted for their preternatural coarseness. Then monstrous heads were clapped upon diminutive bodies, as the vehicles of conundrums at which Holywell - Street might stare, or coaches were upset in order to show the stout proportions of the female passengers, or bedrooms and other sanctuaries were invaded to make sport of every secret of our mortal state, from the sacred endearments of connubial affection to the purgative efficacy of the Cheltenham Waters. Alas, for our revered ancestors! they were simple-minded men, on whom the delicacy of Leech would probably have been wasted."[3]

3. Lucas, S., *Mornings of Recess,* 1864, Vol. 2, pp. 205-208.

T. N. FINDS RUNNING AFTER HIS QUADRUPED VERY LABORIOUS. HE RESTS HIMSELF ON A STILE, AND HAS ANOTHER QUIET WEED.

The fat ladies, overturned coaches and secrets of the closet, obviously refer to the works of Rowlandson and that artist comes in for trenchant criticism too from W.P. Frith. "That Rowlandson had a certain very coarse humour, a facility in grouping masses of figures in large compositions, and a power of investing faces and figures for which he had no authority in nature, cannot be denied; but there is always an intense vulgarity, in which the man seems to revel with as intense a pleasure."[4] The exaggeration of Gillray, the figures of Rowlandson that "had no authority in nature" loomed large for the Victorians when judging these artists. Where was the observation in any of them, where was the instruction in looking at the world as it actually was? Leech *had* this naturalism, he needed no exaggeration, his duty was to portray impressions of society, not prejudices about it. Richard Westmacott Junior RA, who wrote to Hole after the artist's death, put it like this: "It would be a great omission not to notice also with high praise Mr Leech's exquisite feeling for landscape. No real judge of art, no just observer of nature can be insensible to the taste shown in the characteristic introduction of backgrounds in his country scenes — nor to the fine judgement and elegant feeling with which these were always treated — His touches were slight; but what he indicated was of the best — true to nature and to its place."[5]

It is true that John Ruskin in his earliest notice of Leech in *Modern Painters,* 1850, refers to him as a "caricaturist" and brackets him with Cruikshank, but later on this view is considerably modified. In 1884 he credits Leech not only for the "natural simplicity and aerial space" in his works, but for introducing "the great softening of the English mind" that made way for the designs of Walter Crane, Randolph Caldecott and Kate Greenaway.[7]

But wasn't Leech consciously imitating the work of a bygone age in some of his engravings and therefore acknowledging a debt to the old School? His most famous parody of the eighteenth century masters was published in *The Illustrated London News* at Christmas 1856. The companion wood engravings are "Foxhunters in the 'Good' Old Times" and "Foxhunters regaling in the present Degenerate Days". The first, which is really the one to concern us here, is a clever pastiche of the works of Bunbury and Woodward with which Leech was obviously familiar. Gordon Tidy refers to this engraving as "Fieldingesque or Smollettesque" though it is not Hogarthian as he suggests. "Should any novelist", writes Tidy, "desire to open an eighteenth century story with an inn scene where, after a day's hunting, some members of the hunt were met to spend what, in the eighteenth century, was apparently thought to be a most enjoyable evening, let such a writer come to this woodcut for his models."[8] The rubicund faces and coarse postures are all there, only spoilt by a horrified woman at the door, who would never have been there in the original. Turn to "Foxhunters regaling in the present Degenerate Days" and it not only shows Victorian decorum, tamed huntsmen standing elegantly in a drawing-room, but the new style of realistic drawing of which Leech clearly felt a part. In fact the first

4. Frith, op. cit., Vol. 2, p. 98.

5. Tallents Collection.

6. Ruskin, J., *Modern Painters,* IV, Appendix 1. 1856, p. 471.

7. Ruskin, J., *The Art of England,* pp. 144-145 and 179.

8. Tidy, Rev. Gordon, *A Little About Leech,* 1930, p. 71.

An illustration by Gavarni from Gavarni in London, *1850.*

9. Evans Letters, Harvard University, MS Eng 1028. Letter from W.H. Bradley (Cuthbert Bede), 17 September, 1884.

10. Silver, "Art Life of J.L.", *Art Journal,* pp. 115-120.

11. Henry Silver Diary, *Punch* Office, 11 May, 1864.

12. Ribeyre, Felix, *Cham Sa Vie Et Son Oeuvre,* 1884, p. 181.

13. de Goncourt, Edmond and Jules, *Gavarni L'Homme Et L'Oeuvre,* 1879, p. 310.

illustration was not taken up with the enthusiasm of a man who felt himself part of the caricature tradition, but rather reluctantly at the suggestion of Cuthbert Bede.[9]

The last word on this subject could be left to Silver who above all considered that Leech had taken the whole comic press with him in a new direction. "It may be said with perfect truth that Leech was the first artist working with a pencil who could manage to be comical without ever being coarse. There is no trace in his works of the extravagance of Gillray, the vulgarity of Rowlandson, or the fanciful, fantastic drolleries of Cruikshank; and, unlike these caricaturists, he abstained from drawing what was needlessly uncouth. He first showed it to be possible for an artist to be funny without painting deformity; and, with all his gift of humour, he never tried to win a laugh by drawing men misshapen or of an ape-like type."[10]

If Leech's roots were definitely not in the mainstream of the caricature tradition, neither did they derive at all from the British genre painters of the 1820s and 1830s whose works he obviously saw. These would appear to be a more attractive source for his works to spring from, the paintings were in a narrative context, their groupings were intricate and episodic, their subjects in a similar, if a more sentimental idiom. But Leech found little satisfaction there either, the artists did not "carry the subjects home in their eye". His recorded comments on one famous painting perhaps stands for the whole lot. "J.L. thinks Wilkie forced and unnatural," Silver confided to his diary, "his Scotch Blindman's buffer painted from a London drayman, his colour poor and his treatment niggling."[11]

In his well known lectures "The Art of England" Ruskin criticised John Leech and other illustrators for their lack of Continental awareness. Like so many of his contemporaries, Ruskin was quite oblivious of Leech's grounding in French art, his continuing interest in French work and his familiarity with the French capital. One of only two or three humorous artists to benefit from this contact, it proved the single most significant factor in his development, largely because he was too young at the time of his Parisian tutelage to have drunk deep from the excesses of British caricature. Although we shall probably never know who Leech's Parisian instructor was, the artist *was* personally acquainted with "Cham", Comte Amedée de Noé, at a fairly early date. He was introduced to the great French caricaturist at Thackeray's house about 1843, after one of that artist's frequent visits to England to see his sister. This meeting is specifically referred to in the earliest biography of Cham and there may well have been others, when views were exchanged.[12] It would also seem most unlikely that Leech failed to meet the other Parisian giant, Gavarni, who was in this country from 1847 to 1851 and was an acquaintance of Thackeray, Dickens, Mowbray Morris and Tom Taylor. Gavarni's time in London and Scotland was particularly fruitful, but he shocked cultivated society by wishing to draw the street folk of London and the crofters of Scotland, rather than elegant high life (margin illustration).[13] Gavarni expressed a tremendous admiration

THE HUSBAND AS HE OUGHT TO BE,

Angelina. "WELL, LOVE—HOW DO YOU THINK I LOOK? DO YOU LIKE THE DRESS?"

Edwin. "I THINK IT'S PERFECTLY CHARMING.—I NEVER SAW YOU LOOK BETTER?"

AND

AS HE OUGHT NOT TO BE.

(Isn't it so, my Dears?)

Angelina. "WELL, E.,—YOU DON'T SAY A WORD ABOUT MY DRESS?"

Edwin. "EH? WHAT? OH! UGH!—H'M—BEAUTIFUL, BEAUTIFUL, BEAUTIFUL!"

14. Filon, op. cit., p. 260.

15. Now in the collection of Sterling and Francine Clark Art Institute, Williamstown.

for Hogarth but much more for George Cruikshank. Gavarni later explained the Cruikshank series "The Drunkards Children" to the de Goncourt brothers — "Peu à peu, en ecoutant Gavarni, l'admirateur nous donnait de son admiration." But what was this enthusiasm from across the Channel that ignored Leech and the new generation of caricaturists but lauded the rather outdated style of Cruikshank? If it does nothing else, this paradox does explain something about Leech. Gavarni's pleasure in Cruikshank's work was in the details of the story, the powerful way in which it was presented, and its moral content, *not* in the *drawing*. He would almost certainly have regarded Leech and his contemporaries as not serious enough commentators on society and merely as hangers on to the coat-tails of the bourgeoisie. Although this was far from the truth, it was what a radical Frenchman was likely to see, at once warming to the more profound social motives in Cruikshank's temperance engravings. Leech, on his part, had been strongly influenced by the drawing, the naturalism, the larger scale of French work, but not essentially by *French humour*. He had taken the situational comedy to his heart but worked out themes that were wholly English. A perceptive Frenchman like Filon was also able to see that the captions in Leech sometimes have a directness and terseness like Parisian satire. "Un très grand nombre des desseins donnés au *Punch* par l'artiste représentent de peintes scènes de la vie privée, à deux ou trois personnages, au-dessou desquelles on lit, en général, un bout de dialogue, à la manière de Cham ou de Gavarni. Ce sont de simples esquisses, mais l'effet en est presque toujours agréable et l'intention facile à comprendre."[14] But generally these Continental traits went unrecognised and many Victorians though comparing Leech with his French contemporaries, remark only on the difference in content, failing to observe the similarities in style.

The breadth and universality of the English illustrator must have been the underlying reason for his being brought together with his most distinguished French contact, Edouard Manet. We do not know who introduced them, but it is likely that the meeting took place in Paris in the summer of 1862 when Leech was on his way to south-west France. The occasion was marked by Manet's presenting the English artist with a delightful little ink drawing of a lady cashier sitting in a restaurant, perhaps dashed off in the very café or hotel where they were sitting.[15] The picture is inscribed simply and warmly "à John Leech E. Manet". One can well understand a mutual admiration between the two men, Manet's free spontaneous drawing has exactly that verve and excitement that we find in the best of Leech, that sense of capturing the passing minute, that desire to understand modern life by glimpsing. An unpublished watercolour by Leech which dates from about 1862 (Colour Plate 40 page 133), mirrors Manet's sketch in a quite uncanny way. If we look further at Manet's major works of the early 'sixties there are other similarities. "La chanteuse des rues" for example is caught, confronted and captured in a way that Leech would fully appreciate, set down in the fraction of a second between one busking location and another.

Manet is full of these little moments in the back of his paintings, the maid frozen into passivity carrying a coffee pot in "Le dejeuner dans l'atelier" and the absorbed distant woman in his "Portrait de Zacaharie Astruc". Leech's art was anything but insular and there is probability that Manet recognised this.[16]

One of the most interesting links in this subtle chain of interchanges and influences is provided by the work of the French illustrator Edouard Riou 1833-1900. Riou had considerable contact with the English press, worked for *The Illustrated Times* in 1859 and was a spasmodic contributor to *Petit Journal Pour Rire* in his role as social caricaturist. In the late 1860s Riou's languid pictures of high life included a set entitled "Le Sport Pour Rire" in which he investigates the crowds at a race course, one of which is shown below. Riou's hand has, it is true, that peculiar French softness and his horses that febrile tautness that make them more like lines of energy than actual creatures, but his compositions come straight from Leech. There are groups of swells, groups of jockeys and most illuminating of all, two carriage subjects which take as their viewpoint the same 'camera' sweep as Leech's wood engravings of the

16. *Manet 1832-1883,* Catalogue of the exhibition held at the Galeries nationales du Grand Palais, Paris, 22 April to 1st August 1983, No. 61.

Illustration from 'Le Sport Pour Rire' by Edward Riou, 1833-1900, for Journal Pour Rire *c.1867.*

Colour Plate 39. Scene in a train. Chalk and slight watercolour, 7 x 4½ins.
Private Collection

"Please Sir! Youre treading on my Toe"

Colour Plate 40. Girl at a writing desk. Watercolour, 5 x 5ins. Private Collection.

233

STICK-MEN.

A quels signes l'observateur reconnaît qu'il ne se trouve point dans Covent-Garden, ni même à la porte de *Nicholson's tavern*, et qu'il y a dans les airs des émanations de lord britannique.

Illustration from 'Voyage Dans Les Rues de Londres' by Bertall, 1820-1882. Illustration for Journal Pour Rire, *c.1867.*

Derby! The landau in which the Parisian shopkeeper and his family loll and lounge in painful imitation of their betters is a delightful pastiche of the English humorist. An even more telling piece of Franco-British plagiarism from the same magazine is found in Riou's jolly little sequence "La Nouvelle Generation". There, cocksure children are placed in adult roles, a cheeky boy quizzes a handsome woman, a future academician pulls a long nose at his school-master; it is Leech's "Rising Generation" of ten years before with a Gallic lens. One finds also the caricaturist Bertall (Albert d'Arnoux), 1820-82, travelling to England at the same time and satirising in "Voyage Dans Les Rues de Londres" the same subjects that Leech had popularised, absurdly snobbish flunkies and small swells with large neckties, neither very typical scenes from French comic genre (see margin illustration).

The fact that Leech's humour had nothing overtly sexual in it and did not exhibit anything of the *double entendre* was seen as a great solace by the strait-laced Victorians. It was perfectly true that *double entendre* was the be all and end all of French satirical magazines under the Second Empire, but *Punch* readers could expect such sauciness from the *other* side of the channel. In a rather prudish paragraph, Samuel Lucas commends John Leech because he never "puts improper notions in the minds of our young ladies" but goes on to talk more interestingly of the differences in the national humours in the 1860s.

"The most scrupulous mammas may be certain that 'Punch's Sketch-book' will contain no intimation that there is a seventh commandment, or that some naughty people are in the habit of breaking it. What the satirist foregoes in the deprivation of this topic can be appreciated by those who remember the space it occupies in the caricatures of our neighbours on the other side of the Channel. It is hardly too much to say that it is there the principal theme to which the draughtsman devotes his art, and for which subscribers look as for their daily *viaticum.* Unhappy Monsieur Cornard, he serves the 'Charivari' *in perpetuum,* as Jenkins, Jeames, Briggs, and other harmless varieties have served successively the turn of 'Punch'. The husband of Leech sometimes swears a little if he cannot 'get his wife's things together', but he is never perplexed by finding a staylace in a bow which he himself had fastened in a knot in the morning. So also of the *enfants terribles* of the English and French caricaturists. There is a striking difference in the nature of their revelations. The English youth has no recollection of canes in mamma's dressing-room; the little English girl never asks if the moustache-brush picked up in that sacred shrine is intended as a hearth-brush for her little doll's house, and neither of them are ever sent to play in the dining-room under circumstances which induce their suspicious fathers to address them to their astonishment as 'enfants malheureux'!" [17]

Silver must surely have had that same difference in mind when he wrote that Leech's work was transparently pure. "His art was never tainted by the humours of Gavarni or the drolleries of 'Cham'. Though an admirer of their cleverness, he cared little for their works,

17. Lucas, op. cit., pp. 205-208.

and showed his good taste by avoiding their chief highway to success. Pure-minded himself, he had no liking for a Frenchy style of subject which might shock Mrs Grundy."[18] This caring "little for their works" referred in every case to the content, not to the manner in which they were executed. Holman Hunt too remembered unfortunate comparisons being made with Gavarni, but dismisses them. "Time, which tries all things justly, will scarcely now bring forward the Frenchman — whose wit was nothing if not immoral — as the rival to John Leech, who found so many cheery, kindly, and healthy facts in the world, and uncurtained its actors mostly as they appeared under the innocent perplexities of life, but never as gracing vicious act with attractive colour."[19]

Leech's more private side, often overlooked, also had its origins in French illustration. The artist delighted in making small comic drawings for private circulation, little grotesques sketched on a scrap of paper or the back of an envelope, circulated among the family circle or to amuse a child. A considerable private collection[20] of these are all on blue paper with ink lines heightened here and there with colour (two examples are shown below). The subjects show anthropomorphic household utensils and vegetables punning to each other and playing with words, the real kernel of mid-nineteenth century wit! Leech has clearly been influenced by Grandville's *Public and Private Life of Animals,* 1842, as well as by the *singeries* of Thomas Landseer. This probably led a critic in 1872 to reflect that his work showed "indications of a study of and admiration for the grotesqueries of the old *Comic Annuals* of Hood".[21]

18. Silver, "Art Life of J.L.", op. cit., pp. 115-120.

19. Holman Hunt, W., *Contemporary Review,* 1888, p. 353.

20. Martin Horrocks' Collection.

21. Leech albums, Bodleian Library, MSS Eng misc e 946/1-7, unnamed newspaper, about 1872.

Off to the Wars. — after Hobbyma.

The Hampshire Cup Winner

Two ink and watercolour sketches showing Leech in his more relaxed style, probably drawn to amuse family circle or friends. Left, 5 x 4ins.; above, 4¼ x 5¾ins. Private Collection.

HOW YOUNG GENTLEMEN FROM SCHOOL GO
TO SEE A PANTOMIME NOW-A-DAYS.

As far as we know Leech never had a single pupil; Cruikshank instructed a number of young artists including Leech and the dramatist Watts Phillips was his accredited protégé, but John Leech was too self-effacing and reticent to want a following. Whether he wanted it or not, it certainly came once his published works were established, not in the form of pupils but of conscious and unconscious imitators both professional and amateur. Leech's postbag must have been filled with pleas for help as his name became famous, aspiring caricaturists wanting advice, young hopefuls needing an introduction to the great men of *Punch*. We know that he was punctilious in answering all these letters himself and as in the case of one correspondent mentioned by Frith, sometimes paid a sum of money to a deserving artist or sent a present of his books.

In 1859, a young Etonian sent *Punch* a humorous incident "Dreadful For Young Oxford" which he had overheard at a dance. Young Oxford, diminutive and full of himself, complains of the dearth of female society, to which his partner retorts "What a pity you didn't go to a girl's school instead!" This caption duly appeared under a brilliantly characterised Leech drawing. The Etonian hoping for some pecuniary advantage wrote to Leech, who replied somewhat drily that *Mr Punch* felt that he had done *enough* by supplying the illustration for the joke, but nevertheless he, John Leech, would enclose two guineas. The money Leech suggested should buy gloves "for the young lady". Leech also sent him two volumes of *Life and Character*.

The Etonian also fancied himself as something of a caricaturist and a lively correspondence with Leech ensued, the artist sending his young friend advice and the boy posting back sketches for an opinion.

"32 Brunswick Square
June 11 1859

"My dear Sir,
I am very busy, so you must excuse a rather short note. Your sketches I have looked at carefully, however, and I have no hesitation in saying that they show a great perception of humour on your part. They seem to me to be altogether very good; and I have no doubt that with practice you might make your talent available in *Punch* and elsewhere. I don't know about your taking lessons, except from Nature, and learn from her as much as possible. Try your hand at some initial letters — if drawn on the wood clearly, so much the better — and I will, with great pleasure, hand them to the editor of *Punch*. 'The Pleasures of Eton' is capital; the style, I take it, founded a little upon Doyle's works. I would not do that too much. You have quite cleverness enough to strike out a path of your own, and with my best wishes for your success.
Believe me
Yours faithfully
John Leech"[22]

22. Frith, op. cit., Vol. 1, p. 135.

Studious Boy. "JOHNNY!—I ADVISE YOU NOT TO BE A GOOD BOY!"
Johnny. "WHY?"
Studious Boy. "BECAUSE IN BOOKS ALL GOOD BOYS DIE, YOU KNOW!"

It was typical of Leech's generous spirit that he should end up by inviting the Etonian to his home in the holidays and presenting him with wood engraving blocks on which to pursue his efforts. The letter also reveals the artist's distrust of anything approaching a formal training and his antipathy to any sort of slavish copyism. Nature alone had been his instructor and nothing was going to make him deviate from that.

From the end of the 1840s and for the following twenty years, the pages of *Punch* are filled with social 'cuts, domestic scenes, country house subjects, many of which seem to have been inspired by Leech if they are not actually his hand. Silver says that he was really the inventor of "social 'cuts" and the "headmaster of the school of humorous artists"[23] so this influence was great. One of the first to adopt this sincerest form of flattery was W.M. Thackeray, whose pleasant weak sketches adorn early *Punch* numbers. Signed with a tiny pair of spectacles, his engravings are always ideal with their text but hardly forceful enough to stand on their own. In his initial letters and some larger 'cuts such as those to "Punch's Prize Novelists" and "Brighton in 1847" where a frisky horse bucks under an intrepid equestrian, he rests quite heavily on his friend.

In 1851 *Punch* enlisted another social caricaturist, Captain Henry R. Howard, whose subject matter and style was to closely resemble Leech's for fifteen years. Howard, a country gentleman and amateur was asked to contribute his sketches on the wood block rather than on paper, presumably for reasons of speed and convenience like the professionals. As he was not familiar with the method, Leech was asked to instruct him.[24] If it is strange that an artist of his standing should have had to do this sort of hack work, it is no less strange that he should have been expected to redraw contributions of the Revd W.F. Callaway some years afterwards.[25] Howard's understudying of Leech led to some confusion of style and even signature. In the course of some years Leech complained to Lemon that Howard's sign-manual — the Manx legs — was too similar to his own wriggling signature, a rather over-stated charge. it is much more likely that our artist saw such a close approximation in subject matter in Howard's work, that he felt a stop had to come to it somewhere. Howard was persuaded to change his sign-manual to a trident and continued to use this for as long as he worked on the paper. In the early 'sixties his skits on crinolines and footmen are very nearly vintage Leech, but even at best his girls are less beguiling and his urchins less whole-heartedly impish. If Howard's work was always distinguishable from Leech's, the same thing was not always true of Julian Portch. Portch, a self-taught artist from a very poor background, contributed social 'cuts to *Punch* from 1858 to 1861. They are nearly always signed by a script "JP" but his children, young ladies and street characters often bear a striking resemblance to Leech's. There was no animosity over this gentle plagiarism, and when Portch was dying of rheumatic fever in 1863, Leech was probably a subscriber to a fund for him.[26]

A rather different kind of imitation had appeared in 1860 when the

23. Silver, "Art Life of J.L.", op. cit., pp. 115-120.

24. Spielmann, M.H., *The History of "Punch"*, 1895, pp. 475-477.

25. ibid., p. 498.

26. Silver Diary, 16 December, 1863.

YOUTHFUL HUMANITY.

Mamma :—"Poor Arthur has got the face-ache, Willy."
Willy :—"Ah! then hadn't we better put him out of his misery at once?"

An illustration after Leech which appeared in Fun, *1865.*

satirical magazine *Fun* was launched. This was a deliberate attempt to copy *Punch's* success *in toto,* it had the same format, the same type, and in fact numbered some disaffected Punchites on its staff. The social cartoons never rose to the heights of the original, but several were closely derived from Leech's work (margin illustration), both in drawing style and subject matter. Leech was well aware of this and fulminated against this knavery at a *Punch* dinner on 12 February, 1862. Thackeray seems to have taken this rivalry in his stride, referring to the new publication as "Funch". Silver records that "WMT looking at 'Funch' observes how they copy Leech and his early efforts in feminine development".[27] Such travesties did nothing to diminish Leech's reputation, in fact they enhanced it, for the originals were so much richer in imagination.

When Charles Keene arrived on *Punch* in 1852, it was probably not recognised what an important artist had joined their ranks; in 1860 he joined the Table. He was without question a less inventive artist than Leech, but also undoubtedly a much stronger draughtsman. Perhaps *Punch* needed that strength at the time to act as foil to Leech's immediacy of line and Tenniel's finesse. Keene also had the unlimited advantage of walking in to an established genre of "social cutting" which Leech had created single-handed; there was nothing much left for him to do other than develop that brilliant draughtsmanship. As Silver wrote, Keene was heavily "indebted" to Leech[28] and the latter, despite contrary reports, helped the young man along, speaking of his work "with the very highest praise".[29] The difference in the drawing was what most struck Du Maurier and explains why, though he admired Leech, he actually sat at the feet of Keene.

"Leech, no doubt, had a good natural hand, that swept about with enviable freedom and boldness," writes Du Maurier, "but for want of early discipline it could not execute these miracles of skill; and the commands that came from the head also lacked preciseness which results from patiently acquired and well-digested knowledge, so that Mr Hand was apt now and then to zigzag a little on its own account — in backgrounds, on floors and walls, under chairs and tables, wherever a little tone was felt to be desirable — sometimes in the shading of coats and trousers and ladies dresses." But he adds, "There is no difficulty in reading between Keene's lines; every one of them has its unmistakeable definite intimation; every one is the right line in the right place."[30]

The clear style of what Ruskin calls "unbroken lines" and meticulous hatching became the accepted way of drawing for *Punch* from the 1860s to the 1880s in the hands of Keene and Du Maurier. Although as Ruskin realised the technique was greater than Leech's, their obtaining an even tint in laying dark over light for transparency and light over dark for opacity, could have something mechanical about it. "When . . . a number of Mr Du Maurier's compositions are seen together, and compared with the natural simplicity and aerial space of Leech's, they will be felt to depend on this principle too absolutely and undisguisedly; so that the quarterings of black and white in them sometimes look more like a chess board than a

27. ibid., 5 March, 1862.

28. Silver, "Art Life of J.L.", op. cit., p. 120.

29. Henry Silver, "Home Life of J.L.", *Art Journal,* Vol. 16, 1893, p. 167.

30. Du Maurier, George, *Social and Political Satire,* 1898, p. 84.

31. Ruskin, J., "The Art of England — The Fireside", *The Works,* Vol. 33, 1908, pp. 358-359.

32. Silver Diary, 25 January, 1860.

33. *Royal Academy Commission, Minutes of Evidence,* 13 March, 1863, pp. 185-186.

34. Ruskin, J., *Catalogue of the Exhibition of Outlines . . .*, op. cit.

picture."[31] In neither case were the worlds inhabited by Du Maurier and Keene totally their own, the homely street types of Keene had been pioneered by Leech in the 1840s and he had stormed High Society long before George Du Maurier arrived there. The fact that he straddled these two nations, did sometimes give cause for anxiety in his later work. Shirley Brooks was obviously worried about the old "natural simplicity" of the illustrations when he cautioned Leech not to "get aristocratic in his girls' noses, and to give up drawing cuddle-able girls".[32] Above all he had made the role of the humorous artist respectable to both artists and Society, by the 1880s Keene's work was acknowledged by Continental draughtsmen, Du Maurier's by the most influential figures in the land.

When in 1863, Millais had been interviewed by the Royal Academy Commission under the chairmanship of Lord Stanhope, his answers about the fair representation of the other arts in the institution were unequivocal.

"Does the Academy, in your opinion, at present include all branches of art as far as it would be desirable to include them," asked Lord Hardinge.

"No," replied Millais, "it seems to me desirable that all great artists (whether oil painters or not does not seem to me to signify) should be members of an institution like the Royal Academy. I think, for instance, that Mr John Leech, one of the greatest artists of the day, should be a member; Mr Hunt, the water-colour painter, is another instance."

"Are Mr Hunt and Mr Leech the only names which suggest themselves to you at present?" continued Lord Hardinge.

"They seem to me", replied Millais, "pre-eminently men who, amongst others, should be members of the Academy of England."[33]

Leech was certainly the first British humorous artist of his time to be considered for that kind of honour in that sort of company.

Within a decade of his death, Leech's work was not only being copied by the artists of the humorous weeklies, but by more serious students. Ruskin's purchase of the outlines, referred to in the previous chapter, was to be the foundation of a study collection at Sheffield; the critic added his comments on their value at the time:

"I will not indeed have any in Oxford while I am there, because I am afraid that my pupils should think too lightly of their drawing as compared with their other studies, and I doubt their studying anything else but John Leech if they had him to study. But in our servile schools of mechanical drawing, to see what drawing was indeed, which could represent something better than machines and could not be mimicked by any machinery, would put more life into them than any other teaching I can conceive."[34]

When George Evans was collecting material for his projected biography of the artist in the early 'eighties, he received a letter from Leech's old colleague Cuthbert Bede, which showed how deep Leech's influence was on a new generation of illustrators. "I have bought every copy of the Illd News (also The Graphic) from its very commencement to the present day," Bede wrote to him, "and have a great many bound volumes. But I cut out those 2 engravings and also all the others done by Leech in the Illd News — and gave them to my eldest son, Cuthbert, who is studying Art at S. Kensington and the Academy and does hunting scenes very cleverly."[35]

The only artist that I can discover, who was directly helped by Leech[36] and went on to some considerable success in his idiom was Miss Georgina Bowers, afterwards Mrs Bowers-Edwards. She must have come under his influence in the early 1860s and supplied initial letters and vignettes to *Punch* from 1866 to 1876. From 1880 onwards she drew for a series of album books, issued in landscape quarto size, which carried on the tradition of *Pictures of Life and Character,* although in this case they told a complete story. The most famous were *Canters in Crampshire,* and *Mr Cropp's Harriers,* both dating from around 1880, *Across Country,* 1882, and *Hunting in Hard Times* with its colour illustrations, of a year or two later. Miss Bowers' illustrations lack the vitality and character of Leech, but she did have the advantage of living in the colour printing revolution and apparently enjoyed the profitable Christmas card trade of the 1880s.

There is a superficial resemblance between Miss Bowers' album books and Randolph Caldecott's work, but temperamentally and

35. Evans Letters, op. cit. Letter from W.H. Bradley, 17 September, 1884.
36. Spielmann, op. cit., pp. 529-530.

An illustration from Hunting in Hard Times *by Georgina Bowers, 1889.*

imaginatively he is in another class. Caldecott's England was the same England that Leech knew and loved but bewitched by a sort of nostalgic genius. The farmhouses, haystacks, hedges and ditches of Leech's illustrations to Surtees are full of an earthy beauty, which places them unquestionably in the real world. Caldecott's scenery and architecture are carefully observed but slightly ethereal, life is seen through the distorting mirror of costume, story-book and the legends of the good old days. Nevertheless, Caldecott's huntsmen, horses and dogs have tremendous vigour and in such illustrations as "The Three Jovial Huntsmen" (below left), he seems to have looked fairly closely at his great predecessor. Writing to a friend in 1882, Caldecott said, "I was much interested in your remarks about Du Maurier. He is great: but cannot be compared to Leech in 'passion'. To descend to detail — Leech's women were dolls; but his men were suggestions of finer individuals than du M's. The latter would have been as happy in following out one of several other bents — Leech must have drawn."[37] It was one powerful and natural draughtsman recognising the abilities of another.

An intriguing question is whether Caldecott had seen any of Leech's original watercolours based on his illustrations. Although rather rare today, they show a pastel effect in their tones and washes which is quite different from the somewhat strident colouring of the hand-coloured plates. A sheet of Leech watercolours studies could

37. Quoted in *Yours Pictorially, Illustrated Letters of Randolph Caldecott,* 1976, edited by Michael Hutchins, p. 93.

Left, "The Three Jovial Huntsmen", illustration by Caldecott for The Graphic, *1880. Above, Jorrocks as seen by Aldin for* Jorrocks on 'Unting, *1909.*

LATEST WAR NEWS
" We'll soon 'ev the Kaiser pinched nah,—the copper's gorn from our court !"

An illustration to Ragamuffins; Sixty-Five Drawings, *by G.L. Stampa, 1916.*

easily be confused with preparatory designs for a Caldecott picture book (Colour Plates 39 and 40, page 233).

In many ways Leech meets with his next great successor Cecil Aldin, in the pages of Caldecott's *Old Christmas,* and *Bracebridge Hall,* 1876. The figure and animal drawing in these seem to be precursors of the Aldin style with its bold outline and intricate compositions based on poster art. It was really Surtees however that introduced Leech to the young novice Aldin in the late 1880s. Aldin was a student at the School of Animal Painting run by Frank Calderon at Midhurst, Sussex, and it was there that he first read *Handley Cross,* becoming enraptured by the author and the artist.[38] In 1912 Aldin illustrated his version of *Handley Cross or Mr Jorrocks Hunt,* published by Edward Arnold and issued in two volumes. He had already designed for *Jorrocks on 'Unting,* a small book published in 1909. But Aldin's vision of the fat sportsman was already his own (see illustration bottom right page 241), far more the stout farmer than the stout grocer which Leech had let him be.

Other late Victorian artists had inherited a little of Leech in their make-up, John Sturgess, that prolific and wiry equestrian illustrator of the 1890s, has some of his compositions; G.H. Jalland, a versatile sporting artist, had a little of his humour. Besides Aldin, the most notable follower was G.D. Armour, who as well as being an extremely strong pen and ink draughtsman, had Leech's great passion for horse-flesh and his eye for the minutest detail in dress and landscape. But Armour unlike Leech was not a *universal* observer, he was only dragged into the town unwillingly and as *Punch* editors discovered was unwilling to draw motor cars! Armour, incidentally,

38. Heron, Roy, *Cecil Aldin, The Story of a Sporting Artist,* 1981, p. 17.

had brought out his version of *Handley Cross* in 1908. Leech's urchins, who had delighted thousands of Victorian readers, continued to have their place in *Punch* too. They can be found in both Keene and May, but one suspects the most happy inheritor of the tradition is G.L. Stampa who decorated the pages of the magazine with cockney children before and after the First World War (illustration opposite).

Had John Leech's oil sketches been known to some of these artists, they might have been influential, but after the 1862 exhibition they sunk into obscurity. In fact when Professor Bodkin published his *The Noble Science — John Leech in the Hunting Field,* in 1948, he doubted whether many of them had survived. The one artist who would have appreciated those oil sketches would have been Sir Alfred Munnings PRA, those sparkling hunting landscapes with the purples and whites in the skies, rich greens of the verdure and everywhere the scarlet of hunting coats. The last word can be safely left with him — "How Leech must have enjoyed and lived in the pictures and its making, giving vent to his unquenchable humour and stored-up knowledge and memories. What brilliant invention!"[39]

39. Bodkin, Thomas, op. cit., preface by Sir Alfred Munnings.

Indignant Master of Hounds. "NOW, YOU SIR! MIND THE HOUND! HE'S WORTH FORTY TIMES AS MUCH AS YOUR HORSE."

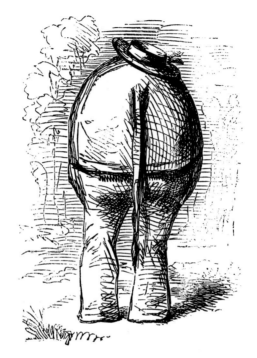

BACK VIEW OF THE ELEPHANT AT THE ZOOLOGICAL GARDENS.

APPENDIX
BIBLIOGRAPHY OF THE
WORKS OF JOHN LEECH

AUTHOR'S NOTE: This bibliography is based on the Grolier Catalogue of 1914, originally edited by Stanley Kidder Wilson. I have further amended it in the light of my own researches. Each entry commences with the author of the titles listed (in square brackets where not identified on the title page), or the title only where Leech is the author, followed by the wording on the title page. Printing notes follow and then details of the Leech illustrations which may be found in the book. Where cross references are made in italics they refer to the main body of the present work.

1835-6

1 [ETCHINGS AND SKETCHINGS, By A. Pen, Esq....]
Quarto.

The following description is from F.G. Kitton's biography of Leech: "He was eighteen years of age when he published his first work, entitled 'Etchings and Sketchings by A. Pen, Esq.', which bore this characteristic motto...

That noble lady,
Or gentleman that is not freely merry,
Is not my friend.

This little work, published at the price of '2s. plain, 3s. coloured,' consisted of four quarto sheets, covered with clever sketches, slightly caricatured, of cabmen, policemen, street-musicians, donkeys, broken-down hacks, and many other oddities of London life. Most of these sketches, however, were very incomplete, and were mere suggestions of heads of half-length and full-length figures." *(See p. 29.)*

2 DROLL DOINGS ... London, W. Spooner, 377 Strand. Printed by L.M. Lefevre. [1837-38]
Folio.

A series of coloured lithographs. Each plate, with one exception, has "Droll Doings", followed by its number, at the top, and all have explanatory text and publisher's address below. Those exhibited at the Grolier Exhibition were: No. 12: Well, Lucy dear; No. 13: Well! I declare now; No. 14: A tender question *(see p. 37)*; No. 15: The rivals; No. 16: A hem — Waiter!; No. 17: Revenge; No. 20: Going the whole hog; No. 21: Envy; No. 23: Long looked for happiness; No. 24: Why! hollo Muggins; Unnumbered plate: The kitchen dresser; No. 26: The Morning Call.

The plates are signed variously "J. Leech", "J. Leech delt.", "J.L. Delt", the leech followed by "delt", and the leech in bottle followed by "delt". Plate No. 23 has both the leech in the bottle and the leech followed by "delt". *(See pp. 31, 32).*

3 FUNNY CHARACTERS ... London. Published by W. Spooner, 377 Strand. [1837-38]
Folio.

A series of coloured lithographs. Each plate has "Funny Characters", followed by its number, at the top, and explanatory text and publisher's address, sometimes with the addition of Lefevre's name as printer, below.

The words "published by" are omitted on most of the plates, and some have "William Spooner" instead of "W. Spooner". The numbers and partial titles of plates exhibited are: No. 1: Please sir I'm comed to have my hair curled; No. 2: A penny hawanner; No. 3: Come, Maria, do walk faster; No. 4: Kicking

up a dust; No. 5: Who are you? No. 6: Astonishing a native; No. 7: The consumptive patient; No. 8: Hollo! who are you? No. 9: O cry here's a posty; No. 10: Sentiment interrupted; No. 11: Hollo! you feller, Take your wheelbarrow away; No. 12: Rural enjoyment in winter; No. 17: Oh my! How sweetly pretty!! No. 18: Did you ever? No. 19: Oh my goodness gracious!! What a nice young man! No. 22: Now then Julier; No. 23: Come old fellow dont be stingy; No. 35: Ladie's Men; No. 36: Well! pray who are you? *(See p. 37.)*

The plates are signed variously with Leech's initials, the leech followed by "delt.", and different forms of the leech in the bottle followed by "delt". *(See pp. 31, 32.)*

4 THE HUMAN FACE DIVINE AND DE VINO. London. Published by William Spooner, 377 Strand Printed by L.M. Lefevre, Newman St. [1837-38]
Quarto.

A lithograph of similar character to those of the three series of 1835 (Nos. 2, 4, and 9). It consists of the half-length figures of a pretty woman and an intoxicated man; signed "J.L. delt" in script. *(See pp. 31, 35.)*

5 [HUMOROUS SKETCHES] Published by W. Soffe, 380, Strand. [1837-38]
Folio.

A series of 12 coloured lithographs, without general title, but with explanatory text and publisher's address at the foot of each pl., sometimes with the addition of Lefevre's name as printer. *(See p. 32.)*

Partial titles of pls.: Starring it; Companions in misfortune *(See p. 33)*; Well Boy what does Mr. Snip say?; Presuming on a short acquaintance; Portrait of a young man wot keeps a horse; I say Bob! let's turn back; A left tenant; Constancy *(See p. 36)*; Come Jerry darling; Holiday examination; Will I what? (This plate has the address changed to "388 Strand".)

A further pl. belonging to the series shows a London policeman and a small boy with the partial title "Now, then, young feller". This is referred to by Cuthbert Bede in *Notes & Queries,* July-Dec., 1884, pp. 166-7

1836

6 BELL'S LIFE IN LONDON And Sporting Chronicle ...
Folio.

Leech's woodcuts for *Bell's Life* and its supplementary *Gallery of Comicalities.* The following series appear: Ups and Downs of Life; or, Vicissitudes of a Swell (14 woodcuts); Amateur Originals (18 woodcuts); The Boy's own Series (14 unnumbered woodcuts); Features of Insolvent Life (12 woodcuts, none of them signed); Paris Originals (15 woodcuts); Studies from Nature (10 woodcuts); Sketches from Nature (21 wood-cuts apparently belonging to this series); London Particulars (Nos. VII and X signed by Leech).

7 J.P. HARLEY as The Strange Gentleman [c.1836]
Octavo.

Coloured lithograph. A portrait of John Pritt Harley as he appeared in the leading part of Dickens' play, *The Strange Gentleman,* in 1836 and 1837.

8 [TOM SMART AND THE CHAIR; Leech's design for an illustration for Dickens' *Pickwick Papers.* (In the Victoria Edition of *Pickwick Papers,* London, Chapman and Hall, 1887, Vol. I, facing p. 203.)]
Octavo.

The first seven plates for *Pickwick Papers* were the work of Robert Seymour, who committed suicide before the publication of the second number in 1836. Leech was among those who applied, unsuccessfully, for the task of carrying on the work of illus. The design which he submitted, illus.'' Tom Smart and the Chair'', was first published in the Victoria Edition of *Pickwick Papers,* 1887. *(See p. 30.)*

1837

9 HOOK, THEODORE. Jack Brag. By The Author Of ''Sayings and Doings,'' — ''Maxwell,'' &c. In three Volumes ... London: Richard Bentley ... 1837.
Octavo. Three vols.

Two etched pls. (including frontis.) by Leech in each vol.; a total of six pls., as in the list of illus. The pls. were reproduced in the collection of Etchings [1850]. (See no. 101.) *(See p. 40.)*

1838

10 AMERICAN BROAD GRINS: Edited By Rigdum Funnidos, Gent. [Quotation] With Humorous Illustrations. London: Robert Tyas ... J. Menzies, Edinburgh. MDCCCXXXVIII.
Twentyfour-mo. Original limp brown cloth cover, gold stamped; yellow end-papers and gilt edges.

Four etched pls. (frontis. and facing pp. 14, 43, and 58) by Leech, entitled: An American Audience; The Fascinating Editor; A touch of the Sublime; Absence of Mind. The signature on the frontispiece is a pen stroke to represent a leech, followed by the word ''fecit''. The other three signatures are ''J Lh''. Some copies have a grey cloth cover.

11 AMERICAN BROAD GRINS: Edited By Rigdum Funnidos, Gent. With Humorous Illustrations. London: Robert Tyas ... Edinburgh ... Dublin. MDCCCXXXIX.
Twentyfour-mo. Original limp brown cloth cover, gold stamped (same as that of preceding number).

In this edition the anecdotes are entirely rearranged with additions and omissions. The illus. are the same as in No.10.

12 DIX, JOHN. Local Legends And Rambling Rhymes. By John Dix ... With Illustrations, by ''A. Pen.'' ''Ipse DIXit.'' Bristol: George Davey ... MDCCCXXXIX.
Sixteenmo. Original green cloth binding, gold stamped; yellow end-papers. Author's presentation copy.

24 lithographs (including frontis. and pictorial title-page) lithographed by Lavars & Ackland. The frontis. is signed ''J. L.'', and it seems possible that all the illus. are by Leech. On p. vii, there is a humorous allusion to ''A. Pen''.

13 WILLIS, N.P. Pencillings By The Way. By N.P. Willis, Esq ... A New Edition. London: John Macrone ... MDCCCXXXIX.
Duodecimo.

Frontis. and engraved title by C.H. Weigall, and two etched plates (French Foolery ..., facing p. 2, and German Sentiment, facing p. 160) by Leech. This is the 1st edition with Leech's plates. The work first appeared in *The New York Mirror,* and was published in editions of one and three vols. in 1835. An edition of 1844 contains, in addition to the pls. of the present edition, a portrait of Willis used as a frontis., while the pl. by Weigall faces p. 305.

1840

14 [BARHAM, R.H.] The Ingoldsby legends Or Mirth And Marvels by Thomas Ingoldsby Esquire London. Richard Bentley. MDCCCXL J.S. Gwilt. Invt.

— The Ingoldsby legends Or Mirth And Marvels by Thomas Ingoldsby Esquire Second Series London Richard Bentley M DCCCXLII C. Cook, Sculpt.

— The Ingoldsby legends Or Mirth And Marvels by Thomas Ingoldsby Esquire Third Series London Richard Bentley MDCCCXLVII. Cook Sc.
Octavo. Three series. Original brown stamped cloth binding; yellow end-papers. The stamped cover design of Series I is unlike that of Series II and III.

Series I: Engraved title by J.S. Gwilt, and six etched plates (three by Leech, two by Cruikshank, and one by Dalton). Series II: Engraved title by C. Cook, seven etched plates (three by Leech and four by Cruikshank), three woodcuts in text, and initial letters. Series III: Engraved title by Cook, two portraits of R.H. Barham, and four etched plates (two by Leech and two by Cruikshank).

Titles of Leech's eight plates: The Canterbury Ghost; Hamilton Tighe; ''That's him''; The Black Mousquetaire; The Auto-da-fé; The Confession; Little Jack Ingoldsby entering the Cellar; The Housewarming.

The first issue of the 1st edition, with p. 236 of Series I blank, and a slip with verses referring to the blank page. In the first issue of the 2nd Series the pls. precede the various pieces which they illustrate. They were afterwards rearranged according to a scheme outlined by the author in a letter preserved in a copy of the first issue.

Many of the legends appeared in *Bentley's Miscellany* and the *New Monthly Magazine. (See p. 40.)*

15 [BARHAM, R.H.] The Ingoldsby Legends ... With Sixty Illustrations By George Cruikshank, John Leech, And John Tenniel. London Richard Bentley ... 1864.
Octavo. Original red cloth binding, gold stamped; green end-papers and gilt edges.

Woodcut frontis. and numerous woodcuts in text by Cruikshank, Leech, and Tenniel. The frontis. and five illus. are by Leech; five of his earlier subjects are redrawn on wood with slight changes, and one new one (A Lay of St. Gengulphus) is added. The plate called The Confession is omitted, and The Black Mousquetaire and The Wedding Day (Little Jack Ingoldsby entering the Cellar) are here illus. by Cruikshank.

16 BENTLEY'S MISCELLANY. Vol. VIII [-XXV, and XXXIII-XXXV]. London: Richard Bentley ... 1840 [-1854].
Octavo. Vols. VIII-XXV, and XXXIII-XXXV, the only ones with illus. by Leech.

Pls., portraits, and woodcuts by George Cruikshank, Leech, Crowquill, and others. Leech's illus. are as follows:

Vol. VIII: Three etchings (Ingoldsby Legends, 1; Stanley Thorn, 2) and six woodcuts, illus. A Disinterested Review.

Vol. IX: Seven etchings (Stanley Thorn, 3; The Porcelain Tower, 2; Rumfuskin, 1; Ingoldsby Legends, 1).

Vol. X: Ten etchings (Richard Savage, 9; Ingoldsby Legends,

1) and seven woodcuts (An Apology for Noses, 1; The Porcelain Tower, 4; The Lady's Maid, 1; Ode to Taglioni, 1).

Vol. XI: Six etchings (Richard Savage) and thirteen woodcuts (Comicalities of the Feelings, 3; Some account of a great Singer, 2; Mr. Nosebody, 1; Old Green, 1; Speculations on Marriage, 1; Visit to Greenwich Fair, 5).

Vol. XII: Seven etchings (Richard Savage, 3; Mr. Ledbury, 4) and three woodcuts (Mr. Ledbury).

Vol. XIII: Seven etchings (Mr. Ledbury).

Vol. XIV: Seven etchings (Mr. Ledbury).

Vol. XV: Twelve etchings (The Fortunes of the Scattergood Family, 8; Physiology of London Life, 1; Mike Leary, 1; My Creole Cousin, 1; A Legend of Revolution, 1).

Vol. XVI: Eleven etchings (The Fortunes of the Scattergood Family, 6; An old Dog, 1; A Tale of the Wars of Marlborough, 1; Smoking Robin, 1; The House in the Terrain, 1; The Benefits of Snuff-taking, 1).

Vol. XVII: Twelve etchings (The Marchioness of Brinvilliers, 9; The Polkaphobia, 1; The wet Blanket, 1; St. Silvester's Night, 1).

Vol. XVIII: Eleven etchings (The Marchioness of Brinvilliers, 6; The old House in the Gungate, 1; Story of a Picture, 1; The opal Set, 1; The little velvet Shoes, 1; Dick Sparrow's Evening "out", 1).

Vol. XIX: Six etchings (Brian O'Lynn, 5; The Mermaid, 1). The "tea-table" cut on p. 464, which is repeated in Vol. XX, p. 154, has been ascribed to Leech, but seems doubtful.

Vol. XX: Nine etchings (Brian O'Lynn, 5; Mr. Ledbury, 2; Captain Spike, by J. Fenimore Cooper, 1; The Gipsey's Baptism, 1).

Vol. XXI: Five etchings (Miss Perkapple, 1; Thefts from the Percy Reliques, 2; Brian O'Lynn, 1; Doings at Stamford Hill 1.

Vol: XXII: Three etchings (How Mr. Straggle ate Whitebait, 1; Mr. Richard Jones and the Polka, 1; The wandering Fiddler, 1).

Vol. XXIII: Three etchings (The Lucky Grocer, 1; What Tom Pringle did with a £100 Note, 1; A Yankee amongst the Mermaids, 1).

Vol. XXIV: Seven etchings (Horrible Delusions, 1; The Widow outmanoeuvred, 1; A most unfeeling ... Assault, 1; The Luck of Inigo Dobbs, 1; The Golden Fleece, 1; Dr. Dodge, 1; The two Mr. Smiths, 1).

Vol. XXV: Two etchings (The Coroner's Clerk).

Vol. XXXIII: Six etchings (Aspen Court).

Vol. XXXIV: Three etchings (Aspen Court).

Vol. XXXV: One etching (Aspen Court).

Bentley's Miscellany was begun in 1837, under Dickens' editorship, and ran until 1868 (64 Vols.). It was published in monthly parts in an illus. wrapper designed by George Cruikshank, whose illus. for the magazine ceased with Vol. XIV, 1843. After Vol. XXXV, 1854, the Miscellany was not illustrated. *(See p. 40.)*

17 [CARTOONS] Is this the General Post, Sir? [and] The Regicide Pot Boy ... Published by R. Tyas ... June 13 [and] 20, 1840.
    Folio.

    Two lithographic cartoons. *(See p.40.)*
    A copy of the former is in the National Postal Museum, London.

18 [LEIGH PERCIVAL.] The Fiddle Faddle Fashion Book And

Beau Monde A La Française enriched with numerous Highly Coloured Figures Of Lady-Like Gentlemen, Edited by The Author Of The Comic Latin Grammar, The Costumes and other Illustrations By John Leech. London: Chapman & Hall ... Price 3/6 [1840].
Folio. Original white pictorial paper wrapper, with the same design as the engraved title.

Engraved title and four plates by Leech all coloured by hand. The plates contain over fifty figures and heads, caricaturing the absurd fashion books of the period. They are signed with Leech's full name, the leech in bottle, or both. *(See pp. 39, 41, 139.)*

19 [HALIBURTON, T.C.] The Clockmaker; Or, The Sayings And Doings Of Samuel Slick, Of Slickville. [Quotations] Third Series. London: Richard Bentley ... M.DCCC.XL.
    Octavo. Original maroon stamped cloth binding; yellow end-papers.

    Five etched plates (including frontis.) by Leech: Only a remarkable Development; Behind the Scenes; The Black Brother; Patriotism; What do you think of Socialism? (The first and second series appeared in 1837 and 1838 and contained no illus. by Leech.)

20 [LEIGH, PERCIVAL.] The Comic English Grammar; A New And Facetious Introduction to the English Tongue, By The Author Of The Comic Latin Grammar. Embellished With Upwards Of Fifty Characteristic Illustrations by J. Leech. London: Richard Bentley ... 1840.
    Octavo. Original maroon stamped cloth binding; yellow end-papers.

    Etched frontis. (showing pedagogical scenes and figures) and 49 woodcuts in text by Leech, as in the list of illus. Most of the woodcutting was done by T. Gilks. *(See pp. 15, 40, 42.)*

21 [LEIGH, PERCIVAL.] The Comic Latin Grammar; A new and facetious Introduction To The Latin Tongue. With Numerous Illustrations. London: Charles Tilt ... MDCCCXL.
    Octavo. Original maroon cloth binding, gold stamped; yellow end-papers.

    Eight etched pls. (including frontis.) by Leech, as in the list of etchings, and 55 woodcuts in text by Leech, who signed those on pp. 14, 17, 19, 24 and 136. The design on the cover is not repeated in the text. Many of the designs were repeated with changed titles in *Merry Pictures by the Comic Hands,* 1857 (see no. 134). *(See pp. 32, 40, 42.)*

    A 2nd edition appeared the same year with a caricature of the author by Leech as a frontis. A new edition, very similar to the 2nd was published in 1848 (see no. 22).

22 [LEIGH, PERCIVAL.] The Comic Latin Grammar... New Edition. London: David Bogue ... MDCCCXLVIII.
    Duodecimo. Original green cloth binding, gold stamped; yellow end-papers.

23 [LEIGH, PERCIVAL.] The Comic Eton Grammar. With Numerous Illustrations, From Designs by John Leech, Alfred Crowquill, Etc. London: Ward and Lock ... [n.d.]
    Sixteenmo. Original yellow pictorial boards; white end-papers, with advertisements printed in blue.

    54 woodcuts in text by Leech. Another edition of Percival Leigh's *Comic Latin Grammar,* with changed title. The etchings are omitted, but the same woodcuts are used, with the exception of that at the end of the intro. which is not repeated in this edition. The portrait does not appear, though mentioned in the preface, which is the same as that of the 2nd edition. Although it is undated, it probably appeared later than *Paul Prendergast* (see No. 24) as the text sheets are the same as in the latter work, and the error in the title, which attributes some of the illus. to Crowquill, is probably due to the appearance of his name in the title of *Paul Prendergast.*

24 [LEIGH, PERCIVAL.] Paul Prendergast; Or, The Comic Schoolmaster. (In Three Parts.) Comprising A New and Facetious Introduction To The English Language; Arithmetic; And The Classics. Illustrated with 230 Comic Designs by Leech, Alfred Crowquill, &c. London: Ward & Lock ... [1859]
Sixteenmo.

A collection comprising *The Comic English Grammar* (No. 20), *The Comic Eton Grammar* (No. 23), and *The Comic Cocker,* illus. by Crowquill.

Chambers assigns the date 1850 to this. It is here accompanied by Nos. 1 and 2 of a sheet called *The Humorist* in which most of the illus. appearing in the three parts of *Paul Prendergast* are reproduced

25 THE LONDON MAGAZINE, Charivari, And Courrier Des Dames ... With Illustrations ... London: Simpkin, Marshall And Co.... 1840.
Octavo. Two Vols. (Vol. I, Nos. I-VI; Vol. III, Nos. VII-X).

Etched pls. by Leech, H.K. Browne, and "Gillray the younger", woodcuts. The pls. facing pp. 274, 359, 407, and 443, and the woodcut on p.492, in Vol. I, and the pls. facing pp, 4, 77, 133, and 203 in Vol II, are by Leech. One (Davie Diddledoft, Vol. II, facing p.77) is signed "Jack Leech done it".

Leech's pls. illus. The Diurnal Revolutions of Davie Diddledoft; with the exception of the caricature, Vol. I, facing p. 407. Everitt and Thornber also ascribe to Leech the caricature of Benjamin D'Israeli, Vol. I, facing p.484.

26 [MULREADY ENVELOPE PARODY.] Design For The New Postage Envelopes. This Design has (most respectfully of course) been submitted to Government by an aspiring Artist Mul-led-al-ready. His [signature of leech in bottle] Mark. London, Published by Messrs... May 6th, 1840.
Quarto.

A lithographic parody of Mulready's envelope. Leech's "first popular hit was an adroit pictorial parody of the inappropriate design which Mulready prepared in 1840 for a universal envelope. Leech's imitation (copied in Kitton, Leech, 1883, p.16) was very funny, and his assumption upon it of the device (a leech in a bottle) which he afterwards made so well known, gave rise to a curious misunderstanding on Mulready's part..." *Dictionary of National Biography. (See p. 42, 43.)*

27 [MULREADY ENVELOPE PARODY.] Fores's Comic Envelopes No. I. [Design] London. Published by Messrs. Fores... [1840].
Oblong thirtytwo-mo.

There are slight differences in the design and the explanatory text is omitted.

28 [STYLES, PETER.] The Bachelor's Walk in a Fog, Written by Himself, Peter Styles Gentleman. [Vignette] With Fifteen Illustrations. London 1840. Sherwood, Gilbert, And Piper...
Octavo. Original green boards, with the 14 illus. reproduced in a border of small medallions, and Leech's initials, as illustrator, formed by the figures of two children, with heads as periods.

15 lithographs (including title-page) by Leech.

1841

29 COCKTON, HENRY. Stanley Thorn. By Henry Cockton, Esq.... 1841.
Octavo. Three vols. Original maroon, stamped cloth cover bound in.

Vols. I-III contain respectively four, six and five etched plates (including frontis.) by Leech, George Cruikshank, and Alfred Crowquill; a total of 15 pls., eight of them by Leech entitled: Vol. II: Mr. Bouncewell and his Colleagues "trying it on"; Canvassing, Chairing the Member; Vol. III: Sir William Wormwell receives Satisfaction; Stanley & his Mother going into their accounts; The Earl and the Professional Gentleman; Capt. Filcher tells Mrs. Gills & her daughter how the Aristocracy behave; Chastisement of Sir William by Amelia's brother.

This first appeared in *Bentley's Miscellany*, Leech's illus. beginning in 1840.

30 HOOTON, CHARLES. Colin Clink. By Charles Hooton, Esq. In Three Volumes...London: Richard Bentley...1841.
Octavo. Three vols. Original maroon stamped cloth binding; yellow end-papers.

Vols. I-III contain respectively eight, five, and three etched pls. (including frontis.); a total of 15 pls. by Leech and one by George Cruikshank (The Gamekeepers attacking the Poachers, Vol I, facing p. 120).

Titles of Leech's pls.: Colin's first Interview with Mr. Palethorpe; The Rebuke; A Father in spite of himself; Mr. Longstaff's Revenge; Cowardly Attack on Colin; Miss Sowersoft's Attention to Mr. Palethorpe; The Struggle; The Inquisitors; Skinwell's Death; Dr. Rowel's Ride home; The Accusation; Mr. Palethorpe amusing himself; "You must be a very brutal fellow..."; Mr. Palethorpe's Jealousy aroused; The unfortunate Attachment.

Colin Clink appeared in *Bentley's Miscellany, 1839-1841,* with no illus. except Cruikshank's one plate.

31 PORTRAITS OF CHILDREN OF THE MOBILITY. Drawn From Nature By J. Leech. With Memoirs And Characteristic Sketches By The Author of "The Comic English Grammar," Etc. [Mock coat-of-arms] London: Richard Bentley...1841.
Square folio. Original light green cloth binding, with leather patch title; white end-papers. Sometimes blond stamped cloth binding with gold title.

Eight lithographs (frontis., and facing pp. 16, 24, 28, 34, 38, 40, and 44) by Leech. Each plate is inscribed "Children of the Mobility", followed by its number.

The text is by Percival Leigh. The work is a parody on a then fashionable publication dealing with the children of the aristocracy. *(See pp. 43, 44, 45.)*

32 CHILDREN OF THE MOBILITY. By John Leech (1841). Reproduced 1875. Richard Bentley and Son.
Square folio. Original brown cloth binding, with title as above in gold; chocolate end-papers.

This consists of reproductions of seven of the original drawings for *Children of the Mobility*, with descriptive pages in facsimile of autograph. Pl. 5 is omitted. A portrait of Leech and "Letter from John Ruskin, Esq." are added.

33 RAMBAUD, YVELING. Little Walks In London By Yveling Rambaud Drawings By John Leech London Longmans, Green, and Co. 1875 All rights reserved
Quarto. Original ornamented green cloth binding; rose end-papers.

This contains reproductions of seven of original drawings for *Children of the Mobility*. Pl. 5 is omitted.

34 PUNCH And London Charivari [Woodcut]...London: Published For The Proprietors...[1841-1864].
Quarto. Vols. I-XLVII, with Punch's Almanacks, 1842-64.

Leech's work for *Punch*, of which for more than twenty years he was "the pictorial pillar", began in the fourth number with No. IV of Punch's Pencillings, entitled Foreign Affairs by [signature, leech in bottle]. The last of his cartoons is "The Weinbrunnen-Schwalbach" (See p. 203), which appeared on Oct. 15, 1864. In all he contributed to the paper, with its yearly Almanacks, above 3,000 drawings, at least 600 of them being cartoons. Most of the smaller woodcuts are reproduced in *Pictures of Life and Character* (see No. 35). The cartoons were published by Bradbury & Evans during the '60s in undated collections called *Early and Later Pencillings. (See pp. 49—50.)*

The Almanacks are found bound up in various series; the one for 1848 was issued on large paper, with coloured illus.

35 PICTURES OF LIFE & CHARACTER [Vignette] By John Leech From The Collection Of Mr Punch. London: Bradbury, Evans, & Co...[1854-1869].
Oblong folio. Five vols. (1st — 5th Series). Original pictorial boards, of various colours, with morocco backs and corners.

These are series of reprints from *Punch*, each vol. containing several hundred woodcuts with descriptive text. All vols. after the 1st (and later issues of the 1st) have the series number added to the title page. The cover design of the 1st series is repeated on all the titles. The covers of the other series have a different design. It has been suggested that copies with half-titles and indexes belong to later issues. When the 1st series appeared Thackeray wrote: "This book is better than plum-cake at Christmas. It is one enduring plum-cake..." (See p. 151.)

The Pictures of Life and Character were republished in three vols. by Bradbury, Agnew and Co., 1886-1887.

36 [SEALY, T.H.] The Porcelain Tower; Or, Nine stories of China. Compiled From Original Sources, By "T.T.T." [Quotation] Embellished By J. Leech. London: Richard Bentley...1841.
Octavo. Original red stamped cloth binding; yellow end-papers.

Three etched pls. (frontis., and facing pp. 19 and 111) and 15 woodcuts in text by Leech, as in the list of illus. The pls. are signed with the leech in bottle signature, which is adapted to represent a Chinaman, the leech being the queue. Several of these stories appeared in *Bentley's Miscellany*, 1840-41.

37 [SEALY, T.H.] Broad Grins From China. [Woodcut] London: Richard Bentley...1852.
Sixteenmo. Original green pictorial boards, with "With illustrations by J. Leech" added to the title; white end-papers, advertising Bentley's Railroad Library.

Woodcut on title-page and 17 woodcuts in text by Leech as in the list of illus. This is another edition of *The Porcelain Tower*, with the addition of the Memoir of the Author and two letters at the end. The subjects of the three etchings have been redrawn on wood and used in the title-page and on pp. 8 and 56, and the 15 woodcuts are the same as in the original edition.

38 WRITTEN CARICATURES: A Sketch Of Peripatetic Philosophy. From Hints In The Paris Charivari. By Captain Pepper. With Numerous Illustrations. By Leech. London: Chapman And Hall...MDCCCXLI.
Twentyfour-mo. Original limp green cloth cover with title in gold; yellow end-papers.

Woodcut frontis. (La Pastorale) and 34 woodcuts in text by Leech. Most of the illus. are signed and are interesting in that they exemplify many signatures used by Leech — "L", both the Roman letter and in script, "J.L." and "J. Leech" in script, "J. Leech" with Roman initials, and the leech in the bottle. The preface is signed "Capsicum Cayenne Pepper, Captain H.M. Invincibles".

1842

39 DANIEL, GEORGE. Merrie England In The Olden Time.

By George Daniel. [Woodcut, Quotation] In Two Volumes... London: Richard Bentley...1842.
Octavo. Two vols.

Vol. I: Four etched plates (including frontis.) by Leech, and seven woodcuts in text. Vol. II: Etched frontis. by Leech, and 16 woodcuts in text. A total of five pls. by Leech, as in the list of illus. The woodcuts are by Thomas Gilks and Robert Cruikshank. This first appeared in *Bentley's Miscellany*, 1840-41, Vols. VIII-IX, without illus.

40 HOOD, THOMAS. The Comic Annual For 1842. By T. Hood. [Woodcut] London: Henry Colburn...1842.
Sixteenmo. Original maroon cloth binding, gold stamped; yellow end-papers and gilt edges.

12 full-page woodcuts not included in pagination, eight cuts in text by Leech, and 16 woodcuts in text by Thomas Hood, as in the list of illus. The wood-cutting was done by W. Folkard and Orrin Smith.

41 HOOD, THOMAS. The Comic Album. By T. Hood [Woodcut] London: Henry G. Bohn...1844.
Sixteenmo. Original red cloth binding, gold stamped; yellow end-papers.

With the exception of the title-page and the omission of four leaves of advertisements at the end, this is identical with No. 40. The woodcut on the title is changed from "Fun" to "A Summer's morn", though the change is not made in the list of illus.

42 THE NEW MONTHLY MAGAZINE AND HUMORIST. Edited By Thomas Hood, Esq...London: Henry Colburn... [1842-1843].
Octavo. 1842, Parts I and II; 1843, Parts I, II, and III (numbered on covers LXV-LXIX).

These vols. contain serially *The Barnabys in America*, by Mrs. Trollope, with nine etchings by Leech. It was published separately in 1843 (see No. 51).

43 WHITEHEAD, CHARLES. Richard Savage. A Romance of Real Life. By Charles Whitehead, Author Of "The Solitary." [Quotation] In Three Volumes...London: Richard Bentley...1842.
Octavo. Three vols.

Vols. I-III contain, respectively, nine, four, and four etched pls. (including frontis.) by Leech, a total of 17 plates as in the list of illus. This copy contains and additional pl., "Ludlow's Madness", Vol. III, facing p. 300, not listed among the illus.

The work first appeared in *Bentley's Miscellany*, Vols. X-XII. The pl. "Ludlow's Madness" appeared in the Miscellany, but was afterwards suppressed. The original steel plates for the etchings are in the possession of the New York Public Library. (See p. 40.)

44 WHITEHEAD, CHARLES. Richard Savage...A New Edition With An Introduction by Harvey Orrinsmith London Richard Bentley...1896.
Octavo.

The intro. concerns Leech and his work. The dates on the pls. are changed to 1896.

1843

45 THE COMIC ALBUM: A Book For Every Table. [Woodcut] London: Wm. S. Orr & Co ...MDCCCXLIII [-MDCCCXLIV].
Quarto. Two vols. The vol. for 1843 is in the original illuminated boards, with fancy blue and white end-papers.

Numerous woodcuts in text by Leech, Crowquill, Hine, and

others. A cut in the vol. for 1843, illus. "The Income Tax" and evidently by Leech, is signed "Leonardo da Vinci delt". Many of the illus. are unsigned, those illus. "The Aerial Burglar", in the vol. for 1844, being the only ones formally ascribed to Leech. A vol. of the *Comic Album* is listed by Chambers under the date 1845.

46 DICKENS, CHARLES. A Christmas Carol. In Prose. Being a Ghost Story of Christmas. By Charles Dickens. With Illustrations By John Leech. London: Chapman & Hall...MDCCCXLIII.
Sixteenmo. Original reddish brown cloth binding, gold stamped; green end-papers and gilt edges.

Four etched pls. (frontis. and facing pp. 25, 78, and 150) coloured by hand, and four woodcuts in text (pp. 37, 73, 119, 164) all by Leech.

Titles of pls.: Mr. Fezziwig's Ball *(See frontispiece)*; Marley's Ghost; Scrooge's Third Visitor; The last of the Spirits. (*See pp. 77, 81.*)

Dickens' first Christmas Story. This is the 1st issue of the 1st edition, with "Stave I" on p. 1 of text. A few copies of this issue have yellow end-papers. The 2nd issue has "Stave One" on p. 1 of text, and yellow end-papers. Another issue has title printed in red and green, yellow end-papers, and "Stave I", and is dated 1844.

47 DICKENS, CHARLES. A Christmas Carol...Philadelphia: Carey & Hart. 1844.
Sixteenmo. Original blue stamped cloth binding; white end-papers.

An early American edition, closely resembling the original. The coloured pls. are reproduced by lithography and the woodcuts appear as full-page illus.

48 THE ILLUMINATED MAGAZINE. Edited by Douglas Jerrold. Vol. I, May to October. [-Vol. III] Published For The Proprietors...MDCCCXLIII[—MDCCCXLIV].
Quarto. Vols. I-III (May 1843-Oct. 1844).

Illuminated titles: pls. and woodcuts by Leech, W.J. Linton, Kenny Meadows, and others. Those by Leech are as follows: Vol. I: Woodcuts on pp. [3], 14, 23, 24, 40, 42, 84, 93, [146], 170, 172, [320]. Vol. II: Two etched plates, coloured by hand, illus. "Tom Houlaghan's Guardian Sprite" and "Legends of Lough Ouel by John L'Estrange", facing pp. 13, [17], 19, 106, 192, [248], [286]. Vol. III: Four etched pls. illus. "The Lost Husband" and "The Adventures of a Scamp", facing pp. [63], 141, 205, 271.

Several of these illus. afterwards appeared in *The Cyclopædia of Wit and Humor*, New York, 1858 (see No. 138).

A 4th vol. of *The Illuminated Magazine* was published, in which H.K. Browne was added to the list of illustrators, but it contains no illus. by Leech.

49 MAXWELL, W.H. The Fortunes Of Hector O'Halloran, And His Man, Mark Antony O'Toole. By W.H. Maxwell... [Quotation] With Illustrations By J. Leech. London: Richard Bentley...Dublin...Edinburgh. [1843].
Octavo. 13 monthly parts, with original buff pictorial paper wrappers.

Two etched pls. in each part, except Parts II, X, and XII, which contain three, one, and three, respectively; a total of 27 pls. as in the list of illus. The first five plates are signed "Dick Kitcat" (Richard Doyle); the others are by Leech. On its completion in parts, the work appeared in vol. form. 19 of Leech's pls. from it were reproduced, omitting the imprint, in the collection of Etchings [1850] (see No. 101).

50 SMITH, ALBERT. The Wassail-Bowl. By Albert Smith. [Quotation] In Two Volumes...London: Richard Bentley...1843.

Octavo. Two vols. Original brown cloth binding gold stamped; yellow end-papers.

Etched frontis. and numerous woodcuts by Leech in each vol.

Titles of frontis., which are signed by the leech in the bottle: The Laudanum Patient; A Night in The Royal George.

Vol. II, "The Physiology of Evening Parties" first appeared in *Punch* in 1842 (see also No. 82). "A visit to Greenwich Fair" was published in *Bentley's Miscellany*, 1841, and several of the other papers had appeared previously. Most of them were reprinted in Smith's *Comic Tales and Sketches*, and *Pictures of Life at Home and Abroad* (see Nos. 119 and 123).

A 2nd edition of *The Wassail-Bowl*, in one vol. appeared in 1844. *(See p. 43.)*

51 TROLLOPE, MRS. [FRANCES]. The Barnabys in America; Or, Adventures Of The Widow Wedded. By Mrs. Trollope... In Three Vols....London: Henry Colburn...1843.
Octavo. Three vols. Original green stamped cloth binding; yellow end-papers.

Vols. I-III contain respectively three, two, and four etched pls. (including frontis.) by Leech, as in the list of illus.; a total of nine pls. The work first appeared in the *New Monthly Magazine*, published by Colburn, in 1842-43 (see No. 42).

52 TROLLOPE, MRS. [FRANCES]. Jessie Phillips. A Tale Of The Present Day. By Mrs. Trollope...London: Henry Colburn...1844.
Octavo. 11 monthly parts, with original green paper wrappers.

Portrait of Mrs. Trollope in Part I, and one etched pl. by Leech in each part; a total of 11 plates by Leech.

All the wrappers are dated 1843, but the date on the title is 1844. On its completion it was issued in one vol., probably late in 1843, although dated 1844 (see also No. 53). Leech's name as illustrator is mentioned in the wrapper-titles, all of which state that the work was to be completed in 12 parts.

53 TROLLOPE, MRS. [FRANCES]. Jessie Phillips. A Tale Of The Present Day. By Mrs. Trollope...In Three Volumes... London: Henry Colburn...1843.
Octavo. Three vols. Original green stamped cloth binding; yellow end-papers.

The pls. are the same as in No. 52, the imprint being cut off, in most cases, to suit the smaller page. There are four in each vol., the portrait of Mrs. Trollope being used as the frontis. of Vol. I. This is set up differently from the edition in parts, the printer being F. Shoberl, instead of Moyes and Barclay. It is probable that it appeared simultaneously with the last numbered parts.

1844

54 HOOD, THOMAS. Whimsicalities, A Periodical Gathering. By Thomas Hood...With Numerous Illustrations, from Designs by Leech. In Two Volumes...London: Henry Colburn ...1844.
Octavo. Two vols. Original brown cloth binding gold stamped; yellow end-papers.

Etched frontis. and numerous woodcuts by Leech in each vol.

Titles of frontis., which are signed by the leech in the bottle: The Laudanum Patient; A Night in The Royal George.

Vol. II, "The Physiology of Evening Parties" first appeared in *Punch* in 1842 (see also No. 82). "A visit to Greenwich Fair" was published in *Bentley's Miscellany*, 1841, and several of the other papers had appeared previously. Most of them were reprinted in Smith's *Comic Tales and Sketches*, and *Pictures of Life at Home and Abroad* (see Nos. 119 and 123).

A 2nd edition of *The Wassail-Bowl*, in one vol. appeared in 1844. *(See p. 43.)*

56 JERROLD, DOUGLAS. The Story Of A Feather. By Douglas Jerrold...Illustrated With A Frontispiece By Leech. London: Published At The Punch Office...MDCCCXLIV.
Sixteenmo.

Etched frontis. (Watch, watch, roared the fellow) and pictorial title-page by Leech. The story first appeared in *Punch* 1843.

57 [LEIGH, PERCIVAL.] Jack The Giant Killer. By The Author Of "The Comic Latin Grammar". With Illustrations by Leech [Woodcut] London: Wm. S. Orr And Co...[c.1844].
Square sixteenmo. Original pictorial boards; yellow end-papers.

12 full-page woodcuts (including frontis.) not included in pagination, printed in black on green background, and seven woodcuts in text, all by Leech. The front cover designed by Alfred Crowquill; the frontis. by Leech is repeated on the back cover.

58 No. 57, with pictorial paper wrapper with same design as the board cover. The fly-leaves, advertising *Comic Nursery Tales*, are printed in red and dated 1844.

59 No. 57, bound in illuminated paper boards, together with *Puss in Boots* and *Hop O' My Thumb*.

60 NURSERY DITTIES From The Lips Of Mrs. Lullaby. With Illustration By J. Leech. London: Grant And Griffith...MDCCCXLIV.
Duodecimo. Original stiff white paper wrapper printed in red.

Woodcut frontis. and five woodcuts in text by Leech.

61 Another edition by the same publisher is dated 1847.

62 PUNCH'S GUIDE To The Chinese Collection. [Woodcut] London: Published At The Office...MDCCCXLIV.
Twentyfour-mo. Original stiff green pictorial paper wrapper.

Two full-page woodcuts (frontis.) and p. [21]), and numerous woodcuts and initials in text by Leech. The cut in the title is repeated on p. 23; the cover-vignette is not repeated in the text.

63 PUNCH'S POCKET-BOOK For 1844 [-1864]...London: Punch Office, 194, Strand. And Sold By All Booksellers. [Price 2s. 6d.]
Twentyfour-mo. 21 vols. Original leather bindings of various colours with pockets and flaps.

Each vol. contains a folded etched frontis. and title by Leech coloured by hand, and numerous woodcuts in the text: the etched titles differ slightly, all except the first having coloured vignettes. In addition, the volumes for 1844-48 have six pls. each etched by Leech. The remaining vols. contain numerous full-page woodcuts not included in the pagination besides the cuts in the text. Leech's name as illustrator appears on the title-page of each vol., that of Richard Doyle being added to the vols. for 1849-51, H.K. Browne's for 1850, and Sir John Tenniel's appearing from 1852-64. Leech's etchings are as follows:

1844: coloured frontis. (Fashions for 1844); Comparisons are odious; Intemperance; The Rivals; Temperance; Home for the Holidays; Pet of the Ballet by Daylight.

1845: coloured frontis. (Farming for Ladies); The Opera; After the Masquerade; Oxford Man ready for his degree; The plain Cook; Midsummer Vacation; A fancy Fair.

1846: coloured frontis. (Hyde Park as it will be) *(See p. 56)*; The Omnibus; The Railway Mania; The Abolition of Gretna; You should try the Camphine; Vell! give me my pint o'beer; I say, Bill, who'd walk who could ride?.

1847: coloured frontis. (The Matrimonial Tattersall's);

Approaching the beseiged lady; All spirits and all vinous liquors flee; Well, if this is Brighting, Joe, give me Whitechapel; Conversations on Cookery; There's such a lovely girl in that carriage; Et Cetera.

1848: coloured frontis. (Converzatione of Ladies) *(See p. 150.)*; I've been and left "The blood-stained Bandit"; Sir Joram à Burton; Please Sir, here's that Major; If things go on like this much longer; Too clever to live; The Lodger-Eaters.

1849-1864: coloured frontis. (Higgledy-piggledy); A social Sketch; Preparatory School for Young Ladies *(See p. 56)*; Progress of Bloomerism; Alarming Prospect; Topsy-Turvy; A Prize-baby Show; The quiet Street; Dressing for the Ball in 1857 *(See p. 141)*; A Substitute for the Sea-side; A Pic-nic in the Drawing-room; Swimming for Ladies; Volunteer Movement; A Croquet Match; Some Sea-side Fashions for 1863 *(See p. 141)*; A rather fast Steeplechase.

The address in the title was changed to "92, Fleet Street", in 1846, and, in 1848, to "85, Fleet Street".

The frontis. appeared collectively in 1866 (?), with text by Shirley Brooks, under the title "Follies of the Year" (see No. 64).

64 FOLLIES OF THE YEAR [Coloured vignette] By John Leech A Series of Coloured Etchings from Punch's Pocket Books — 1844-1864. With some Notes by Shirley Brooks. Bradbury, Evans & Co...[1866?]
Oblong octavo. Original half red morocco binding, with blue cloth sides, gold stamped; yellow end-papers and gilt edges.

Coloured vignette title, 21 etched plates by Leech, coloured by hand, and 21 initials. For titles of pls. see No. 63. The title vignette is repeated on the cover. The pls. are the coloured frontis. of *Punch's Pocket Books,* 1844-64, and are interesting in that they show in one vol. the development of the artist during twenty years.

65 SMITH, ALBERT. The Adventures Of Mr. Ledbury And His Friend Jack Johnson. By Albert Smith...In Three Volumes... London: Richard Bentley...1844.
Octavo. Three vols. Issued in pictorial cloth.

Vols. I-III contain respectively six, five, and seven etched pls. (including frontis.) by Leech, as in the list of illus. There are three woodcuts in Vol. I (pp. 73, 93, and 145) also by Leech.

The work appeared in *Bentley's Miscellany,* 1842-43, Vols. XII-XIV, as Mr. Ledbury's Grand Tour, Second Stage of Mr. Ledbury's Grand Tour, Mr. Ledbury's Adventures at Home and Abroad, and The Adventures of Mr. Ledbury And his Friend Jack Johnson. The character of "Rawkins" was base on the eccentric Mr. Whittle with whom Leech studied medicine for a time. *(See p. 40.)*

1846

66 C.B.C. Hints on Life; And How To Rise In Society. By C.B.C. Amicus. [Quotation, Woodcut] London: Printed For Longman, Brown, Green, And Longmans, Paternoster-Row. 1845.
Duodecimo. Original blue stamped cloth binding; yellow end-papers.

Etched frontis. by Leech. It is in seven compartments, connected by wreaths of smoke.

67 DICKENS, CHARLES. The Chimes: A Goblin Story Of Some Bells That Rang An Old Year Out And A New Year In. By Charles Dickens. London: Chapman and Hall... MDCCCXLV.
Sixteenmo. Original red cloth binding, gold stamped; yellow end-papers and gilt edges.

Frontis. and engraved title by Maclise, and 11 woodcuts in text by Leech, Maclise, Doyle, and Stanfield as in the list of illus. Leech's five woodcuts are on pp. 9, 34, [55], 125, and 174. The wood-cutting was done by Linton. A trial copy of the book is said to exist with the lower part of the woodcut on p.125 differing from that in the published work, showing a curious misapprehension on the part of Leech.

Dickens' second Christmas Story. There are two issues of this 1st edition, the earlier having the names of the publishers engraved upon the cloud in the lower part of the engraved title. In the 2nd they are below it. *(See p. 78.)*

68 DICKENS, CHARLES. The Chimes... Philadelphia: Lea and Blanchard. 1845.
Sixteenmo. Original blue stamped cloth binding; white end-papers.

An early American edition closely resembling the original. The woodcuts appear as full-page illus.

69 DOUGLAS JERROLD'S Shilling Magazine. Vol. I. January to June. [-Vol. IV.] London: Published At The Punch Office... MDCCCXLV [-MDCCCXLVI].
Duodecomo. Vols. I-IV, in 24 monthly numbers [Jan. 1845 — Dec. 1846] with original light grey paper wrappers.

The numbers contain etched pls. by Leech as follows: Nos. I-VIII, one each; No. X, two; Nos. XI-XIII, one each; No. XVI, two; Nos. XVII-XVIII, one each; No. XX, two; No. XXIV, one; a total of 20 pls. A slip in No. IX explains the lack of a pl.

Although the magazine was continued until June 1848 (seven vols.), Leech's illus. cease with No. XXIV. A note on p. [2] of the wrapper of No. XXV states, "It has been deemed expedient — to avoid all future disappointment and the discomfort of future apology — to discontinue the Illustrations."

Leech's pls. illus. *The History of St. Giles and St. James.* It does not seem to have been republished in London until 1851, in the first vol. of Jerrold's collected works, with only one of the plates, "St. James and St. Giles meet as Men" (frontis.). It appeared similarly in the collected works of 1863. An edition in brown paper wrappers, with at least two of the illus. was published by Burgess in New York in 1847. The original steel plates for the etchings are in the possession of the New York Public Library.

70 HODDER, GEORGE. Sketches Of Life And Character: Taken At The Police Court [Woodcut] By George Hodder (Reporter To The Morning Herald.) With Illustrations By Kenny Meadows, Leech, Hine, Hamerton, Henning, and Newman. [Quotation] London: Sherwood And Bowyer... MDCCCXLV.
Duodecimo. Original blue cloth binding; yellow end-papers.

13 full-page woodcuts (including frontis.), and two vignettes, by Leech, Hine, Hamerton, Henning, Meadows and Newman, as in the list of illus.

Titles of Leech's cuts: A Troublesome Guest (frontis.); Political Economy; The Dangers of a Latchkey.

71 PUNCH'S SNAPDRAGONS FOR CHRISTMAS. Illustrated With Four Steel Engravings By Leech. London: Published At The Punch Office... MXCCCXLV.
Sixteenmo. Original white paper wrapper, printed in blue and dated 1844; white end-papers and gilt edges.

Four etched pls. (incl. frontis.) by Leech, all signed with the leech in bottle, entitled: The discovery of Plum Pudding Island; A Game at Snap Dragon; "A very unpleasant day to be out" said the Captain; Snap and the Dragon.

The third pl., illus. the story "Christmas Eve in a Sponging House" was used without the inscription as a frontis. to Mark Lemon's collection of *Prose and Verse,* 1852 (see No. 112).

72 SMITH, ALBERT. The Fortunes Of The Scattergood Family. By Albert Smith... In Three Volumes... London: Richard Bentley... 1845.
Octavo. Three vols. Original maroon cloth binding; yellow end-papers.

Vols. I and II contain, respectively, seven and six etched pls. (incl. frontis.); Vol. III has an etched frontis. but no other plates; a total of 14 plates by Leech.

73 A BECKETT, G.A. The Quizziology Of The British Drama. Comprising I. Stage Passions. II. Stage Characters. III. Stage Plays. By Gilbert Abbott à Beckett. [Woodcut] London: Published At The Punch Office... MDCCCXLVI.
Sixteenmo. Original maroon cloth cover bound in.

Etched frontis. (Stage Passions) by Leech; woodcut on title and seven cuts in text not by Leech.

74 [BARHAM, R.H.] Some account Of My Cousin Nicholas. By Thomas Ingoldsby, Esq... London: Richard Bentley... Edinburgh... Dublin. 1846.
Duodecimo.

Frontis. engraved in line (Sir Oliver Bullwinkle falls in love with Eleanor Skillet) by Leech. The work first appeared in *Blackwood's Magazine,* 1834, and an edition in three vols. was published in 1841. The frontis. was made for the present edition. The original drawing for it is preserved in a copy with the Dublin imprint.

75 DICKENS, CHARLES. The Cricket On The Hearth. A Fairy Tale Of Home. By Charles Dickens. London: Printed And Published For The Author, By Bradbury And Evans... MDCCCXLVI.
Sixteenmo. Original red cloth binding, gold stamped; yellow end-papers and gilt edges.

Frontis. and engraved title by Maclise, and 12 woodcuts in text by Leech, Doyle, Stanfield and Landseer, as in the list of illus. Leech's seven woodcuts are on pp. 17, 51, 61, 89, 103, 120, and [173]. The wood-cutting was done by Dalziel, Swain, and Groves. Dickens' third Christmas Story. *(See p. 79.)*

76 DICKENS, CHARLES. The Battle Of Life. A Love Story. By Charles Dickens. London: Bradbury & Evans... MDCCCXLVI.
Sixteenmo. Original red cloth binding, gold stamped; yellow end-papers and gilt edges.

Frontis. and engraved title by Maclise, and 11 woodcuts in text by Leech, Maclise, Doyle, and Stanfield, as in the list of illus. Leech's three woodcuts are on pp. 28, 60 and 114. The woodcutting was done by Dalziel. On p. 114 occurred Leech's error by which the lady was made to elope with the wrong man *(See p. 82.)*

Dickens fourth Christmas Story. There are four issues of this 1st edition, distinguishable by small differences in the engraved title. *(See pp. 79-82.)*

77 THE ILLUSTRATED FAMILY JOURNAL... With upward Of Two Hundred Illustrations, by Linton, &c. London: Published By J. Clayton.
Quarto. Nos. I (March 8, 1844)-21 (July 26, 1845), bound together, with title-page as above.

Numerous woodcuts in text by Linton, Leech and others. The cut on p.228, illus. "A Nancy Story", is signed by Leech, and one on p. [321], illustrating Rip Van Winkle, seems to be by him (see also No. 88).

78 JERROLD, DOUGLAS. Mrs. Caudle's Curtain Lectures, As Suffered By The Late Job Caudle. Edited from the Original Mss. By Douglas Jerrold. [Quotation] London: Published At The Punch Office... MDCCCXLVI.
Duodecimo. Original stiff paper wrapper, printed in red and green.

Etched frontis. (Mr. Caudle's return from "The Skylark") by Leech. The "lectures" appeared in *Punch*, 1845, with illus. by Leech and others. The frontis. was etched for this edition. *(See pp. 32, 34.)*

79 [Five coloured lithographs supplementing Mrs. Caudle's Curtain Lectures.]
Quarto.

One of these is the same subject as the woodcut by Leech appearing in *Punch,* Vol. VIII, p.135, satirizing Lord Brougham. The others are of quite a different nature, and are entitled: Mr. Caudle's Shirt buttons; Caudle... has been bowed to by a Young Lady; Mrs. Caudle comes in late from Shopping.

80 SMITH, ALBERT. The Marchioness Of Brinvilliers, The Poisoner Of The Seventeenth Century. A Romance of Old Paris. By Albert Smith. London: Richard Bentley... Edinburgh... Dublin... 1846.
Duodecomo. Original brown stamped cloth binding; yellow end-papers.

Etched frontis. (St. Croix upbraiding the Marchioness) by Leech. The work appeared in *Bentley's Miscellany,* 1845, Vols. XVII and XVIII, with fifteen pls. by Leech. An edition with all the pls. was published in 1886. The original steel plates for the etchings are in the possession of the New York Public Library. *(See p. 140.)*

81 SMITH, ALBERT. The Marchioness of Brinvilliers... London: Richard Bentley & Son... 1886.
Quarto.

This edition contains all the pls.

82 SMITH, ALBERT. The Physiology Of Evening Parties. By Albert Smith. With Illustrations By Leech. A New Edition, With Additions And Corrections. London: Richard Bentley... 1846.
Duodecimo. Original white boards printed in brown; yellow end-papers.

Woodcut frontis. and 42 woodcuts in text, all by Leech. The work first appeared in *Punch* in 1842 with different illus. not by Leech. It was included in the 2nd vol. of *The Wassail-Bowl,* 1843, with Leech's illus. This is the first separate edition which contains them.

83 SMITH, ALBERT. The Natural History Of Evening Parties. By Albert Smith. [Woodcut] With Illustrations By Leech. A New Edition. London: D. Bogue... MDCCCXLIX.
Twentyfour-mo. Original stiff blue and white pictorial paper wrapper.

A later edition of No. 82, with the same illus. somewhat differently disposed, the cut on p.21 of the former being here used on the title-page, and not appearing in the text. It is repeated on the front of the wrapper, the back of which bears the illus. appearing on p.47.

1847

84 A BECKETT, G.A. The Comic History Of England. By Gilbert Abbott A'Beckett. [Woodcut] With Ten Coloured Etchings, And One Hundred And Twenty Woodcuts, By John Leech... Published At The Punch Office... MDCCCXLVII. [-MDCCCXLVIII].
Octavo. 20 monthly numbers in 19 (arranged for two vols.), with original green pictorial paper wrappers designed by Leech.

One etched pl., coloured by hand, in each number except the last, which contains two; the numbers of woodcuts in text of No. I-Nos. XIX-XX, respectively, are as follows: sixteen, fourteen, fifteen, twelve, eleven, twelve, ten, six, twelve, twelve, ten, ten, ten, eight, eight, seven, eight, eight, eleven; a total of 20 etchings and 200 woodcuts by Leech, as in the lists of illus., although the title-pages call for 240 woodcuts. The

wrapper design is repeated in the title. The numbers appeared from July 1846-Feb. 1848. *(See pp. 216, 217.)*

85 CHATELAIN, [CLARA] DE. The Silver Swan. A Fairy Tale, by Madame de Chatelain. London: Grant and Griffith... M.DCCC.XLVII.
Sixteenmo. Original green cloth binding, gold stamped; yellow end-papers and gilt edges.

Four full-page woodcuts (frontis. and facing pp. 57, 101, and 114) by Leech, entitled: The mysterious Stranger; Kaspar's Reception by his Neighbours; A warm Discussion; The Departure of Kaspar's Fortune. The wood-cutting was done by Linton.

86 CHATELAIN, [CLARA] DE. The Silver Swan. A Legendary Tale. By Madame De Chatelain, Author of "Merry Tales for Little Folks," Etc. With Illustrations By John Leech. London: Griffith and Farran... [1847].
Sixteenmo. Original red cloth, gold stamped; yellow end-papers and gilt edges.

A later edition with the illus coloured by hand. Some copies are bound in white cloth.

87 THE HAND-BOOK OF JOKING: Or, What To Say, Do, And Avoid. By Two Of The Joneses. With An Illustration by J. Leech. London: Grant and Griffith... 1847.
Twentyfour-mo. Original light green stamped cloth binding, with title in gold on front cover; cream-coloured end-papers.

Woodcut frontis. (The Mal-a-propos Joke) by Leech (not signed).

88 THE ILLUSTRATED PARLOUR MISCELLANY. [Woodcut] London: J. Field... 1847.
Octavo. Original brown stamped cloth binding; yellow end-papers.

Four full-page woodcuts (those on pp. [121] and 193 probably by Leech), and numerous cuts in text, some of them by Kenny Meadows. The cut on p. [121], illustrating Rip Van Winkle, had appeared in *The Illustrated Family Journal* (see No. 77).

89 MAXWELL, W.H. Hillside And Border Sketches. With Legends Of The Cheviots And The Lammermuir. By W.H. Maxwell... [Quotation] In Two Volumes... London: Richard Bentley... 1847.
Octavo. Two vols. Original green, stamped cloth binding; yellow end-papers.

Etched frontis. by Leech in each vol. (Unexpected Appearance of Claudine Dubreton, and Mrs. Robson startled at the Apparition of her late Husband); and seven and eight woodcuts by G. Measom in Vols. I and II respectively.

1848

90 DICKENS, CHARLES. The Haunted Man And The Ghost's Bargain. A Fancy for Christmas-Time. By Charles Dickens. London: Bradbury & Evans... 1848.
Sixteenmo. Original red cloth binding, gold stamped; yellow end-papers and gilt edges.

Frontis. and pictorial title by Tenniel, and fourteen woodcuts in text by Leech, Tenniel, Stanfield, and Stone, as in the list of illus. Leech's five woodcuts are on pp. 34, 48, 68, 130, and 145. The wood-cutting was done by Smith and Cheltnam. Dickens' fifth and last Christmas Story. *(See pp. 82, 178.)*

91 FORSTER, JOHN. The Life And Adventures Of Oliver Goldsmith. A Biography: In Four Books. [Portrait] By John Forster,... London: Bradbury & Evans... And Chapman & Hall... 1848.
Octavo. Original green cloth binding, gold stamped; yellow end-papers and gilt edges.

Numerous woodcuts in text by Leech, Clarkson Stanfield and others. Those on pp.652 and 675 are signed by Leech. A 4th edition, *The Life and Times of Oliver Goldsmith,* appeared in 1863.

92 THE RISING GENERATION. A Series Of Twelve Drawings On Stone. By John Leech. From His Original Designs In The Gallery Of Mr. Punch [Vignette] London: Published At The Punch Office... [1848].
Folio. Original stiff yellow paper wrapper with vignette by Leech.

This consists of 12 coloured lithographs of precocious youths, with ''The Rising Generation'' at the top of each pl. and descriptive text and address below, with the names of the lithographers, Maclure, Macdonald and Macgregor. The woodcut originals appeared in *Punch* in 1847. *(See pp. 82-83.)*

93 SMITH, ALBERT. The Struggles And Adventures Of Christopher Tadpole At Home And Abroad. By Albert Smith... Illustrated by Leech. London: Richard Bentley... 1848.
Octavo. 16 monthly parts, with original buff pictorial paper wrappers.

Portrait of Albert Smith by Baugniet in Part XVI; two etched plates, by Leech, in each number except Parts IX, X, XV, and XVI, which contain respectively one, three, none, and four, explanatory slips being found in Parts X and XV; a total of 32 pls. by Leech as in the list of illus.

On its completion in parts, the work appeared in vol. form bound in pictorial cloth. 26 of the pls. were reproduced, omitting the imprint, in the collection of Etchings [1850](see No. 101). Other editions of the work were published in 1854 and 1864.

1849

94 CROSLAND, MRS. CAMILLA TOULMIN. Toil And Trial: A Story of London Life. To Which Are Added The Iron Rule; And A Story Of The West End. By Mrs. Newton Crosland. [Late Camilla Toulmin]... [Quotation] With A Frontispiece By John Leech. London: Arthur Hall, Virtue, & Co... MDCCC.XLIX.
Duodecimo. Original light brown paper wrapper.

Woodcut frontis. (The Husband declares himself) by Leech. It is not signed and not included in the pagination.

95 JERROLD, DOUGLAS. A Man Made Of Money. By Douglas Jerrold. With Twelve Illustrations On Steel By John Leech. London: Published At The Punch Office... 1849.
Octavo. Six monthly numbers, with original light green and white pictorial paper wrappers.

Two etched plates by Leech in each number, a total of 12 plates, as follows: Mr. Jericho when can you let me have some money?; The Dream; A Family Picture; The Man made of Money shows his want of feeling; The Duel; Basil's Practical Joke; The Perforated Bank Note; Excitement of the Man of Money; The Bride-groom!; The Pauper & Man of money; ''And there stood Jericho''; The end of the Man of Money.

The numbers appeared from Oct. 1848 — March 1849. On its completion it appeared in vol. form bound in black cloth. The original steel plates for the etchings are in the possession of the New York Public Library.

96 TUPPER, M.F. The Crock of Gold, And Other Tales. By Martin Farquhar Tupper... A New Edition, With Illustrations by John Leech. London: Arthur Hall, Virtue & Co... MDCCCXLIX.
Duodecimo. Original brown embossed cloth binding, yellow end-papers.

Woodcut frontis. for each division (The Dismissal; The Tête-à-tête; and The Introduction) by Leech. *The Crock of Gold* first appeared in 1844.

97 BROWNE, W.Y. Fun, Poetry, And Pathos; Or, The Cornucopia: A Miscellany. By William Young Browne. With An Illustration By John Leech. [Quotation] London: Effingham Wilson... 1850.
Duodecimo. Original red cloth binding, gold and blind stamped; yellow end-papers.

Etched frontis. [The Elves in Windsor Forest] by Leech. The poem which the frontis. illustrates appeared, without the plate, in *Bentley's Miscellany* in 1845, signed ''W.Y.B.''.

98 [FLY LEAVES. By John Leech Punch Office 1850]
Quarto.

Six numbered lithographs, with letterpress, dealing with the adventures of ''Mr. G''.

99 A HOLIDAY BOOK For Christmas And The New Year: Embracing Legends, Tales, Poetry, Music, Sketches Of Manners And Customs, Games And Sports, Etc. London: Ingram, Cooke, And Co... [c. 1850]
Folio. Original white cloth binding, with glazed paper sides, with Christmas emblems and illuminated title, ''A Book for Christmas and the New Year''; yellow end-papers and gilt edges.

Coloured frontis. and title, numerous full-page woodcuts, woodcuts in text, and initial letters by Meadows, Browne, Foster, Leech, and many others, engraved by the Dalziels, Linton, and others. Some of Leech's most important illus. are on pp. 48, 49, 80, 81, 87, and [135].

100 THE ILLUSTRATED LONDON NEWS... 1850 [-1860].
Folio. Vols. XVI, etc.

The following illus., most of them full-page woodcuts, are signed by Leech: Jan. 5, 1850: London Ice-Carts. Dec. 21, 1850: Punch & Judy at Christmas; There is no deception, Ladies; Where you should not dine on Christmas Day; The Young Man who is alone in London, on Christmas Day. Nov. 29, 1851: The Wedding Party at Mrs. Byers's. Jan. 17, 1852: Arms Found. May 21, 1853: Pony Races on Black Heath. Dec. 24, 1853: Going to the Pantomime. Dec. 23, 1854: Very fond of it. Feb. 10, 1855: Hunting in the Holidays. May 5, 1855: Her Majesty's Buckhounds at Salt Hall — The Last Day of the Season. July 7, 1855: ''The Demonstration'' in Hyde Park. Dec. 22, 1855: The Boys in the Snow. Feb. 23, 1856: Fox Hunters regaling in the ''good'' Old Times; Fox Hunters regaling in the present ''degenerate'' Days. *(See p. 229.)* April 26, 1856: Very Polite. May 10, 1856 (Supplement): Eight hours at the Sea-side. Sept. 6, 1856: Oh my goodness! It's beginning to rain! Nov. 22, 1856: The first day of the Season. Feb. 14, 1857. Skating in Hyde Park. April 18, 1857: Close of the Hunting Season. Sept. 26, 1857: Part of Scarborough. Dec. 19, 1857: A Real Christmas Day. April 24, 1858: The supposed incurable Horse. Nov. 10, 1860: The Exmoor Pony Fair at Bampton, Devon. Dec. 22, 1860: ''The house on fire on Christmas Eve''; The Font and the Flowers. The number for Nov. 10, 1864, contained a portrait of Leech.

101 JOHN LEECH'S ETCHINGS, From Jack Bragg... From Christopher Tadpole. By Albert Smith... From Hector O'Halloran. By W.H. Maxwell... The two last works are Published by William Tegg... [c.1850].
Quarto. Original illuminated boards; yellow end-papers.

This consists of 51 etched pls. by Leech, as listed on the title-page, each pl. being followed by an unnumbered leaf with descriptive text printed on one side of the leaf. The imprint is omitted from the Christopher Tadpole and Hector O'Halloran pls. (see Nos. 49 and 93).

There are several issues of the etchings both with and without text. An edition containing 53 pls. has a separate table of contents, and title-page reading as follows: Etchings by John Leech [leech in bottle] London: William Tegg.

102 "YOUNG TROUBLESOME": Or [Coloured vignette] Master Jacky's Holidays. London: Bradbury & Evans... [1850].
Oblong Duodecimo. Original yellow boards; white end-papers.

This consists of etched title and 11 pls. (comprising 25 etchings) by Leech, coloured by hand. There is a half-title, with "Persons represented" on verso. Dr. John Brown lists a sequel to this, called "Master Jacky in Love", but no copies have been found by later students of Leech.

103 [AYTOUN, W.E., and MARTIN, THEODORE.] The Book Of Ballads. Edited By Bon Gaultier. A New Edition, With Several New Ballads. Illustrated By Alfred Crowquill, Richard Doyle, And John Leech. London: Wm. S. Orr And Co... [1851].
Duodecimo. Original blue cloth binding, gold stamped; yellow end-papers and tilt edges.

Woodcut frontis. illuminated title-page, numerous woodcuts in text and small cuts at the corners of each page, by Crowquill, Doyle, and Leech. The poems entitled Little John and the Red Friar, The Rhyme of Sir Launcelot Bogle, and The Lay of the Lover's Friend have illus. by Leech, those on pp. 178 and 192 being signed by him. Most of the wood-cutting was done by F. Dalziel.

This collection of ballads was issued with the Crowquill illus. in 1845. Both the 1845 edition and one of 1849, illus. by Crowquill and Doyle, contain a tail-piece by Leech showing that he had a small connection with the early editions.

104 "COMING HOME". A Comic Panorama. Drawn By "Leech". Delineating, With Irresistible Humour, The Fun, Mishaps, And Queer Occurrences, To which the votaries of Sport are subjected 'Coming Home' From The Races... London: Renshaw And Kirkman... [1851].
Oblong twentyfour-mo (6ft. 6ins. x 4½in.). Original blue cloth binding, gold stamped, with paper patch illus. by Leech on front cover; grey end-paper, bearing title.

A folding coloured woodcut, signed "J. Leech [three times] Smyth Sc.", printed on grey paper in four divisions and pasted together.

105 GOLDSMITH, OLIVER. The Traveller, By Oliver Goldsmith. With Thirty Illustrations Designed Expressly For The Art-Union Of London. 1851.
Quarto.

Frontis. (portrait of Goldsmith) and 33 full-page woodcuts by various artists. No. XXVI is by Leech.

106 THE LADIES' COMPANION And Monthly Magazine [Woodcut] Volume the Third London: Bradbury And Evans... [1851].
Quarto.

Vol. III, Feb.-July 1851 (accompanied by the numbers for March, May, and July, with original pink paper wrappers).

Four etched plates (facing pp. 73, 121, 150, and 247) by Leech coloured by hand, and two coloured costume pls. and woodcuts in text, not by Leech.

Titles of Leech's pls: The new Dress; Mrs. Berligan at the Opera; More frightened than hurt, King Radbob's Daughter.

107 THE MONTH. A View Of Passing Subjects And Manners, Home And Foreign, Social And General. By Albert Smith & John Leech. July, 1851 [-December, 1851], Published At the Office Of "The Month"... [1851].
Square sixteenmo. Six monthly numbers, July-Dec. 1851 (all published), with original brown, pictorial paper wrappers, designed by Leech.

Etched frontis. in each number, 23 full-page woodcuts, and 77 woodcuts in text, all by Leech. Titles of the six etchings: Mr. Simmons's Attempt at Reform; Charade Acting; The Little

Party; The Doctor's Mishap; The Domestic Difficulty; Mr Marshall "is not mad".

On p. [49] is the caricature of Thackeray as "Mr. Michael Angelo Titmarsh, as he appeared at Willis's Rooms in his celebrated character of Mr. Thackeray". Several of the full-page cuts represent "Belles of the Month".

108 THE RAGGED SCHOOL UNION MAGAZINE [Quotations] Volume III. London: Parthidge & Oakey... [1851].
Octavo. Vol. III.

This vol. contains a frontis. attributed to Leech. It is divided into compartments showing different phases of child life.

109 RECORDS OF THE GREAT EXHIBITION Extracted From Punch. [Printed by William Bradbury... Oct. 4, 1851.]
Folio. A newspaper of eight pages.

Numerous woodcuts from Punch, by Leech and others. At the top of p. [I] is Leech's woodcut "The Great Derby Race" which first appeared as a double-page illus. in *Punch,* Vol. XX, pp. [214-215].

1852

110 A BECKETT, G.A. The Comic History Of Rome By Gilbert Abbott A'Beckett. Illustrated by John Leech. Bradbury and Evans... [1852].
Octavo. Ten monthly numbers in nine, with original green pictorial paper wrappers, designed by Leech.

One etched plate, coloured by hand, in each number except the last which contains two; the numbers of woodcuts in text of No. I-Nos. IX-X, respectively, are as follows, thirteen, twelve, ten, nine, ten, ten, nine, eight, seventeen; a total of ten etchings and 98 woodcuts by Leech, as in the lists of illus. The wrapper design is repeated in the title. The numbers appeared from May 1851-Feb. 1852.

111 A BECKETT, G.A. The Comic History Of Rome... [Woodcut] Illustrated By John Leech. London: Bradbury, Agnew, & Co. Ltd. [1897-1898].
Quarto.

This late edition was published in parts with coloured pls.

112 LEMON, MARK. Prose And Verse. By Mark Lemon. London: Bradbury And Evans... 1852.
Sixteenmo. Original drab, stamped cloth binding; yellow end-papers.

Etched frontis. by Leech, illus. "Christmas Eve in a Sponging House", pp. 209-219. The story appeared in *Punch's* Snapdragons for Christmas", 1845, which bore the inscription, "A very unpleasant day to be out...". In its present state, the inscription is erased and "Frontispiece. Page 216" is substituted.

113 MILLER, THOMAS. Picturesque Sketches Of London, Past and Present. By Thomas Miller... With Numerous Engravings... London: Office Of The National Illustrated Library... [pref. d.1852.]
Duodecimo. Original green embossed cloth binding; yellow end-papers.

Woodcut frontis. and pictorial title, numerous full-page woodcuts, not included in the pagination, and woodcuts in text. The cut on p.285 is signed by Leech, and those on pp. 286 and 287 seem to be by him.

114 PAUL, H.H. Dashes Of American Humour, By Henry Howard Paul, With A Preface By J.B. Buckstone, Esq. Illustrated by John Leech. London: Piper Brothers and Co... 1852.
Octavo. Original blue stamped cloth binding; yellow end-papers. The title on the back of the cover is "Yankee Stories", which is used also for the running title.

Eight etched plates (frontis. and facing pp. 43, 69, 120, 131, 172, 193, and 232) by Leech entitled: Jonathan Homebred at the Zoological Gardens; Dan Suggs and the Sarpint; The Down Easter Rehearsal; Mr. Profile's Great Catch; A Row at Miss Nibbles's; The Robbery; Colonel Crickley's Horse; Lost! a black cat. Chambers says that this was first issued in parts.

115 PAUL, H.H. Dashes Of American Humor... New York: Garrett & Co... 1853.
Duodecimo.

An early American edition. The illus. are copied on wood, and are differently arranged, Dan Suggs and the Sarpint being used as a frontis.

116 REACH, A.B., and BROOKS, SHIRLEY. A Story With a Vengeance; or, How many Joints may go to a Tale. Inscribed To The Greater Number Of Railway Travellers, And Dedicated To The Rest. By Angus B. Reach And Shirley Brooks. [Woodcut] With A Steel-Engraving By John Leech, And Ten Cuts By Smyth. London: 227 Strand [1852].
Duodecimo. Original brown pictorial paper wrapper.

Etched frontis. (An "Eligible Situation" in Regent Street) by Leech, and ten woodcuts in text, some of them signed by Charles Keene.

117 REACH, A.B., and BROOKS, SHIRLEY. A Story With A Vengeance... Second Edition, Revised... London: Nathaniel Cooke... [n.d.]
Duodecimo.

In this 2nd edition, Leech's frontis. is redrawn on wood, and there are additional full-page woodcuts by Keene (?).

118 SEALY, T.H. Broad Grins from China, 1852 (see No. 37).

119 SMITH, ALBERT. Comic Tales And Sketches. By Albert Smith... London: Richard Bentley... 1852
Sixteenmo.

21 woodcuts (including initials) in text by Leech, most of them signed. All of these articles had appeared in *The Wassail-Bowl*, 1843 (see No. 50).

120 SMITH, ALBERT. Comic Tales And Pictures Of Life... London: David Bryce... [1861?]
Sixteenmo.

A cheap edition of No. 119 and 124 paged continuously. It contains all the illus.

121 STOWE, MRS. HARRIET BEECHER. Uncle Tom's Cabin; Or, Life Among The Lowly. By Harriet Beecher Stowe. London: H.G. Bohn... 1852.
Duodecimo.

Frontis. and eight full-page woodcuts not included in pagination. The one facing p.4 (Eliza's Child dancing to amuse Mr. Haley) is signed by Leech.

1853

122 THE FIELD Or Country Gentleman's Newspaper... 1853.
Folio.

The following woodcuts by Leech, appeared in the first two vols. of *The Field*, his work beginning in No. I, Jan. 1853: "Gone away", A Day in the Snow; The first Open Day; After the Race; The State of the Country;... It's very good Landing; The Canter; The early part of the Season; "Fly em, Charley", A Way; the Way of going to the Derby. *(See p. 118.)*

123 SMITH, ALBERT. Pictures Of Life At Home And Abroad. By Albert Smith. London: Richard Bentley... 1853.
Sixteenmo.

17 woodcuts (including initials) in text by Leech. All of these articles had appeared in *The Wassail-Bowl*, 1843 (see No. 50). See also No. 120.

124 [SURTEES, R.S.] Mr. Sponge's Sporting Tour. By The Author Of "Handley Cross", "Jorrocks's Jaunts" Etc. Etc. [Woodcut] With Illustrations By John Leech. London: Bradbury And Evans... 1853.
Octavo. 13 monthly numbers in 12 with original brown pictorial paper wrappers designed by Leech.

One etched plate, coloured by hand, in each number except the last which contains two; woodcuts in Nos. I-XII-XIII, respectively, seven, nine, seven, six, eight, eight, six, seven, seven, seven, ten; a total of 13 etchings and 89 woodcuts by Leech, including five cuts (on pp. 129, 165, 182, 227, and 296) not mentioned in the list of illus. The cut on p. 225 is used also on the title-page. *(See pp. 96-109, 141, 149.)*

On the completion of the work in numbers, it appeared in vol. form bound in pictorial cloth as announced among the extra advertisements in the last number. A reprint was published by Bradbury, Agnew & Co. in 1888 (undated).

125 Another edition, 1860 with original brown cloth binding and gold stamped.

126 BERKELEY, G.F. Reminiscences Of A Huntsman. By The Honourable Grantley F. Berkeley. With Illustrations By Leech. London: Longman, Brown, Green, And Longmans. 1854.
Octavo. Original red cloth binding; dark red end-papers with advertisements.

Etched frontis. coloured by hand and three etched pls. (facing pp. 17, 73, and 81) all by Leech entitled: "I implored them to have the street door opened", How to preserve Pheasants; A Shindy — Eton to the rescue; Old John Baldwin and his Prisoner.

127 FULLOM, S.W. The Great Highway: A Story Of The World's Struggles. By S.W. Fullom... With Illustrations On Steel, By John Leech. [Quotation] In Three Volumes... London: Longman, Brown, Green, And Longmans. 1854.
Octavo. Three vols. Original blue cloth binding, gold stamped; yellow end-papers. Author's presentation copy.

Etched frontis. by Leech in each vol. (Guilty or not guilty; The Return; and An unexpected Meeting).

128 FULLOM, S.W. The Great Highway... Second Edition, Revised. London... 1854.
Octavo. Three vols. in one. Original blue stamped cloth binding; yellow end-papers.

In this 2nd edition the pagination of each vol. is separate and is the same as in the 1st edition. The pls. are the same. The vols. sometimes appear separately.

129 SURTEES, R.S. Handley Cross; Or, Mr. Jorrocks's Hunt. By The Author of "Mr. Sponge's Sporting Tour", "Jorrocks's Jaunts," Etc. Etc. [Woodcut] With Illustrations By John Leech. London: Bradbury And Evans... 1854
Octavo. 17 monthly numbers with original brown pictorial paper wrappers designed by Leech.

One etched plate, coloured by hand, in each number; woodcuts in Nos. I-XVII, respectively, eight, eight, seven, six, seven, seven, five, six, six, five, six, five, six, four, two, five, six; a total of 17 etchings and 99 woodcuts by Leech, including 15 initial letters not mentioned in the list of illus. The cut on p.409 is used on the title-page.

The numbers appeared from Mar. 1853 — Oct. 1854. On its completion the work was published in vol. form bound in red pictorial cloth. A reprint was published by Bradbury, Agnew & Co. in 1888 (undated). *(See pp. 109-118.)*

1856

130 FULLOM, S.W. The Man Of The World; Or, Vanities Of The Day. By S.W. Fullom... In Three Volumes... "It's a mad world, my masters." — *Old Play.* London: Charles Joseph Skeet... 1856.
Octavo. Three vols. Original maroon cloth binding lettered in gold; green end-papers.

Vols. I-III contain, respectively, three, two, and two etched plates (including frontis.), a total of seven plates by Leech, as in the lists of illus.

131 [RUFFINI, GIOVANNI.] The Paragreens On A Visit To The Paris Universal Exhibition. By The Author Of "Lorenzo Benoni", And "Doctor Antonio". With Illustrations By John Leech. Edinburgh: Thomas Constable And Co. Hamilton Adams And Co., London. MDCCCLVI.
Duodecimo. Original blue cloth binding, gold stamped; yellow end-papers.

Five full-page woodcuts (frontis. and facing pp. 28, 111, 176, and 228), by Leech without titles. The wood-cutting was done by Swain. Some copies are bound in light green cloth.

132 ST. JOHN, BAYLE. Legends Of The Christian East. By Bayle St. John... London: Addey And Co... MDCCCLVI.
Duodecimo. Original pictorial white cloth binding; white end-papers.

The design on the cover is signed with a monogram "J.L." and is attributed to Leech.

1857

133 BERKELEY, G.F. A Month In The Forests Of France. By The Hon. Grantley F. Berkeley. London: Longman, Brown, Green, Longmans, & Roberts. 1857...
Octavo. Original red stamped cloth binding; yellow end-papers.

Two etched pls. (frontis. coloured by hand, and facing p. [I]) by Leech. The pls. represent hunting scenes but have no titles.

134 MERRY PICTURES By The Comic Hands H.K. Browne, Crowquill, Doyle, Leech, Meadows, Hine, And Others. London: W. Kent & Co... [1857].
Oblong quarto. Original brown pictorial boards, red leather back.

This consists of lithographed title by Alfred Crowquill, and 43 numbered leaves, printed on one side only, each leaf containing numerous woodcuts, with descriptive text, by Leech and others, as enumerated in the title.

Several of Leech's illus. for *The Comic Latin Grammar* (see No. 21) are reproduced with added or altered inscriptions.

135 [PROWER,— .] The Militiaman At Home And Abroad; Being The History Of A Militia Regiment, From Its First Training To Its Disembodiment; With Sketches Of The Ionian Islands, Malta, And Gibraltar. By Emeritus. With Illustrations By John Leech. London: Smith, Elder & Co... 1857.
Octavo. Original red cloth binding, gold stamped; dark blue end-papers.

Two etched pls. (frontis. and facing p. 37) by Leech entitled: The Bugler; The Old Friends at Southsea.

1858

136 BALMANNO, MRS. Pen And Pencil. By Mrs. Balmanno. [Woodcut] New York: D. Appleton & Co... 1858.
Octavo.

Etched frontis. and numerous woodcuts in text by various artists; the cut on p. [251] illus. "the Child's Evening Prayer", is by Leech.

137 THE CYCLOPAEDIA OF WIT AND HUMOR; Containing Choice And Characteristic Selections From The Writings Of The Most Eminent Humorists Of America, Ireland, Scotland, And England. Illustrated with Twenty-four Portraits on Steel, and many Hundred Wood Engravings. Edited by William E. Burton... [Quotation] New York: D. Appleton And Company... London... 1858.
Quarto. 24 monthly numbers (arranged for two vols.), with original brown pictorial paper wrappers.

24 portraits and numerous woodcuts in text. Cuts by Leech are found on pp. 520 (copy on wood of Tom Houlaghan's Guardian Sprite, appearing in *The Illuminated Magazine,* Vol. II), 726, 862, 864, 945, 946, 991, 1103, 1119.

Most of Leech's illus. are copies of those in *The Illuminated Magazine,* 1843-1844 (see No. 48), with a few from *Punch.*

138 AN ENCYCLOPAEDIA OF RURAL SPORTS... By Delabere P. Blaine, Esq. A New Edition, Revised And Corrected. [Woodcut] Illustrated By Above Six Hundred Engravings On Wood By R. Branston From Drawings By Leech, Alken, T. Landseer, Dickes, Etc. London Longman, Brown, Green, Longmans, & Roberts. 1858.
Octavo.

Numerous woodcuts in text by Leech, Alken, T. Landseer, Dickes and others. Editions appeared in 1840 and 1852. The preface of the present vol. contains the following note: "This edition will be found to be embellished with many additional engravings, from drawings by Mr. John Leech." It was published the same year in three vols.

139 GREENWOOD, FREDERICK. The Path Of Roses. By Frederick Greenwood. With Illustrations By Birket Foster, John Leech, Noel Humphreys, James Danby, Harrison Weir, &c., &c. London: Charles H. Clarke... [c.1858].
Octavo. Original light green cloth binding, gold and blind stamped, with floral medallion in center of upper cover; yellow end-papers.

Numerous woodcuts in text, by Leech and others; that on p.67 is signed by Leech. The story first appeared in *Tait's Magazine.*

140 SMITH, ALBERT. The English Hotel Nuisance. By Albert Smith. [Quotation] Second Edition. London: Bradbury And Evans... 1858.
Sixteenmo. Original buff pictorial paper wrapper.

Two full-page woodcuts (frontis. and p. [33]) by Leech and two woodcuts in text. This first appeared in 1855.

141 SURTEES, R.S. "Ask Mamma"; Or, The Richest Commoner In England. By The Author Of "Handley Cross", "Sponge's Sporting Tour", Etc. Etc. [Woodcut] With Illustrations By John Leech. London: Bradbury And Evans... 1858.
Octavo. 13 monthly numbers with original brown pictorial paper wrappers designed by Leech.

One etched pl. coloured by hand, in each number; woodcuts in Nos. I-XIII, respectively, eight, seven, six, five, five, four, five, five, six, three, four, six, six; a total of 13 etchings and 70 woodcuts by Leech, including one cut (on p. 195) not included in the list of illus. The cut on p. 225 is used on the title-page.

On the completion of the work in numbers, it appeared in vol. form bound in pictorial cloth. A reprint was published by Bradbury, Agnew & Co. in 1888 (undated). *(See pp. 114, 118-119, 149.)*

1859

142 FRANCIS, FRANCIS. Newton Dogvane. A Story Of English

Country Life. By Francis Francis. With Illustrations by Leech. In Three Volumes... London: Hurst And Blackett, Publishers, Successors To Henry Colburn... 1859. The right of Translation is reserved.

Duodecimo. Three vols. Original dark rose cloth binding; yellow end-papers.

Etched frontis. by Leech, coloured by hand, in each vol. (Newton distinguishes himself in a minuet; Mr. Chilliwun preparing for the Field; The Chalk Pit). Some copies have the plates uncoloured. It was reprinted in 1888.

143 [HALIBURTON, T.C.] Nature And Human Nature. By The Author Of "Sam Slick, The Clockmaker"... London: Hurst And Blackett... 1859.
Duodecimo.

Frontis. engraved in line (Female colleges) by Leech.

Both this and No. 145 belong to Hurst and Blackett's Standard Library of Cheap Editions of Popular Modern Works. The frontis. of The Old Judge, also by Haliburton, in the same series, is sometimes attributed to Leech but does not seem to be by him.

144 [HALIBURTON, T.C.] Sam Slick's Wise Saws And Modern Instances; Or, What He Said, Did, Or Invented... London: Hurst And Blackett... 1859.
Duodecimo.

Frontis. engraved in line (The House without Hope) by Leech.

145 HOLE, S.R. A Little Tour In Ireland. Being A Visit To Dublin, Galway, Connamara, Athlone, Limerick, Killarney, Glengarriif, Cork, Etc. Etc. Etc. By An Oxonian. With Illustrations By John Leech. [Quotation] London: Bradbury & Evans... 1859.
Duodecimo. Original green cloth binding, gold stamped; yellow end-papers and gilt edges.

Folding etched frontis. coloured by hand, four full-page woodcuts facing pp. 31, 84, 141, and 209, and 33 woodcuts in text, all by Leech.

At p. 141 is a representation of Leech. "It is a back view of him, riding with very short stirrups a rakish Irish pony, listening to a barefooted master of blarney". — *Dr. John Brown.*

The author was the Rev. S. Reynolds Hole, Dean of Rochester Cathedral and Leech's friend and biographer, with whom he made the journey to Ireland. (*See pp. 188-190.*)

146 HOLE, S.R. A Little Tour In Ireland By An Oxonian (S. Reynolds Hole, Dean Of Rochester) With Illustrations By John Leech [Quotation] New Edition London: Edward Arnold... 1892...
Quarto. No. 25 of an edition of 100 copies on large paper.

New edition with dedication to John Leech, and new preface and list of illus. added.

147 MILLS, JOHN. The Flyers Of The Hunt. By John Mills... Illustrated By John Leech. [Quotation] "The Field" Office, Strand; And Ward And Lock... London. 1859.
Octavo. Original blue cloth binding, gold stamped, orange end-papers.

Five etched plates (including frontis.) by Leech, coloured by hand, as in the list of plates entitled: "There's nothing to stop yer"; "And fell head foremost..."; Puffy Doddles lectured in the Saddle Room; Sir Digby presenting the brush...; "Pompous, silent, and grand..."; The Match.

Some copies have the illus. uncoloured.

148 ONCE A WEEK. An Illustrated Miscellany Of Literature, Art, Science, & Popular Information. Volume I. July to December,

1859 [-Volume V, June to December, 1861]. London: Bradbury & Evans... [1859-1861].
Octavo. Vols. I-V.

Numerous woodcuts by Browne, Du Maurier, Keene, Leech, Millais, Tenniel and many others. According to the lists of illus. Vol. I has 32 designs by Leech, Vol. II, 46, Vol. III, seven, Vol. IV, one, and Vol. V, four.

Leech's work begins on pp. 1-2 of Vol. I, with illus. to a rhymed programme of the magazine, by Shirley Brooks. An article on "The Public Schools of London" has a cut (Coach-tree, Vol. III, p. 98) (*see p. 21*) and other articles on London life are illus. by him. A large number of his designs are for "Divorce a Vinculo" and "The Science of Matrimony" in Vol. II.

1860

149 MR. BRIGGS & HIS DOINGS. Fishing. [Woodcut] By John Leech. London. Published By Bradbury And Evans... [1860].
Folio. Original brown pictorial paper wrapper, with design by Leech and title as above.

This consits of 12 coloured lithographs, with title above each plate and explanatory text and publishers' names below. The eleventh plate is divided into two pictures. The first woodcuts depicting Mr. Briggs and his various doings appeared in *Punch* in 1849, and for some time he continued to be a favourite subject with Leech and the readers of *Punch*. (*See pp. 71-75.*)

150 SURTEES, R.S. "Plain Or Ringlets?" By The Author Of "Handley Cross", "Sponge's Sporting Tour", "Ask Mamma", Etc. Etc. [Woodcut] With Illustration By John Leech. London: Bradbury And Evans... 1860.
Octavo. 13 monthly numbers in 12 with original brown pictorial paper wrappers.

One etched pl. coloured by hand, in each number except the last, which contains two, one of them a pictorial title; woodcuts in No. I-Nos. XII-XIII, respectively, six, four, five, four, six, five, four, five, three, three, three, six; a total of 13 etchings and 54 woodcuts by Leech, including ten initial letters not mentioned in the list of illus. The cut on p. 155 is used in the printed title-page.

On the completion of the work in numbers, it appeared in vol. form bound in pictorial cloth. A reprint was published by Bradbury, Agnew & Co. in 1888 (not dated). (*See p. 118.*)

1861

151 MILLS, JOHN. The Life Of A Foxhound. By John Mills... Second Edition. London: Longman, Green, Longman, And Roberts... 1861.
Octavo. Original maroon cloth cover bound in.

Four etched pls. (including frontis.) by Leech, coloured by hand, as in the list of illus. entitled: The meet; "Head and Hands will beat Heels"; A Curious Finish; "Hold har-r-r-d!".

The 1st edition appeared in 1848. This is the first with Leech's illus.

152 PENNELL, H.C. Puck On Pegasus: By H. Cholmondeley Pennell. Illustrated By Leech, Phiz, Portch, And Tenniel. With A Frontispiece By George Cruikshank. Engraved By Dalziel Brothers, Joseph Swain, John Swain, & E. Evans. [Quotation] London: John Camden Hotten, Piccadilly. 1861.
Octavo. Original violet cloth binding, gold stamped; chocolate end-papers.

Etched frontis. by George Cruikshank, 12 full-page woodcuts not included in pagination, and numerous woodcuts and initials in the text by Leech, Browne, Portch, and Tenniel. The full-page cuts on pp. 37, 53, and 132 appear to be by Leech.

153 PENNELL, H.C. Puck On Pegasus... Fourth Edition...
London Routledge... 1862.
Octavo. Original red cloth binding, gold stamped; cream-coloured end-papers.

In this 4th edition the full-page cuts are introduced into the text.

1862, 1865

154 [SKETCHES IN OIL.] The Originals (From "Punch") Of Mr.
John Leech's Sketches In Oil. Exhibited At The Egyptian Hall,
Piccadilly. [1862].
Quarto.

"Though essentially a worker in black and white, Leech...
had a strong desire to try his skill at colours. In 1862 he essayed
a series of so-called 'Sketches in Oil', which were exhibited at
the Egyptian Hall, Piccadilly, in June and the following
months. (See Chapter Eight). These consisted of copies of a
selection of his *Punch* drawings, which had been ingeniously
enlarged, transferred to canvas, and coloured lightly in
oils....."

155 MR. JOHN LEECH'S GALLERY of Sketches In Oil. From
Subjects in "Punch". Exhibited At The Auction Mart Gallery,
Near The Bank of England... Admission One Shilling. Price
Threepence. [n.d.].
Octavo. Stitched.

On p. [8] is the following note: "The Secretary in attendance at
the Room will give information respecting the limited number
of subjects from Mr. John Leech's Gallery of Sketches in Oil
which it is proposed to publish. (See advertisement.)"

On p. [18] is an announcement that a limited number of
Sketches in Oil would be reproduced to the order of
subscribers, followed by two lists of works to be reproduced
under the divisions, "Hunting. The Noble Science. Ten
Incidents," and "Sports and Pastimes. Ten Subjects". A
subscription blank for the two series, at £10. 10s. each, is
inserted. (For lists see No. 156.)

156 [HUNTING; and SPORTS AND PASTIMES.] Published by
Thos. Agnew & Sons. London, Manchr. & L'pool, Jany 2nd.,
1865 [-1866].
Folio. The former series issued in orange wrapper, the latter in magenta.

23 reproductions in colour of Sketches in Oil as advertised in
Catalogue (see No. 155) with three additional Hunting prints,
making that series number 13 and Sports and Pastimes, ten.
Two of the additional prints (Stop a bit Master Reginald; and
One of Multum in Parvo's "going" days) are dated Oct. 22
1866. Leech's name and title or explanation of subject, in
facsimile of Leech's handwriting, appear under each print. *(See
p. 204.)*

The subjects of the reproductions are as follows, each subject
being followed by a reference to the original source from which
it was enlarged:

HUNTING: A Frolic home after a Blank Day (*Punch's
Almanack* for 1859); Come Hup! you ugly brute (Surtees,
R.S., *Handley Cross*, No. IV); "Hold hard, Master George"
(*Punch*, Vol. XXXVI, p. 120) *(See p. 175.)*; Where there's a
Will there's a Way (*Punch*, Vol. XXXVI, p. 60); A Friendly
Mount (*Punch*, Vol. XXXII, p.34); Gone away! (*Punch*, Vol.
XL, p. 120); The Noble Science (*Punch's Almanack* for 1858);
Our Friend Mr Noddy (*Punch's Almanack* for 1857); A
Capital Finish (*Punch*, Vol. XXXVIII, p. 74); "Don't move
there, we shall clear you" (*Punch's Almanack* for 1854) *(See p.
197.)*; "Stop a bit, Master Reginald" (*Punch*, Vol. XXXVIII,
p. 16); No Consequence (*Punch*, Vol. XXIX, p. 228); One of
Multum in Parvo's "going" days (Surtees, R.S., *Mr. Sponge's
Sporting Tour*, No. IV).

(The last three are not mentioned in the advertisement. The
second, third, sixth and twelfth prints, as listed above, were
issued later, without the publisher's name, in a portfolio
lettered Four Masterpieces by John Leech.)

SPORTS AND PASTIMES: The Mermaid's Haunt (*Punch's
Almanack* for 1858) *(See p. 195.)*; A Cavalier (*Punch's
Almanack* for 1857); None but the Brave deserve the Fair
(*Punch's Almanack* for 1858); "Yes, my dears, the sea breeze
after bathing is beneficial to the back hair" (*Punch's
Almanack* for 1858); A shocking Young Lady, indeed (*Punch:
Vol. XXXVIII, p. 242); Scene at Sandbath (*Punch*, Vol. XLI,
p. 116); The Fair Toxophilites (*Punch*, Vol. XXXV, p. 24) *(See
p. 219.)*; A nice Game for two or more; (*Punch*, Vol. XLI, p.
66); The Old Fox Hunter (*Punch*, Vol. XXXVI, p. 258); Not a
bad idea for warm weather (*Punch*, Vol. XXXIII, p. 54).

1863

157 THE GARDENERS' ANNUAL FOR 1863. Edited By The
Rev. S. Reynolds Hole. With A Coloured Illustration By John
Leech. London: Longman, Green, Longman, Roberts, &
Green. 1863.
Sixteenmo. Original green paper wrapper.
Etched frontis. (A Garden Subject...) by Leech coloured by
hand.

1865

158 SURTEES, R.S. Mr. Facey Romford's Hounds. By The
Author of "Handley Cross," "Mr. Sponge's Sporting Tour,"
"Ask Mamma," Etc. Etc. [Woodcut] With Illustrations By
John Leech And Hablot K. Browne. London: Bradbury And
Evans... 1865. [The Right of Translation is reserved.]
Octavo. 12 monthly numbers, with original brown pictorial paper
wrappers designed by Leech.

Two etched pls. coloured by hand, in each number, those in
Nos. I-VII by Leech, the remainder by Hablot K. Browne; a
total of 24 pls. (14 by Leech and ten by Browne), as in the list
of plates. The woodcut on the title-page is by Browne.

The author died shortly after the appearance of the first
number of this publication, and Leech died, at the age of forty-seven,
during its publication (see Chapter 10), the work of illus. being
carried on by H.K. Browne. The numbers appeared from May
1864 -April 1865. On its completion the work was published in
vol. form bound in pictorial cloth. *(See pp. 111, 119.)*

159 ONE HUNDRED AND SEVENTY DESIGNS AND
ETCHINGS By John Leech... London: Richard Bentley...
1865.
Folio. Two vols. Original maroon stamped cloth binding; yellow end-papers.

Each vol. contains title and contents (two leaves) in addition to
the etchings, which are reproductions on India paper, without
imprint, of the various pls. issued by Bentley.

1869

160 LEIGH, H.S. Carols Of Cockayne By Henry S. Leigh.
[Woodcut] With Numerous Illustrations By Alfred Concanen
And The Late John Leech. London: John Camden Hotten...
1869.
Duodecimo. Original green cloth binding, gold stamped; dark grey end-papers and gilt edges.

Numerous small woodcuts in text and initials by Leech and
Alfred Concanen, most of them signed by the latter.

Bibliography

Bodkin, Thomas, *The Noble Science. John Leech in the Hunting Field*, 1948. (Introduction by Sir Alfred Munnings.)

Brown, John, "John Leech", *The North British Review*, March, 1865, Article VIII, pp. 213-244. Includes illustrations and a list of Leech's works.

Brown, John, *Leech's Etchings. Characteristic Sketches of his illustrations ... also Thackeray and his Writings*, for private circulation (n.d.).

Brown, John, *John Leech and other Papers*, Edinburgh, 1872. Includes a facsimile of a sketch of John Leech as the jolly tar, by himself. This work was also published without the illustrations, and with Dean Hole's reminiscences (including facsimile) appended. A fifth edition of this was published in 1884.

Chambers, C.E.S., *A List of Works containing Illustrations by John Leech*, Edinburgh, 1892.

Dolman, Frederick, "John Leech and his Method", *The Strand*, March 1903, pp. 158-164.

Du Maurier, George, *Social Pictorial Satire*, London and New York, 1898, pp. 9-156. Includes Frontispiece "Mr and Mrs Caudle" and a list of illustrations. It was based on an article in *Harper's New Monthly Magazine*, February, 1898, pp. 331-344.

Evans, Edward B., *A Description of the Mulready Envelope*, 1891.

Everitt, Graham, *English Caricaturists ... of the Nineteenth Century*, 2nd edition, London, 1893, pp. 407-409. Includes illustrations and a list of Leech's works. The first edition appeared in 1886.

Frith, W.P., *John Leech, his Life and Works*, London, 1891. Two volumes.

Hole, S.R., *The Memories of Dean Hole*, London, 1892.

Holman Hunt, W., "Reminiscences of John Leech", *The Contemporary Review*, 54, July-December 1888, pp. 335-353.

Humorous Masterpieces, London and Glasgow, 1905. Includes illustrations by John Leech.

Kitton, F.G., *Charles Dickens by Pen and Pencil*, London, 1890, in thirteen parts.

Kitton, F.G., *John Leech, Artist and Humourist: a biographical Sketch*, London, 1883. Includes illustrations and a list of Leech's works, pp. 64-67.

Kitton, F.G., *John Leech*, London, 1884 (Redway's Shilling Series). A new revised edition from which most of the illustrations and the list of works are omitted.

"Obituary of John Leech", *The Cornhill Magazine*, December, 1864, pp. 743-760. Illustrations.

Osgood Field, W.B., *John Leech On My Shelves*, privately printed, 1930 (Munich). Includes introduction, pp. 13-18, illustrated books, pp. 21-230, drawings, pp. 241-254, etchings and woodcuts, pp. 257-306. Republished by Collectors' Editions, New York, 1970.

Rose, June, *The Drawings of John Leech*, London, 1950.

Saint-Gaudens, Homer, "John Leech", *The Critic*, October, 1905, pp. 358-367. Includes illustrations.

Silver, Henry, "The Art-Life of John Leech", *The Magazine of Art*, Vol. XVI. "The Home-life of John Leech", *The Magazine of Art*, Vol. XVI.

Sturgis, Russell, "John Leech", *Scribner's Monthly*, February, 1879, pp. 553-565.

Thornber, Harry, John Leech, London (nd.). Reprinted from the *Manchester Quarterly*, 1890.

Tidy, Rev. Gordon, *A Little About Leech*, London, 1931.

Wilson, Stanley K., *Catalogue of An Exhibition of Works By John Leech*, New York, 1914. The catalogue of an exhibition held from January 22 — March 8, 1914, at the Grolier Club. Only 240 copies were printed.

INDEX

Indexer's note: John Leech is referred to throughout the index as JL. Page numbers in bold indicate an illustration. There is a separate index of cartoon subjects on page 265.

INDEX OF "PUNCH" CARTOON SUBJECTS

Antique Collectors' Club

The Antique Collectors' Club was formed in 1966 and now has a five figure membership spread throughout the world. It publishes the only independently run monthly antiques magazine *Antique Collecting* which caters for those collectors who are interested in increasing their knowledge of antiques, both by increasing the members' knowledge of quality as well as in discussing the factors which influence the price that is likely to be asked. The Antique Collectors' Club pioneered the provision of information on prices for collectors and still leads in the provision of detailed articles on a variety of subjects.

It was in response to the enormous demand for information on "what to pay" that the price guide series was introduced in 1968 with the first edition of *The Price Guide to Antique Furniture* (completely revised, 1978), a book which broke new ground by illustrating the more common types of antique furniture, the sort that collectors could buy in shops and at auctions, rather than the rare museum pieces which had previously been used (and still to a large extent are used) to make up the limited amount of illustrations in books published by commercial publishers. Many other price guides have followed, all copiously illustrated, and greatly appreciated by collectors for the valuable information they contain, quite apart from prices. The Antique Collectors' Club also publishes other books on antiques, including horology and art reference works, and a full book list is available.

Club membership, which is open to all collectors, costs £11.50 per annum. Members receive free of charge *Antique Collecting,* the Club's magazine (published every month except August), which contains well-illustrated articles dealing with the practical aspects of collecting not normally dealt with by magazines. Prices, features of value, investment potential, fakes and forgeries are all given prominence in the magazine.

Among other facilities available to members are private buying and selling facilities, the longest list of "For Sales" of any antiques magazine, an annual ceramics conference and the opportunity to meet other collectors at their local antique collectors' club. There are nearly eighty in Britain and so far a dozen overseas. Members may also buy the Club's publications at special pre-publication prices.

As its motto implies, the Club is an amateur organisation designed to help collectors to get the most out of their hobby: it is informal and friendly and gives enormous enjoyment to all concerned.

For Collectors — By Collectors — About Collecting

The Antique Collectors' Club, 5 Church Street, Woodbridge, Suffolk